Death in the Diaspora

Studies in British and Irish Migration

Series Editors: T. M. Devine, University of Edinburgh, and
Angela McCarthy, University of Otago

Showcasing the histories of migration into and out of Britain and Ireland from the seventeenth century to contemporary times and their impact at home and abroad

From the 1600s to the current day, millions of British and Irish migrants have sought new lives around the world. Britain and Ireland have also received returning migrants and other newcomers of diverse ethnicities. This series will examine the causes, consequences, representations and legacies of these movements on the homelands, the migrants and the destinations in which they settled. The series incorporates not just the inward and outward movement of people, but of ideas, products and objects. It specifically encourages transnational and comparative cross-disciplinary approaches across groups, space and time.

Titles available in the series:

New Scots: Scotland's Immigrant Communities since 1945
Edited by T. M. Devine and Angela McCarthy

Death in the Diaspora: British and Irish Gravestones
Edited by Nicholas J. Evans and Angela McCarthy

edinburghuniversitypress.com/series/bims

Death in the Diaspora
British and Irish Gravestones

Edited by Nicholas J. Evans and Angela McCarthy

EDINBURGH
University Press

In fond memory of historians of the British and Irish diasporas:
David Fitzpatrick (1948–2019)
and Eric Richards (1940–2018)

Edinburgh University Press is one of the leading university presses in the UK. We publish academic books and journals in our selected subject areas across the humanities and social sciences, combining cutting-edge scholarship with high editorial and production values to produce academic works of lasting importance. For more information visit our website: edinburghuniversitypress.com

© editorial matter and organisation Nicholas J. Evans and Angela McCarthy, 2020, 2022
© the chapters and their several authors, 2020, 2022

Edinburgh University Press Ltd
The Tun – Holyrood Road
12 (2f) Jackson's Entry
Edinburgh EH8 8PJ

First published in hardback by Edinburgh University Press 2020

Typeset in 10.5/13pt Sabon by
Servis Filmsetting Ltd, Stockport, Cheshire

A CIP record for this book is available from the British Library

ISBN 978 1 4744 7378 1 (hardback)
ISBN 978 1 4744 7379 8 (paperback)
ISBN 978 1 4744 7380 4 (webready PDF)
ISBN 978 1 4744 7381 1 (epub)

The right of the contributors to be identified as authors of this work has been asserted in accordance with the Copyright, Designs and Patents Act 1988 and the Copyright and Related Rights Regulations 2003 (SI No. 2498).

Contents

List of Figures and Tables	vii
The Contributors	ix
Acknowledgements	x
Series Editors' Introduction	xii

1 Introduction – Death in the Diaspora: British and Irish Gravestones
   Nicholas J. Evans and Angela McCarthy 1

2 Forgetting and Remembering: Scots and Ulster Scots Memorials in Eighteenth-century Ulster, Pennsylvania and Nineteenth-century New South Wales
   Harold Mytum 14

3 Imposing Identity: Death Markers to 'English' People in Barbados, 1627–1838
   Nicholas J. Evans 52

4 Looking for Thistles in Stone Gardens: The Cemeteries of Nova Scotia's Scottish Immigrants
   Laurie Stanley-Blackwell and Michael Linkletter 81

5 Scottish Headstones in Ceylon in Comparative Perspective
   Angela McCarthy 108

6 Irish Memorialisation in South Australia, 1850–99
   Janine McEgan 127

7 Memorialising the Diasporic Cornish
   Philip Payton 155

8 Documents in Stone: Records of Lives and Deaths of Scots Abroad and in Scotland 176
John M. MacKenzie

9 Conclusion 201
Angela McCarthy and Nicholas J. Evans

Index 206

Figures and Tables

FIGURES

2.1	Ulster Scots settlement and Presbyterian burial grounds surveyed	27
2.2	Pennsylvania memorials with heraldic devices	28
2.3	Pennsylvania memorials with waisted sides	30–1
2.4	Pennsylvania memorials with crowns and mortality symbols	34
2.5	Presbyterian Kiama region memorials with Ulster origins stated	37
2.6	Memorials in the Presbyterian section, Rookwood, Sydney	38–9
2.7	Bar graph of stated places of origin by country, Presbyterian section memorials, Rookwood, Sydney	41
2.8	Irish symbols on Roman Catholic memorials	42
3.1	The chest tomb to William Arnold	54
3.2	The gravestone of John Smith of Liverpool	59
3.3	The memorial tablet to Thomas Withers	64–5
3.4	A marble relief plaque of King's Lynn	68
3.5	A replica marble gravestone in Bridgetown Jewish Cemetery	72
3.6	Marble gravestone in a smaller Jewish cemetery at Bridgetown	73
4.1	Catholic symbols on Ann Chisholm's headstone	90
4.2	Gaelic inscription on Bard John MacLean's headstone	92
4.3	Thistle motifs on headstones of Catherine Ross McKay and Donald McKay	95
4.4	Thistle, scroll, rosette, bible and hand motifs on David McIntosh's headstone	96

4.5	Cross and thistle motifs on Hugh Cameron's headstone	98
4.6	Folk image on base of Mary McPherson's headstone	100
5.1	The headstone of James Taylor, 'the father of the Ceylon tea enterprise'	110
5.2	The headstone of James McPherson at Garrisons Cemetery, Kandy	115
5.3	The headstone of Archibald MacPhee MacNeill at Trinity Church, Nuwara Eliya	117
5.4	Mr. David Reid, Sir W. Johnstone and Mr Shand enjoy their tea!	121
6.1	Towns of the Clare Valley region of South Australia	131
6.2	Irish vs non-Irish: change over time of introductory phrases in inscriptions	137
6.3	Engraved stone of the Sacred Heart on Ellen Crowe's grave, 1895, Undalya Catholic Cemetery	139
6.4	Michael Dermody's Irish Catholic grave 1861, St John's Cemetery, Kapunda	141
6.5	Newgrange, Co. Meath, showing triskele designs on entrance stone	143
6.6	Fahey headstone 1858, Navan Catholic Cemetery	145
6.7	Sketch of motifs on the top section of the O'Sullivan headstone 1863, Navan Catholic Cemetery	146
6.8	Sketch of the O'Brien headstone, 1860s, Navan Catholic Cemetery	147
7.1	The lonely grave of Annie Trevithic[k], near the entrance to the Blinman copper mine in the northern Flinders Ranges	167
7.2	The gravestone of William Tremaine in the cemetery at Silverton	170
8.1	The monument to Jonathan Duncan, Governor of Bombay	184–5
8.2	The tomb of John Alexander Bannerman, Governor of Penang	189
8.3	The tomb of Philip Dundas, Governor of Prince of Wales Island (Penang)	191
8.4	The gravestone of the missionary Revd William Ross, Abernyte Kirkyard, Perthshire	195

TABLE

2.1	Symbols frequently occurring on memorials in Scotland	22

The Contributors

Nicholas J. Evans is Lecturer in Diaspora History at the University of Hull, England.

Michael Linkletter is Sister Saint Veronica Professor of Gaelic Studies, St Francis Xavier University, Canada.

Angela McCarthy is Professor of Scottish and Irish History and Director of the Centre for Global Migrations, University of Otago, Dunedin, New Zealand.

Janine McEgan is a postgraduate researcher in Cultural Heritage Management, Department of Archaeology, Flinders University, Adelaide, Australia.

John M. MacKenzie is Visiting Professor Emeritus of Imperial History, University of the Highlands and Islands, Scotland.

Harold Mytum is Professor of Archaeology and Director of the Centre for Manx Studies, University of Liverpool, England.

Philip Payton is Professor of History, College of Humanities, Arts and Social Sciences, Flinders University, Australia.

Laurie Stanley-Blackwell is Professor of History and Principal Investigator of the SSHRC project 'Centering Death', St Francis Xavier University, Canada.

Acknowledgements

We have both always been interested in roaming around cemeteries but our collaboration in this area began at the University of Aberdeen in 2002 when we were both research fellows at the Research Institute for Irish and Scottish Studies. Many Sundays we would ramble around St Machar's Churchyard where we were struck with the extensive references to Scottish family members in assorted overseas destinations. We began to compile registers of monumental inscriptions from various Scottish cemeteries but had to put these aside due to other commitments.

When, in 2015, Nick was part of a team receiving an Arts and Humanities Research Council UK grant for a project called 'Remember Me: The Changing Face of Memorialisation', we elected to hold the last seminar in our 'Scotland's Diasporas in Comparative International Perspective' series (the joint initiative of Angela McCarthy, Sir Tom Devine and Nicholas J. Evans) on diaspora gravestone memorialisation. We are grateful to the Economic and Social Research Council UK for funding that three-year (2014–16) seminar series, of which this is the sixth book publication. We thank National Museums Scotland for providing the stimulating environment within which the event took place and all those speakers and chairs who participated. Regrettably, Bill Jones, who presented on Welsh memorialisation, was unable to contribute to this collection. We thank Dr Lisa Marr for her care in preparing the index for this volume and the Centre for Global Migrations at the University of Otago for funding Lisa's work. We are also deeply thankful to Les O'Neil for his magic work preparing the map on page 131.

We dedicate this book to two historians of migration, and of Ireland, Scotland and Australia: David Fitzpatrick (1948–2019), who was Angela's PhD supervisor, and Eric Richards (1940–2018). Both David and Eric, at one time, travelled around New South Wales examining the graves of Irish migrants in Australia.[1] The legacy of their work on migration continues to inspire friends and colleagues.

Nicholas J. Evans and Angela McCarthy

NOTE

1. Philip Payton, 'Eric Richards: Emigrant and historian', in Philip Payton (ed.), *Emigrants and Historians: Essays in Honour of Eric Richards* (Mile End, SA: Wakefield Press, 2016), p. 5.

Series Editors' Introduction

The antiquarian examination of gravestones and other death markers dates back to Victorian times. But this pioneering study of memorialisation practices moves beyond earlier transcription and cataloguing practices to provide fresh and intriguing perspectives on how British and Irish people remembered their dead, both at home and abroad.

Unlike previous studies, it focuses especially on the British Empire across three centuries and five continents and the ways in which migrants who settled across the Empire and their descendants from England, Scotland and Ireland commemorated relatives and friends who had passed away.

A key aspect of the book is the enlightening comparisons which are drawn by the different authors, not simply between the different ethnicities but also between the distinctive regions of the source countries from which the migrants moved in their search for new opportunities overseas. The study is also emphatically multidisciplinary in approach. Insights are derived from a focus on archaeology, textual analysis, material composition, symbolism, memory and ethnicity. The specific themes of memorialisation are set within the national histories of the peoples of the British Isles in the attempt to draw meaning from the inscriptions and ornamentations of grave markers.

Much of general significance can also be learned from the questions the contributors attach to their evaluations of these monuments in the Americas, South Asia, Australia and New Zealand. How much can gravestones tell us about those in the past whose names do not appear in document-based historical works, those whom, as the editors of the volume put it, 'are often written out of history'? To what extent did death cultures change over time and space? How far are they another route into understanding the national identities of migrants? What do gravestones tell us about the collective survival of their memories from the homeland? The varied answers which are given by the contributors to these questions illustrate the value of evidence derived from these historical artefacts as a means to interrogate the past other than through conventional written sources.

Because of this, the book should have wide appeal, not only to those interested in death studies but also to scholars of the British Empire from before the Union of England and Scotland in 1707 until its decline in the 1960s. Students of British and Irish diasporas, national identities and memory will also find much of value in these pages.

T. M. Devine and Angela McCarthy

1

Introduction – Death in the Diaspora: British and Irish Gravestones

Nicholas J. Evans and Angela McCarthy

On 12 October 2019 newspapers around the world reported that more than forty tombstones in the British cemetery at Haifa in Israel had been desecrated.[1] Journalists in *The Jerusalem Post* noted, 'Some of the graves were knocked over, while others were covered in graffiti and several with painted swastikas. Three of the graves were completely destroyed.'[2] The incident was not the first such act of violence on a British cemetery in Israel, as just two years previously the Templar Cemetery, neighbouring the British cemetery, had also been attacked.[3] As the press coverage revealed, 'The cemetery contains more than 300 graves of British, Australian, Canadian and Indian soldiers, as well as troops from other former British colonies, who died fighting in Israel during both world wars.'[4] While damage to Jewish graves has been long associated with anti-Semitic feeling across Western Europe since before the Second World War, the desecration of non-Jewish graves, especially those to non-military personnel, is unusual in peacetime.[5] Such vandalism serves to show the enduring social, political and religious importance of memorials to long-dead colonial men, women and children in the twenty-first century.[6] Headstones and memorial tablets erected during the era of European imperialism, the focus of this volume, are not only public statements about the deceased and those erecting such markers, but are also testaments to the emotional relationships between the dead and the living.[7]

This introduction serves to provide an overview of the historical expansion of headstones and epitaphs in the commemorations of death and as part of the development of broader death landscapes during the period of British overseas imperialism between c.1608 and 1960. While death markers were erected by the grieving, their longevity as harbingers of identity reveal much about changing attitudes to death and remembrance in the time since they were erected. After examining the ways that previous scholars have interpreted such memorials, we highlight this volume's specific contribution to both death studies in general and diaspora studies more specifically. In doing so, we demonstrate the abundance of memorials at home and abroad that scholars, genealogists and communities can explore.

COMMEMORATING DEATH IN BRITAIN, IRELAND AND EUROPE

Following the Protestant Reformation in the sixteenth century, Catholic influence upon death rituals in the Western world gradually eroded. Changing attitudes to death marked the secularisation of death culture in Europe, leading to the birth of permanent burial spaces and death markers – whether memorials or epitaphs – that changed the death landscape in perpetuity.[8]

The Protestant Reformation not only altered the afterlife of the deceased, but marked a change in attitudes in life, with 'a growing emphasis on the unique individual' which 'created increasing problems when that individual died, and . . . this helps explain changes in how the dead were commemorated'.[9] This transformation meant less of a focus on the afterlife and more consideration for those left behind. The needs of the bereaved were just as important as preserving the memory of the deceased. A fitting or good death included not only a committal but also appropriate mourning rituals in art forms varying from word to art, from stone to print. Fundamentally, gravestones were used to mark burial plots.[10]

Profound social and economic change, especially after the widespread political unrest of the seventeenth century, also engendered the expansion of the middle class. Wealth creation not only enabled material gain but also provided the middle classes with the ability to emulate, both inside and outside of the church, practices of remembrance that had once been the preserve of the elite.[11] The demise of earlier ritual surrounding the disinterment of the 'oldest graves' when a graveyard became full, mainly by the end of the seventeenth century, also helped to stabilise the churchyard plot as the principal and perpetual place of burial.[12] Memorialisation in perpetuity motivated the gentry and aspiring middling classes to expend more money on permanent death markers. The architecture of the afterlife was a powerful tool and demonstrated what Thomas W. Laqueur has recently called the 'work of the dead'.[13] While aristocratic landowners had long filled the most significant burial spaces inside of churches, including in crypts or vaults, the churchyard plot became the only real estate 'normal' people purchased.[14] That they retained ownership of this land beyond their inevitable mortality made it an important part of the life cycle from the beginning of the seventeenth century. The poor, meanwhile, often shared their final resting place with others in the same plot with a pauper burial. Class consciousness was as profound in death as it had been in life.[15] Class was part of remembrance spaces with the burial landscape offering a cornucopia of difference to be observed for parishioners and visitors alike for centuries to come.

It was not until the beginning of the eighteenth century, however, that widespread change in memorialisation practices can be observed between Catholic and Protestant memorialisation ritual.[16] Among strongholds of Catholic Europe – especially Spain, Italy and France – over-elaborate forms of artistic celebration of death transformed the death landscape. Meanwhile, across Western Europe, death culture – especially within parts of Germany, Holland and Britain – witnessed a more conservative democratisation of memorialisation ritual. There, more modest memorials and epitaphs were being erected to remember Protestant Europeans while Catholic European memorials were seemingly overburdening the death landscape with their elaborate and often ostentatious structures.[17] Moreover, freed of the need to prolong the spiritual life of the deceased, the worldly attainments of the deceased were being publicly proclaimed on above-ground death markers outside of the church, as well as on memorial tablets on the walls inside of churches and cathedrals. No longer was death a private ritual; the deceased's life was now told to public audiences beyond the privacy of the home or church, especially on headstones, 'the commonest form of grave-monument'.[18]

Further transition took place in Britain during the nineteenth century.[19] Burials in public cemeteries from the 1820s began to replace the final resting place of the deceased in church graveyards: 'By the 1850s, the virtual monopoly of the churchyard in accommodating the last remains of the deceased had been irrevocably broken.'[20] Crucially, the large, often landscaped, cemeteries on the outskirts of towns and cities were mostly outside of church control: 'In towns and cities all over Britain, the laying out of cemeteries broke the centuries-old pattern of burial provision, sometimes in a matter of less than a decade.'[21] Disease pandemics, such as Britain's cholera epidemic of 1848–9, completed the divorce from the dead's traditional association with the church.[22] A raft of new legislation throughout the 1850s reinforced this shift, leaving the churchyard as a relic of an earlier era, and presenting the cemetery as a new canvas to display the architecture of the afterlife.[23]

The globalisation of the death industry during the long nineteenth century transformed memorialisation practices too. The greater availability of different materials, the mechanisation of stonemasons' work and greater access to funds also popularised stone commemorations.[24] Both at 'home' in Britain and Ireland and abroad in the diaspora, those with sufficient wealth projected onto the world an agreed account of the deceased. Statements in the secular language of the state displayed on stone – invariably marble, sandstone, granite, or slate – the deceased's key achievements and relationships to the people erecting the memorial. Freed of the restrictive hierarchy of pre-Reformation control, memorialisation practices changed significantly.[25] The secularisation of the language of memorials and their form, mirroring cultural rather than religious trends, transformed what stones looked like.[26] The mourners, normally family but sometimes augmented by kinship or fraternal groups, ascribed the life that needed mourning; they became a mnemonic tool that preserved the memory of the deceased but also reflected the class of the deceased.[27] Visiting the grave, too, became a form of pilgrimage that protracted the deceased's memory, eclipsing society's earlier need to preserve only their spiritual journey.[28]

The production of more diverse headstones and memorial tablets reflected a shift from local to national and international sources of production.[29] Death markers, like other associated ways of remembering the dead such as death cards, samplers, and later newspaper advertisements, were one of many 'new' ways of culturally remembering the dead. They were part of what Beverley Lemire describes as the remaking of the material world in which, for our purposes, headstones were part of a broader change in global consumer cultures.[30] Crucially, the agency of those Lemire termed as 'common people' transformed cultural habits far beyond the metropole, as death culture became one of many 'exercises for public display'.[31] While the sometimes limited memorials to poorer people may have been produced locally, headstones and memorial tablets for discerning mourners could be sourced from distant shores. Not only were memorials transported across ever larger distances over land and sea, but styles and form collectively played a role in 'civilising' remote burial spaces.[32] Epitaphs acted as social statements, yet they remain relevant for communities, even in the face of physical erosion and the detachment of features.[33]

How far, though, can we discern different memorialisation practices within Britain and Ireland and their diasporas? Situated on the western littoral of what had been Catholic Europe, the four nations of Britain and Ireland had different experiences of death culture in the aftermath of Reformation, despite unification of the two kingdoms of England

and Scotland in 1603, and the political union of all four kingdoms in 1801. Stark religious differences among the four nations would remain noticeable until the twentieth century.

For England, the Anglican Church changed some, but not many, practices towards the dead and retained an influence over the form and content of memorials in the only place people 'wanted' to bury their family and friends: the parish churchyard. Clerics played a central role in the administration of the dead, including allocating a space for an internment. Even after the Reformation, spaces within the Anglican Church were expensive, yet those outside in the surrounding churchyard were often limited. Though charged with providing space within the parish, clerics also had some control over the form, style and content of memorials. Reflecting the increased use of the vernacular language in worship after the Reformation, the use of Latin on memorials quickly disappeared. The educational role of the church, especially through Sunday school and parish schools, helped the growth in literacy by the eighteenth century so that more people could read what memorials said. When space ran out by the beginning of the mid-nineteenth century, the church still provided spaces inside the church for memorial tablets, provided they met with clerical expectations. Until the growth of urbanisation witnessed the emergence of a largely secular England by 1851, the Anglican church remained at the heart of village life and thereby village death.

For the Welsh, death became a personal matter after the Reformation. The deceased was not always acknowledged with a grave marker, a practice considered by many as ostentatious. Welsh gravestones were also distinguished through their use of the Welsh language, particularly in Nonconformist burial grounds in urban and rural graveyards. This usage typically included an epitaph or quotation from the Bible. Bilingual stones also demonstrated a knowledge of the Welsh language.[34] This points to a knowledge of Welsh among those commemorating the deceased, and a recognition that others would also understand such ritual.[35] Welsh gravestones were often made from locally sourced slate before the importation of marble and granite in the twentieth century.[36] Unlike other parts of Britain, the Welsh were also less inclined to record occupations on grave markers.[37]

In Scotland, the kirk was no longer involved in the burying or remembrance of the departed after the Protestant Reformation. Ministers may have been asked to officiate at the time of death, but the committal of the deceased was a secular matter. Here, growing Scottish literacy, disproportionate to other parts of the British nation, meant that headstones after c.1715 were more detailed than other parts of the four nations, with noticeable regional, if not local, variance between differing kirkyards. In Kincardineshire during the seventeenth century, for instance, heart motifs were common.[38] Yet the domination of the English language in death culture for most parts of the country denoted the cultural suppression of Scots and Gaelic, even if the Scots dialect was still evident on some graves.[39]

Finally, Ireland, especially after the violent Scottish plantations of Ulster during the seventeenth century, was a society divided in life and death. While the Ulster Scots brought with them freedoms in mourning associated with the Reformation, most of Ireland remained entrenched with Catholicism. Marking Catholic deaths through grave art was unusual. This, though, denoted the growing difference between Ireland and other Catholic nations within Western Europe. Irish headstones are more frequently seen to have complex biographies that extended over generations than those of England, Scotland and Wales.[40] Ulster Scots stones did not replicate the extensive variations of symbols found in Scotland.[41]

COMMEMORATING DEATH IN THE BRITISH AND IRISH DIASPORAS

Changes to death cultures by the British and Irish overseas did not occur in isolation. Instead, the dominant cultural influence of Europe transformed parts of the world affected by the European conquest, trade and settlement taking place from the 1470s onwards. The influence of Puritan settlers in colonial America ensured that changing memorialisation practices in Europe eventually reached all parts of the British World, and not just America.[42]

English and, to a lesser extent, Scottish memorial practices far beyond Europe began to dominate burial traditions in the New Worlds where the British settled. The genesis of that tradition was profoundly influenced by the English Protestant settlement of colonial America from 1608 where English settlers attempted to settle Jamestown. The failure of the Jamestown settlement did not, however, diminish 'British' ambitions to settle overseas. In the ensuing three and a half centuries, English, Scottish, Welsh, Irish and Ulster Scots overseas cemented the British and Irish traditions of both burying and then remembering the dead. While some Catholic, Nonconformist, and even Judaic practices were also exported, 'deathways facilitated communication among peoples otherwise divided by language and custom'.[43] The Protestant tradition of a 'good death' left an abundance of material culture in the churchyards and cemeteries of most British and Irish communities overseas.

It was in this elementary aspect of death that behavioural norms for disposing of the dead became identifiable with the British. Before the erection of churches, administrative buildings and permanent housing were established, the British overseas made organised provision for their dead. The loss of 52 out of 102 English settlers at Jamestown by the first winter of 1620 made the founders of each settlement very conscious of the need to quickly establish a safe and fitting place for burying men, women and children.[44] English provision mirrored other failed settlements, including by the Scottish at Darien, where 1,500 out of 2,800 Scottish settlers died during the doomed project.[45] Both failures illustrate not only the inevitability of death but also the centrality of ensuring a fitting committal for some of the earliest British settlers overseas.

After the emergence of Britain's command of the sea by 1815, *Pax Britannica* enabled not only people to settle different spaces around the world, but the movement of materials from Britain to remember the dead. Stones and words shaped in Britain were transported overseas. As Robert Hutchinson found, Britain's East India Company arranged for blank marble headstones to be on hand for transhipment to India, in anticipation of the need to memorialise remote Britons dying in tropical climates.[46] By the middle of the nineteenth century, words, designs and structures for less elaborate memorials were also bound for secular cemeteries in Ceylon, Canada, South Africa, Australia and New Zealand. While the work of Julie Rugg has explained how cemeteries transformed death landscapes in Britain during the 1820s and 1830s, such ideas on managing the dead also altered the way the British Empire organised death and thereby remembrance overseas. As early as 1827, for example, this included the creation of a new cemetery outside of Freetown, Sierra Leone.[47]

Even so, as Elizabeth Buettner reminds us, European practices were also influenced by cross-cultural contact with other parts of the world. South Asia played 'a pioneering role in what ultimately became predominant trends in European burial practices and commemoration of the dead alike'.[48] Erik Seeman, meanwhile, points to the various cross-cultural encounters colonial Americans had with indigenous Americans, Jews and other Christians.[49] Early death practices in New Zealand's churchyards and cemeteries also took on their own salient features, influenced by new materials and diverse environmental features. Unfamiliar with the new suburban cemeteries appearing in Britain, migrants in the Antipodes replicated instead their familiar 'home' parish churchyards.[50]

Faith and ethnicity led to the creation of separate burial areas within cemeteries, divided by fences, hedges and fauna that have now often disappeared.[51] As such, New Zealand's cemeteries had sections for Catholics, Anglicans, Jews, Chinese and the 'general' population, whereas in Britain such divides were generally only between consecrated and non-consecrated.[52] Only over time did they come to resemble such public cemetery burials as were held back in Britain and Ireland.[53] Even so, materials continued to differ, reflecting the availability of diverse materials throughout the country, such as Oamaru stone in Dunedin.[54] From the 1870s onwards, however, mass-produced headstones became more widespread and marble and granite took over from slate, sandstone, limestone, wood and cast iron.[55]

THIS VOLUME

Scholarly interest in memorials, then, is not new but many previous approaches focus on landscapes in isolation, assess artistic forms of elaborate memorials that were atypical, and prioritise forms of elite memorialisation.[56] Such scholarly attention reflected popular interest by antiquarians and genealogists in this architecture of British death culture. As early as 1875 antiquarians were publishing their findings on memorials in the British Caribbean.[57] All the memorials for Scotland before 1855 have been assembled, firstly, by antiquarians and later by family historians because they provide the sole source of death information in Scotland.[58] David Dobson, meanwhile, has published numerous volumes recording Scottish settlement in continental North America.[59] Moreover, as the jewel in the crown of the nineteenth- and twentieth-century Empire, elaborate memorials in India attracted the energies of scholars and heritage professionals following the demise of empire.[60] Continual scholarly and popular interest in gravestones demonstrates what many have described as the ability of stones to speak to new audiences.[61]

This volume advances ideas first raised by Harold Mytum in his 2003 article on death and remembrance in the colonial context.[62] Mytum's work rightly points to the need to expand the study of death culture, not only in his recent survey of the archaeology below ground, but also to consider the 'normal' men, women and children memorialised on headstones and memorial tablets around the British World.[63] So much of the British and Irish footprint on burial landscapes remains underexplored. In this volume, we have built upon the intellectual interest in colonial America and imperial India to encompass British and Irish settlement in Europe, North America, the Caribbean, Africa, Asia and Australasia. Comparative analysis distinguishes the studies here from earlier work and every chapter purposefully compares and contrasts different temporal and/or spatial contexts. Not all cases examined were the dominant place of settlement; remote spaces, such as the Highlands and Islands of Scotland, or the remote spaces in Western Australia, move beyond the metropolitan gaze because a large proportion of 'British' settlers and sojourners who succumbed to an early death had lived rural lives in remote settings.

While the potency of other memorials from Britain's imperial past remain toxic, especially statues and memorials to Cecil John Rhodes, gravestones have not received as much attention, even that of Rhodes in Zimbabwe.[64] Inevitably, there has been significant erosion of memorials and their texts since discernible 'permanent' overseas settlement began in 1608. Many scholars have discussed how sandstone has eroded with the imperial frontier subject to a series of environmental disasters that have removed or hidden the memorials. As Peter Jupp and Glennys Howarth remind us, 'All societies perpetuate their social boundaries after death. Social distinctions, by gender, age, class or ethnicity, have always been identifiable in the degree of investment in the disposal of the dead and in mortality rates.'[65] Family identity was also a 'bulwark against death' and cemented the strong intergenerational ties between families and localities.[66] Maintaining the stones that form the key evidential base of the chapters in this volume was part of this process.

NOTES

1. Tamar Beeri, 'Dozens of tombstones desecrated at the British cemetery in Haifa', *The Jerusalem Post*, 12 October 2019 <https://www.jpost.com/Breaking-News/Dozens-of-tombstones-vandalized-at-the-British-cemetery-in-Haifa-604337> (accessed 30 October 2019).
2. Ibid.
3. Ibid.
4. Ibid.
5. On the attack of Jewish graves, see Tony Kushner, 'Anti-semitism in Britain: Continuity and the absence of a resurgence?', *Ethnic and Racial Studies*, 3:3 (2013), p. 446. The first battlefield cemetery to British casualties in the Crimean War was attacked in June 2019. See Hannah Lucinda Smith, 'Graves of Britain's Crimean War dead are desecrated, exploited and forgotten', *The Times*, 16 June 2019 <https://www.thetimes.co.uk/article/graves-of-britains-crimean-war-dead-are-desecrated-exploited-and-forgotten-5ljjq8fr8#> (accessed 30 October 2019).

6. Harold Mytum, 'Artefact biography as an approach to material culture: Irish gravestones as a material form of genealogy', *Journal of Irish Archaeology*, 12/13 (2003–4), p. 124; Stephen Deed, *Unearthly Landscapes: New Zealand's Early Churchyards, Cemeteries and Urupā* (Dunedin: Otago University Press, 2015), p. 11.
7. Harold Mytum, 'The language of death in a bilingual community: Nineteenth-century memorials in Newport, Pembrokeshire', in Roger Blench and Matthew Spriggs (eds), *Archaeology and Language III: Artefacts, Languages and Texts* (London and New York: Routledge, 1999), p. 211; Sarah Tarlow, *Bereavement and Commemoration: An Archaeology of Mortality* (Oxford: Blackwell, 1999).
8. Yvonne Inall and Malcolm Lillie, *Deep in Time: Meaning and Mnemonic in Archaeological Studies of Death* (Hull: University of Hull Remember Me Project, 2018), p. 59.
9. Clare Gittings, 'Expressions of loss in early seventeenth-century England', in Peter C. Jupp and Glennys Howarth (eds), *The Changing Face of Death: Historical Accounts of Death and Disposal* (Basingstoke: Macmillan, 1997), p. 20.
10. Harold Mytum, 'Artefact biography', p. 116.
11. Inall and Lillie, *Deep in Time*, pp. 63–4.
12. J. Mack Welford, 'American death and burial custom derivation from medieval European cultures', *The Forum: Newsletter of The Association for Death Education and Counselling* (September/October 1992), p. 12.
13. Thomas W. Laqueur, *The Work of the Dead: A Cultural History of Mortal Remains* (Princeton, NJ: Princeton University Press, 2015).
14. Deed, *Unearthly Landscapes*, p. 18.
15. Elizabeth Hurren and Steve King, '"Begging for a burial": Form, function and conflict in nineteenth-century pauper burial', *Social History*, 30:3 (2005), pp. 321–41.
16. Cemeteries could demonstrate different approaches to memorialisation by different branches of Christianity. See, for example, Alessandro Gusman and Cristina Vargas, 'Body, culture and place: Towards an anthropology of the cemetery', in Marius Rotar and Adriana Teodorescu (eds), *Dying and Death in 18th–21st Century Europe* (Newcastle upon Tyne: Cambridge Scholars Publishing, 2001), p. 214.
17. Philippe Aries, *Western Attitudes Toward Death: From the Middle Ages to the Present* (Baltimore, Md: Johns Hopkins University Press, 1974), p. 49.
18. Angus Graham, 'Headstones in post-Reformation Scotland', *Proceedings of the Society of Antiquaries of Scotland*, 91 (1957–8), p. 1.
19. Julie Rugg, *Churchyard and Cemetery: Tradition and Modernity in Rural North Yorkshire* (Manchester: Manchester University Press, 2013).
20. Julie Rugg, 'The origins and progress of cemetery establishment in Britain', in Jupp and Howarth (eds), *The Changing Face of Death*, p. 105.
21. Ibid.

22. Deed, *Unearthly Landscapes*, pp. 23, 26.
23. Ibid., p. 95.
24. Harold Mytum, 'Scotland, Ireland and America: The construction of identities through mortuary monuments by Ulster Scots in the seventeenth and eighteenth centuries', in Audrey J. Horning, Nick Brannon, Peter Edward Pope (eds), *Ireland and Britain in the Atlantic World* (Dublin: Wordwell, 2009), p. 236.
25. Inall and Lillie, *Deep in Time*, p. 59.
26. Ibid., p. 59.
27. Paula Vita, 'In keeping with modern views: Publishing epitaphs in the nineteenth century', *Victorian Review*, 25:1 (1999), p. 16.
28. Laqueur, *Work of the Dead*, p. 59.
29. Harold Mytum, 'A comparison of nineteenth- and twentieth- century Anglican and Nonconformist memorials in North Pembrokeshire', *Archaeological Journal*, 159 (2002), p. 235.
30. Beverley Lemire, *Global Trade and the Transformation of Consumer Cultures: The Material World Remade, c.1500–1820* (Cambridge: Cambridge University Press, 2018).
31. Ibid., p. 271.
32. Jennifer Van Horn, *The Power of Objects in Eighteenth Century British America* (Chapel Hill: University of North Carolina Press, 2017), especially pp. 156–213.
33. Harold Mytum, 'Artefact biography', pp. 114–15; Erik R. Seeman, *Death in the New World: Cross-Cultural Encounters, 1492–1800* (Philadelphia: University of Pennsylvania Press, 2010), p. 43.
34. Mytum, 'A comparison', pp. 194, 209, 222.
35. Mytum, 'The language of death', p. 214.
36. Mytum, 'A comparison', pp. 213, 216.
37. Mytum, 'The language of death', p. 461.
38. Mytum, 'Scotland, Ireland and America', p. 237.
39. Ruth McManus, *Death in a Global Age* (Basingstoke and New York: Palgrave Macmillan, 2012), p. 115.
40. Mytum, 'Artefact biography', pp. 113, 117.
41. Mytum, 'Scotland, Ireland and America', pp. 241–3.
42. Seeman, *Death in the New World*.
43. Ibid.
44. Marilyn Yalom, *The American Resting Place: 400 Years of History Through Our Cemeteries and Burial Grounds* (Boston and New York: Houghton Mifflin Company, 2008), p. 6.
45. Mark Horton, '"To transmit to posterity the virtue, lustre and glory of their ancestors": Scottish pioneers in Darien, Panama', in Caroline A Williams (ed.), *Bridging the Early Modern Atlantic World: People, Products, and Practices on the Move* (London: Routledge, 2009), p. 131.
46. Personal correspondence between Nicholas J. Evans and Robert Hutchinson,

28 February 2018. Hutchinson identified that the references within the British Library's archives of the East India Company: IOR/E (EIC general correspondence 1602–1859) and IOR/Z/E, Registers 1753–1858.
47. The National Archives (Kew), MPH 1/881/11, 'Sierra Leone. Plan of Freetown: Town plan showing streets' (1836). The plan, produced for Lieutenant Governor Campbell, includes both a drawing of the 'New Burial Ground' and a note planning to extend the burial provision in an area outside of the main city. The cemetery is the Circular Road Cemetery, Freetown opened in 1827.
48. Elizabeth Buettner, 'Cemeteries, public memory and Raj nostalgia in post-colonial Britain and India', *History and Memory*, 18:1 (2006), p. 10.
49. Seeman, *Death in the New World*.
50. Deed, *Unearthly Landscapes*, p. 56.
51. Ibid., p. 66.
52. Ibid., pp. 71–2.
53. Ibid., p. 10.
54. Ibid., p. 65.
55. Ibid., pp. 65, 105.
56. Howard Colvin, *Architecture and the After-Life* (New Haven and London: Yale University Press, 1991); Barbara Groseclose, *British Sculpture and the Company Raj: Church Monuments and Public Statuary in Madras, Calcutta, and Bombay to 1858* (Newark and London: University of Delaware Press, 1995); Joan Coutu, *Persuasion and Propaganda: Monuments and the Eighteenth-Century British Empire* (Montreal and Ithaca: McGill-Queen's University Press, 2006).
57. James H. Lawrence-Archer, *Monumental Inscriptions of the British West Indies: From the Earliest Date, with Genealogical and Historical Annotations, with Engravings of the Arms of the Principal Families* (London: Chatto & Windus, 1875).
58. See, for example, David Christison, *The Carvings and Inscriptions on the Kirkyard Monuments of the Scottish Lowlands: Particularly in Perth, Fife, Angus, Mearns and Lothian* (Edinburgh: Neill and Co., 1902).
59. David Dobson, *Scottish Immigrants to North America, 1600s-1800s: The Collected Works of David Dobson (Family Archives)* CD-ROM: Vol. 1 (Novato and Baltimore: The Genealogical Pub. Co., 1999); David Dobson, *Scottish Immigrants to North America, 1600s-1800s: The Collected Works of David Dobson (Family Archives)* CD-ROM: Vol. 2 (Novato and Baltimore: The Genealogical Pub. Co., 2011).
60. Groseclose, *British Sculpture and the Company Raj*; British Association for Cemeteries in South Asia, *South Park Street Cemetery, Calcutta: Register of Graves and Standing Tombs: From 1767* (London, 1992).
61. David Rome and Jacques Langlais, *The Stones That Speak: Two Centuries of Jewish Life in Quebec* (Montreal: Baraka Books, 1990).
62. Harold Mytum, 'Death and remembrance in the colonial context', in Susan

Lawrence (ed.), *Archaeologies of the British: Explorations of Identity in Great Britain and its Colonies 1600–1945* (Abingdon: Routledge, 2003), pp. 156–73.
63. Harold Mytum and Laurie Burgess (eds), *Death Across Oceans: Archaeology of Coffins and Vaults in Britain, America, and Australia* (Washington, DC: Smithsonian Institution Scholarly Press, 2018).
64. Paul Maylam, 'Monuments, memorials and the mystique of Empire: The immortalisation of Cecil Rhodes in the twentieth century', *African Sociological Review*, 6:1 (2002), p. 142; Gertrude Makhafola, 'Mugabe takes swipe at Rhodes statue', <https://www.iol.co.za/news/politics/mugabe-takes-swipe-at-rhodes-statue-1842288> (accessed 1 September 2019).
65. Peter Jupp and Glennys Howarth, 'Introduction', in Jupp and Howarth (eds), *The Changing Face of Death*, p. 3.
66. Ibid., p. 4.

2

Forgetting and Remembering: Scots and Ulster Scots Memorials in Eighteenth-century Ulster, Pennsylvania and Nineteenth-century New South Wales

Harold Mytum

Diaspora studies may prioritise what is remembered over what is forgotten, but through migration more aspects of culture are lost or greatly adapted than retained, and often many new cultural traits are absorbed or created, so the relationship between the two is crucial.[1] An archaeological perspective offers a distinctive approach to the material aspects of culture whereby the role of continuity and remembering can be set against a wider set of cultural changes in practice. Migratory peoples take with them material culture from their homeland, but more long-lasting and culturally significant are their already learnt practices, skills and attitudes which affect behaviour in their new environment and which are passed on, however modified, to successive generations. This includes what artefacts are made, by what techniques, and in which style, as well as how those artefacts are used functionally and how they create and recreate meaning. Archaeologists are trained to infer movement, connections, cultural interactions and socio-economic conditions from material remains, and now do this from the remote past right up to the present day. Migrations of the early modern and modern periods are as amenable to archaeological studies as any other, and they provide a distinctive perspective on migration to set alongside those from cultural or art history, or human geography.

For the most recent periods of human history, there are many non-material ways of approaching past societies, and many of the social, economic and ideological structures are already relatively well known and do not require elucidation by archaeology. Historical archaeology can therefore start from a different perspective. For example, we already know of the seventeenth-century migration of Scots to Ulster, when they took place, and in general who was involved.[2] The danger, then, is that the material world is used merely to illustrate what is already known, that is, how academics from other disciplines have incorporated material items in their discussions. This chapter, in contrast, uses material evidence to reveal interactions, processes and cultural change not otherwise recorded, and provides interpretations beyond the traditional historical narrative. It is conceived within a theoretical framework based on relational networks whereby people and things have agency within socio-cultural structures which, with no migration, are largely culturally inherited and may have many conservative self-regulatory features, but on moving to a new location are more fluid and open to transformation.[3]

There is one further issue which requires some attention: how archaeologists choose to make inferences from material culture.[4] The signalling of identity can be either conscious or unconscious. The subconscious 'ways of doing' that form most cultural practices may be perpetuated without its identifying quality being known by the human actors until they are confronted with an alternative. This is part of social memory, the ways of doing which include the design, manufacture and use of material culture and the activities it enables. Social memory, developed by sociologists such as Paul Connerton,[5] but widely applied by archaeologists, is a concept which allows the exploration of the ways by which a group can remember, and how social practices (and for archaeologists the material goods and practices which leave a physical signature) can be perpetuated. However, that perpetuation through repetition does not preclude change, either deliberate or accidental. Both personal and social memory is socially constructed in every present situation at which it is evoked, and the context and nature of that present affects what is remembered and the associative values it contains. Actors may consider that their memories are accurate and authentic, but they may evolve through repetition in different contexts. The process of migration, and the inevitable construction of the culture in very different socio-cultural and environmental contexts, affects what may be remembered, which may veer towards nostalgia,[6] be extremely selective, or may perpetuate horror, as with Holocaust survivors' families experiencing perpetual trauma.[7] The perpetuation of memories involves considerable amounts of forgetting, and some creation and adaptation of recollections; where these have material referents or outcomes, an archaeological approach can consider these processes.

We in the present may identify a past practice as culturally distinctive, but those at the time may not have perpetuated this practice for that reason. Migration often highlights such differences. An unconscious cultural choice in Scotland, where everyone drew from the same

Presbyterian repertoire, became conscious when set against the 'other' of the Catholic indigenous Irish, for example in terms of appropriate clothing or expectations of hospitality. Some Scottish settlers were Catholics, and class identity also cut across religion, so ethnicity or any other single factor, such as class, formed part of a network of relationships that defined any individual's identity – an identity which was fluid and differentially emphasised in various social contexts. A similar set of challenges in even more alien and multicultural environments faced the Ulster Scots settlers in North America and in Australia.

REMEMBERING AND FORGETTING

Memorials mark identities as expressed in a particular locale – the burial ground and the family plot. Only selected features of that person's identity could be expressed in text and monument form and style. Even at the point of monument selection, some things are remembered in that they are signalled, but much else is omitted. The omitted is then often rapidly forgotten. Academics, anxious to demonstrate cultural continuities following migration, have concentrated on what is present and not on what is absent. This chapter attempts to weave, where possible, both present and absent, remembered and forgotten, into the analysis. Both processes are socially and culturally significant, though knowledge once forgotten in one generation inevitably cannot be passed on at a subsequent time. There is therefore a decay rate of the donor culture, but this is neither random nor insignificant.

Connerton has emphasised the importance of forgetting as a positive cultural adaptation.[8] Indeed, the loss of memories and practices associated with a homeland are part of a package of acquisition of new memories and practices that are associated with the diasporic journey itself and the often fluid and short-term changes in circumstance in the process of settling in a new land. Memorials form a valuable category of material culture to explore migrant culture and its relationship to homeland because they serve the same primary function of marking graves, wherever in the world they are erected, and are not as heavily dependent on levels of socio-economic complexity or density of population to be viable. Thus, dispersed colonial contexts may still enable stone memorial production and erection, unlike some powerful cultural practices which require access to a range of products including fragile imports, such as tea drinking. Other practices, such as folk music, may be maintained through the carrying of instruments by migrants, but these have rarely left any early material traces (though the first piano imported to Australia, in 1788, has just been recovered and is to be conserved).[9] Stone memorials, especially on burial grounds which have continued in use to the present day, provide a significant window into the early migrant experience, identity, and cultural behaviour.

Emphasis in this chapter is on the memorials of migrants or their relatively close descendants (generally the first generation that created stone memorials which survive), in early-eighteenth-century Ulster and Pennsylvania, and nineteenth-century New South Wales. Subsequent generations will themselves remember and forget, or even re-remember or revive, cultural attributes including those from a homeland, but these are not the main focus of attention in this study. Scots-Irish or Scotch-Irish terminology was rarely used in the eighteenth century. Rather, this wording is used by North American claimants of that ancestry, and is a product of the later nineteenth and twentieth centuries' desire by Presbyterians to distance themselves from Catholic Irish migrants. Its contemporary manifestation in festivals and events has minimal links to the cultures and practices of the initial Ulster Scots settlers, but has been used by many historians celebrating this particular migrant group.[10]

MEMORIALS

Erecting a stone monument at a gravesite only became a significant cultural practice in the seventeenth century in Britain and Ireland, and indeed was still rare until the early eighteenth century and only began much later than this in many other areas;[11] why different regions initiated external popular memorials when they did has not yet been fully mapped let alone explained, but it is clearly not based on one cause such as wealth, population density, religious denomination or the availability of suitable stone to carve. This study starts near the beginning of this process as some of the early-adopter regions were in Scotland and then Ulster, and so provides an opportunity to explore the process of identity formation in different cultural contexts across the eighteenth and nineteenth centuries.

The seventeenth- and eighteenth-century memorials were generally made according to local folk-art traditions.[12] The elite could sometimes, but not always, commission monuments in more sophisticated styles, and these cosmopolitan styles gradually became more commonly available on less substantial memorials during the eighteenth century. By the late eighteenth century, many memorials were produced in relatively standardised forms as all aspects of the funerary industry grew into a profession. These trends were further developed in the nineteenth century as more industrial processes became incorporated, including the use of imported materials and ready-cut memorials, sometimes even with decoration, produced at quarries with only the inscriptions added locally.[13] North America and, latterly, Australia follow these same overall trends, though there are some regional variations.[14] What is important here is to realise that popular memorial production and choice was not a static phenomenon, but the base line of normative practice was changing over time and this needs to be factored into assessment of the role of migration and remembering and the changes in monument selection. Moreover, although there were global trends in changing commemoration, there were also national variations to which any migrating population would have to adapt.[15]

Grave monuments are not like other categories of evidence available to us in assessing remembering and forgetting in the context of migration. Their most important feature to an archaeologist is that they are both physical – with a material, shape and style – as well as textual (itself physical with style variations in carving, lettering size and layout). For people in the past, their most important feature was that they were a publicly visible statement, a marker of burial for the deceased but chosen by the living and made and viewed by the living.[16] Memorials may in part be about the dead, but they are largely for those still surviving. While monument choice was for the family, memorials formed part of a network of monuments within the commemorative landscape of the burial ground, existing not in isolation but spatially and visibly in relationship with others in a dynamic setting in which gradually more and more monuments were erected. Each monument was selected and erected in the context of what had gone before at that locale. Choosing the same style as others or a different one, being interred in a family group or separated, were decisions based in part on ingrained unconscious cultural practices and also explicitly decided social strategies. This chapter concentrates on monuments as individual artefacts to indicate what was retained and what was forgotten, but the decisions by those commissioning the memorials were made against a rich context of alternatives. Other discussions could focus on issues of standardisation and conformity, the commissioner–carver relationship, or monuments in their burial-scape, but here monuments are considered as discrete items of material culture each created by the combined agency of family and carver. The former wished to remember some parts of their culture and the identity of the deceased, and the latter applied their skills and traditions with the technologies and resources available in that context. The carvers may or may not have shared the cultural tradition of the bereaved, but they had to produce a result satisfactory to the client. The net result is that aspects of identity and memory can be represented in text, form and style but other aspects are omitted or represented in a transformed way which may therefore become re-remembered or forgotten.

Research in the social sciences, history and historical geography has recognised the fluid social construction of identity within Ulster.[17] This chapter offers a theoretically informed archaeological perspective as an addition to this literature. The material culture correlates of ethnicity – items that are considered to have been produced exclusively by that group – have been the concerns of many archaeologists, notably from culture-historical interpretations,[18] with subsequently functionalist claims regarding style and ethnicity becoming more popular in the later twentieth century, with interpretations that emphasised the communicative role of material culture in representing and communicating identity.[19] More recently, post-processual discussions on ethnicity and identity have come to the fore, with more nuanced consideration of claims regarding ethnicity.[20] Different environments, and access to resources, technology and skilled manpower, all affected the perpetuation of traditional housing and agricultural practices by migrant groups. As such, these provide only a partial insight into the desire to retain and remember the culture of the homeland by the migrant actors as they created their new homes and livelihoods. Forgetting how to grow crops that are unsuitable in a different climate is hardly surprising; houses are social spaces where cultural practices may be remembered and perpetuated, but the migrant family unit may not contain the generational spread of the homeland, and the home may have to be made from different materials to be effective in a different climate, or to be part of a landscape populated in a different manner and with people not, initially at least, having an established social network. Memorials do not have the same level of constraint. A source of suitable stone is required, and availability of carvers would affect the quality and elements of the design. Within Scotland, it is clear that geology affects the style of carving but is not the cause of variation in the symbolic repertoire, and memorials can be more or less accomplished from a technical or aesthetic viewpoint but still function quite adequately, socially and emotionally, in their context. This suggests that where there is sufficient disposable income and resources, the production of adequate stone memorials can be undertaken in communities soon after migration. All these may not be available in the early stages of settlement when farmsteads are being established and resources such as suitable stone identified, but by the time that they are, cultural change will already have begun.

If commemorative practice in stone was delayed for several generations, any details of memorials in the homeland may have been completely forgotten or are extremely attenuated. It is unlikely that detailed descriptions of family memorials would have been the subject of fireside stories to be passed on down the generations to act as a catalyst for agency when the opportunity arose. This forgetting assumes, however, no contact with the homeland that, in the case of both Scotland with Ulster, and Ulster with America or Australia, is not the case. Continued movement across the seas of people (largely, but far from exclusively, emigrating), and the interchange of ideas through written correspondence and printed material, created a network of communication that ensured the potential for cultural awareness[21] which could include commemorative practice. Moreover, the movement of carvers would in itself lead to the transfer of mental templates of monuments that would form the basis for the creation of new memorials in a new land. Apprentice carvers who never knew the homeland would learn the techniques and design conventions from their masters and so perpetuate, though with their own interpretation and adaptation, this tradition. These apprentices could be related to migrants or could be others with different ancestry who still learned a distinct style from their master. As carvers worked in regional traditions in Britain and Ireland in the seventeenth and eighteenth centuries,[22] traces of these can be recognised in the migrant communities. By the nineteenth century, the styles were national and indeed international, and different evidence of remembering and forgetting can be identified for migrants of this period.

Many disciplines have used funerary monuments to consider the material effects of migration into North America.[23] Indeed, the Ulster Scots experience has been given particular attention in Ulster[24] and then in America.[25] An extensive study by Daniel Patterson has concentrated on the identification of carvers with Ulster Scots origins,[26] a study situated within the tradition of north-eastern gravestone carver studies.[27] Patterson provides a more cultural and wider historical context than many of the other published carver studies, but still assumes the primacy of the carver in design of the memorials. Most emphasis to date has been concentrated on the products of the secondary Ulster Scots migration from Pennsylvania to the Carolinas as far more memorials survive from this phase.[28] They reveal further shifts in identity and memory, but the analysis here concentrates only on the Ulster experience and its selective remembering and forgetting in the first generations after migration, and therefore only in Pennsylvania. In order to understand the initial Ulster Scots commemorative choices, however, it is necessary to first define the Scottish mortuary traditions with which they were familiar and on which they drew in their new homelands.

THE SCOTTISH MORTUARY TRADITION

Commemoration in graveyards by families beyond the major landowners began in the first half of the seventeenth century in Scotland, and the oldest post-Reformation headstone known in Britain and Ireland is from Dunning, Perthshire, recording a death in 1623.[29] The use of stone ledgers (flat, usually rectangular, slabs covering the grave), was more widespread, however, though as these were larger they would have been more expensive. It was the introduction of the headstone, generally relatively small in the seventeenth and eighteenth centuries, which provided an option for permanent commemoration for those with less resources, and by the mid-eighteenth century this was a relatively common choice among successful tenant farmers and tradesmen in many parts of Scotland.[30] The monuments erected across Scotland demonstrate clear regional differences both in monument shape and relative popularity of motifs. These preferences include coffins in Angus, full figure representations in Peeblesshire, and heart motifs in Kincardineshire.[31] However, this has been only anecdotally recorded and no chronology or detailed spatial analysis of these patterns is as yet available.

While the total range of mortality symbols used in the Scottish repertoire is very wide indeed (Table 2.1), many are regionally specific and even from the eighteenth century onwards more optimistic symbols such as the cherub (or winged soul), and the Glory of God (radiance) appear in most areas, albeit often in combination with mortality symbols. An arrangement with cherub at the top of the stone (indicating the soul heading towards heaven) and mortality symbols at the bottom (representing the abandoned and decaying corpse) is a frequent choice. During the eighteenth century, mortality symbols decline in popularity and cherubs increase, in part as theology shifts to place less emphasis on judgement of sin and more on the salvation of the elect, but only in the nineteenth century do the former stop being chosen, followed a few decades later by cherubs, as flowers and other symbols take over as part of a rise in romantic form of remembrance.[32] A distinctive design feature of a significant minority of early Scottish headstones is also to have some motifs carved on the back of the stone. In some cases, there is only text on one side and symbols on the other, but in other examples

Table 2.1 Memorial symbols. Symbols frequently occurring on memorials in Scotland. Those commonly found in Ulster are marked in bold; those in bold with parentheses are less common.

Mortality Symbols	Other symbols
Angel of Death	Abraham and Isaac
Axe	Anchor
Bell	Angel
Bones	Book
Bow and Arrow	**Cherub**
Coffin	Crown
Corpse	The Glory
Dart Death	Heart
Death-bed scene	**Heraldry**
Death's Head Skull	Portrait
Fall of Man (death) with Adam and Eve	Resurrection scene
Father Time	Rosettes
Green Man	**(Trade symbols)**
Hourglass	
Pick	
Scythe	
Skeleton	
(Snakes)	
Spade	
Spear or lance	
Turf-cutter	
Winged Skull	

the text can be accompanied by decoration with other elements carved on the rear.

Socially significant symbols frequently occur on memorials, notably heraldry in whole or part, or trade symbols, often themselves derived from the coat of arms of the relevant guild.[33] The guilds were powerful in urban contexts, but in rural parishes symbols associated with agriculture and fishing were more common. While the family name was the main indicator of identity, the occupation symbols clearly also played a significant role. Family could also be reinforced by the use of heraldry and, despite the role of the Court of the Lord Lyon in Edinburgh to suppress arms that had not been approved, many were unofficial.[34] These may have had no obvious inspiration or could have been a pun on the family name. They could create an aura of high social standing which may have had no legal status but would indicate an aspiration and affiliation and communicate to the local population who may or may not have known this was not an authentic armorial bearing. Therefore, from the seventeenth century onwards, Scots were aware of the potential of commemorative monuments in stone being placed over graves in burial grounds not just by the major families but by others with disposable income and a desire to demonstrate their commitment to family and place. The popularity of the mortality symbols were indicative of a Presbyterian mindset, with the trade and guild affiliations demonstrating the Protestant virtue of work. Heraldry and text affirmed familial identity, with wives often retaining their maiden names on the memorials and so demonstrating the genealogical connections to the descendants who would visit the grave and memorial. Commemoration was therefore a socially embedded practice in Scotland, and it is not surprising that it was transferred in the mindsets and practices of the Scots who decided to move to Ulster and settle there.

ULSTER

Graveyard memorials were erected relatively early in several parts of Ireland, for example the north of Dublin and in County Wexford,[35] where both Catholics and Anglo-Irish Anglican Protestants erected monuments in regional styles that developed in those localities from the early eighteenth century onwards. Many parts of Ireland, however, have no evidence of a strong monumental tradition until the middle or even late eighteenth century. In the north of Ireland, the commemorative traditions developed differently, and the influence of the Scottish dimension was clear from the start. Both Catholics and Protestants erected memorials from a similar point in time – the early eighteenth century – but they developed their own monumental traditions even if aspects of Scottish funerary culture were taken and adapted by each community for their own purposes. This phenomenon is more complex than just forgetting and remembering; it is rather more one of creation and recreation utilising forms and motifs for related – but at times competing – social strategies.[36]

The Scottish settlers in Ulster show some regional differences in monument form and style within the province, but only a restricted range of symbols were selected (Table 2.1). As yet, there has not been sufficient regional analysis of memorials across the whole province to identify the various regional dynamics, but research at over twenty burial grounds in Fermanagh and Monaghan has revealed intelligible patterns. Of the great range of mortality symbols in Scotland, just five were selected for use on most memorials in this region. The skull, crossed bones, coffin, hourglass and bell were all mortality symbols, and these appear as well as heraldry. The Galbraith family ledgers at Aghalurcher, County Fermanagh, may be similar to reinforce familial identity, but external memorials at that graveyard to other families are also remarkably similar in their own styles.[37] This site, and indeed others in this region, demonstrate wider planter culture through form – particularly the ledger – and the use of heraldry and mortality symbols. Family identity is reinforced through the heraldic device, prominent surname visibility in the commemorative texts, and additionally by the arrangement of graves and their overlying ledgers in rows forming family areas within the graveyard. For some Protestant families these could be extensive and long-lived, emphasising familial success and a genealogical pedigree. These were particularly important as part of the justification of landholding to the whole community as the same burial grounds were used also by the indigenous Catholic families (some of whom had been displaced during the Ulster Plantations from the estates they had owned, to be replaced by the Protestant families commissioning the ledgers) and who still retained some areas of the graveyards for their own use and created their own memorial styles to differentiate themselves from the incomers.[38]

Not only the range of forms but also the carving styles and motif arrangements do not reveal the variation seen in Scotland, but they can be paralleled most closely in Angus on the east coast of Scotland. The Angus memorials frequently display the same array of mortality symbols, often in a line at the base of a ledger with heraldry at the top and a text panel in the centre. The mortality symbols show consistency in selection but their arrangement together and their stylistic treatment is not identical to that in Ulster. This reveals a number of craftsmen all working to a similar mental template of what a memorial should look like. The similarity in Fermanagh and Monaghan suggests one or more carvers coming from this area and recreating these manifestations there. This does not mean that the clients had similar origins, but rather that from their wider Scottish mortuary traditions and expectations these memorials were effective and appropriate. Moreover, within the Ulster settler context it was satisfactory to forget any wider repertoire, and indeed what was remembered by commissioners and within the skill set of the carvers was adapted into appropriate forms for that new setting.

There are, therefore, three key factors that can explain the similarities and differences between Scottish and Ulster commemorative practice. The first is the shared commemorative traditions which create the mental templates of what comprise an effective and appropriate memorial. These traditions are largely (though not exclusively) linked to Presbyterian beliefs and the power of the *momento mori* message that is visible through textual emphasis on the presence of the body and the symbols relating to the burial of the corpse. The other aspect of this template is one that places emphasis on family, visible through heraldry and kinship terms in the texts. The second factor is the limited choice of carver in any one part of Ulster, even more restricted than in Scotland, particularly for the more competent products which could only be afforded by few in this relatively sparsely populated region. This explains the limited repertoire drawn from an Angus carver heritage, pointing to the origins of the producers even if locally born descendants were then trained in this tradition. The shift from Scotland to Ulster meant that only part of the cultural diversity present in the homeland was transferred, a pattern seen widely in archaeologically attested migrations.[39] The third factor is that the planter context provided a different socio-cultural environment where conformity of the incomers was essential in the face of an established, albeit subjugated, Irish Gaelic majority. The Gaelic Irish had their own markedly different cultural, religious and socio-political traditions by which they marked their own family graves with their own distinctive memorials, thus emphasising differences in death as well as in life. The Catholics in this region adopted some of the symbols found on planter stones, but used them in a distinctive manner on denominationally unique memorial forms.[40]

EIGHTEENTH-CENTURY PENNSYLVANIA

Large numbers of migrants from Ulster settled in Pennsylvania from the early eighteenth century onwards, and some moved westwards and established communities on the frontier of European settlement.[41] Some of these settlements established Presbyterian chapels with associated burial ground which survive and in some cases continue in use to this day. The limited amount of research thus far carried out on the Pennsylvania memorials relevant to this study has been with a primary focus on identifying the products of the Bigham family carvers.[42] This family came from Ulster and supplied carved monuments to their fellow immigrants in a number of settlements within the state, though other carvers are known from the variety of designs. Scholars concerned with identifying products of named carvers have the advantage in many parts of New England of more probates surviving within which the memorial commissions are identified and the carvers named, allowing some unsigned stones to be linked to the producers.[43] Unfortunately, the numbers of probates surviving for the areas of Ulster Scots settlement are small. Relatively little use, however, has been made of the evidence for the commissioners from the documentary sources, or the wider material referents that a comparative study of the burial ground assemblages of memorials can reveal. This section provides some results from the second of these approaches, identifying the remembered and repeated Ulster components, Scottish referents not used in Ulster, and new components not present in either homeland. It is based on data collected from five burial grounds linked to congregations with high Ulster Scots membership (Chestnut Level, Derry, Donegal Springs, Great Conewago, and Lower Marsh Creek) with a total sample of *c*.400 recorded memorials (Figure 2.1). The Ulster Scots settlers lived in communities where they may have been the majority, but were also initially in close proximity to native peoples with whom they were antagonistic and, in the longer term, Pennsylvania Dutch settlers with whom they had relationships which were not always amicable.[44] The 'other' therefore shifted from being largely Presbyterian Scottish versus Catholic Irish to one where different Protestant sects from different ethnicities were in play.

The exact date of erection for monuments may not match dates of death, shown by reference to commemorations by known carvers in New England but with death dates before they could have started work.[45] Meanwhile, in Britain and Ireland there are memorials which have explicit erection dates carved on them as well as death dates of those commemorated.[46] Nevertheless, the death dates provide a generalised framework even if some caution has to be exercised and too fine-grained a sequence cannot be assumed.

The burial grounds in Pennsylvania that relate to the earliest appearance of stone memorials are relatively small, some being adjacent to churches, and others being family plots on farms. Many of the latter have been destroyed, sometimes with their memorials moved to a nearby communal burial ground. The Great Conewago church contains some of the most well-known Ulster Scots memorials.[47] A classic example at the most elaborate end of the range of products was that to John Brown (d.1766) which has strong parallels in its decoration with Ulster ledgers (Figure 2.2a). It has a heraldic achievement, but it is an invention in terms of the symbols within the shield. Here are depicted the (red) hand of Ulster, adopted in the seventeenth century as a symbol of Ulster, but also centre stage is the thistle of Scotland. The thistle does not occur on memorials in Scotland or Ulster, and the hand of Ulster is extremely rare, and generally associated with heraldry where it forms a legitimate part. The small crescent moon and star do also occur on Ulster memorials, though more often on headstones rather than on

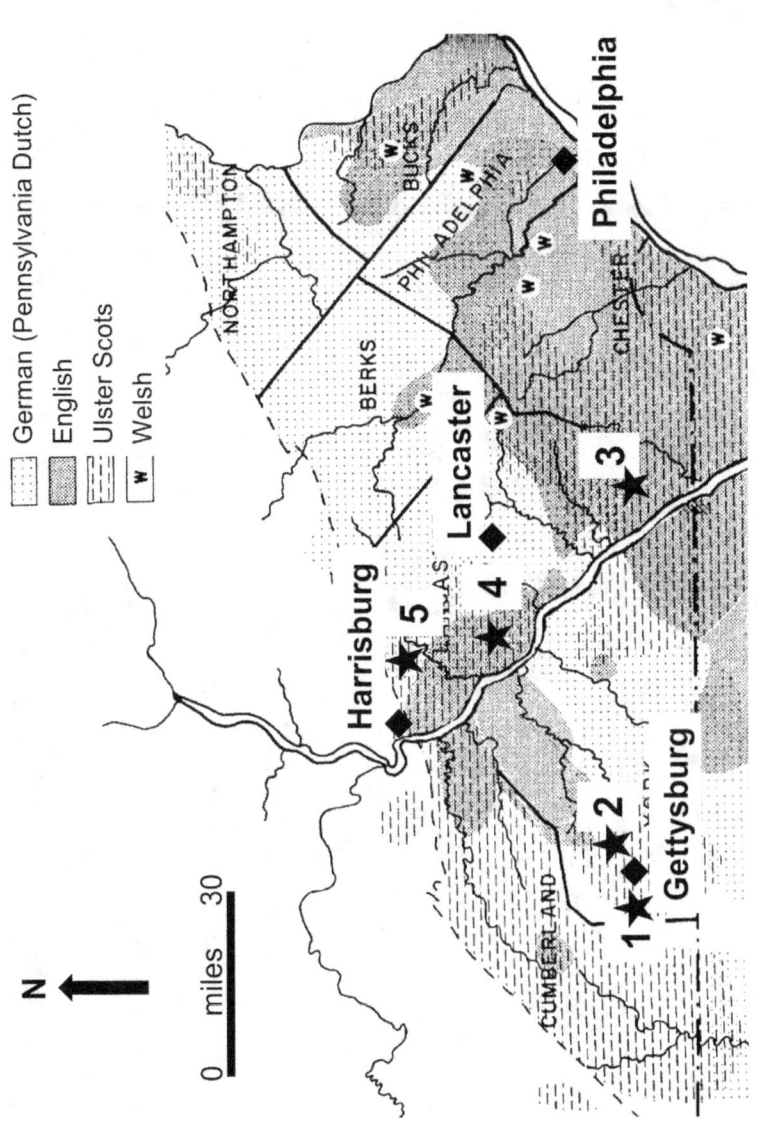

Figure 2.1 Ulster Scots settlement and Presbyterian burial grounds surveyed.
Key: 1 Lower Marsh Creek, 2 Great Conewago, 3 Chestnut Level, 4 Donegal Springs, 5 Derry.
(Artwork: Harold Mytum, base map adapted from Lemon 1972)

Figure 2.2 Pennsylvania memorials with heraldic devices: **a** John Bell, Great Conewago; **b** John Brown, Great Conewago. (Photos: Harold Mytum)

ledgers with heraldry as seen in these Pennsylvania examples. An almost contemporary ledger to John Bell (d.1765) depicts the thistle, but the hand holds a sword and is a distinct heraldic element, and instead of moon and star there is a dove, another completely new element absent from homeland mortuary traditions in the eighteenth century (Figure 2.2b). Patterson demonstrates how the dove was a significant part of the Bigham workshop repertoire, and indeed becomes almost ubiquitous in North Carolina products after the family's move south.[48] It is notable, however, that the dove is already developing in the Pennsylvania output, so rather than remembering common Ulster motifs, new ones are chosen to create new traditions and material identifiers, which then form part of the remembered tradition in North Carolina. While the dove has many meanings on memorials – peace or the Holy Spirit are common attributions given to nineteenth-century depictions – it has been argued that the Pennsylvania and then Carolinas examples represent the dove from the Genesis story of Noah and the ark and may be taken as a symbol of the Presbyterian church and children of grace (members of the elect, like Noah and his family).[49]

Some of the earlier headstone memorials indicate varied attempts at remembering and forgetting. A headstone to John King (d.1727) had a sinuous profile which is similar to some Ulster headstones, and besides a beaded border displayed a central small heraldic device: a lion rampant in a small shield. A fiercer, horizontally depicted lion, with some mantling, forms the design for Martha King (d.1760). These demonstrate motifs from heraldry being extracted, losing their original meaning as part of a composition, to be reproduced as a decoration; whether they carried any meaning or were just associated with the known repertoire of motifs on memorials is unknown. At a similar time, Mary Cord (d.1736) was commemorated with a round-topped, square-shouldered sandstone headstone with text defined by an incised border but beneath were two round-topped arches flanked by tulips which are derived not from Ulster or Scotland, but from the Pennsylvania Dutch cultural tradition. Another feature of that tradition is the 'waisted' headstone shape where the headstone has concave sides, another trait seen at Great Conewago. This burial ground reveals memorials belonging to this Presbyterian congregation being produced by a range of carvers with different cultural traditions, and indeed the Bighams and other Ulster Scots carvers incorporate such motifs into their designs. This can be seen in another early headstone to George Leckey (d.1734); it is in slate and has lettering like other Bigham workshop stones but displays a complex top profile and concave sides (Figure 2.3a) which is paralleled

Figure 2.3 Pennsylvania memorials with waisted sides: **a** Robert Larimer, St Paul's New Chester (Lutheran); **b** Mary Cord, Great Conewago. (Photos: Harold Mytum)

in some numbers at nearby Lutheran burial grounds (Figure 2.3b). This is an example of assimilation and cross-cultural transfer that reflects creativity and the consequent willingness to forget older motifs which no longer hold the same significance. The slate headstone to James Ross (d.1741) has a modified sinuous outline, and displays the hand with sword and some mantling, a precursor to that on the Bell ledger.

Cherubs are relatively rare in Ulster, and they are similarly scarce in Pennsylvania, but Great Conewago has two examples of the sinuous profiled headstones for Shusanna Peters (d.1759) and Hannah Gordon (d.1764); the latter has a 'CG' monogram probably indicating the carver, notably not a Bigham. There are no mortality symbols on any of the memorials at this site, though these were still popular in Scotland and Ulster when the first Great Conewago headstones were being erected. By the time that most of the memorials were being carved, mortality had been superseded by other motifs in the homeland, but at some of the other sites a few mortality symbols appear, though these may be inspired by their continued use on some nearby Lutheran burial ground monuments. It is notable, however, that they do not appear to have been remembered in an Ulster form, and certainly there is no conservatism in the colonial carving styles.

The ways in which the heraldic elements were losing their meaning and association is particularly evident on the headstone for Denis Murphy (d.1747) where the central sheaf of wheat is flanked by foliage, including possibly thistle leaves, with, to the right, a hand in a gauntlet holding a dagger looking like it is ready to cut the plant. That other motifs were adapted is shown on Elizabeth Gall's headstone (d.1758) where a central tulip, now more realistic than in Pennsylvania Dutch symbolism, is combined with foliage and roses.

The less than thirty dated memorials from Great Conewago demonstrate the forgetting, remembering, assimilating and creating all underway in the first and into the second generation of monument makers. The larger sample of around eighty monuments at Lower Marsh Creek reveals a similar pattern, but with many more featuring a centrally placed crown with flanking spirals, though on occasion the latter are replaced with tulips or stars (Figure 2.4a), and are all clearly produced by a different carver. The crown is another symbol not commonly seen in Scotland and even more rarely in Ulster, and even where found is not on the form that it is consistently portrayed on the Pennsylvania stones. The crown, like the dove in the Bigham's repertoire, is an innovation not relying on a remembered set of motifs, but may have been selected to represent the Crown of Righteousness, a significant concept in Presbyterian theology and based on 2 Timothy 4:8. However, the Crown of Life in Revelation 2:10, and James 1:12, and the Crown of Glory (of 1 Peter 5:4) may be what is depicted. The overriding message in a funerary context, however, is likely to have been the crown won in the race of life and for the faith of the deceased, whichever crown may have been intended.

A further eighty eighteenth-century memorials at Chestnut Level reveal a pattern with very few features that could have been derived from an Ulster heritage. There are only headstones for this period at this site, and most are shapes not familiar in Ulster. One memorial boasts a heraldic element similar to some at Great Conewago – in this case a winged griffin – and three memorials have mortality symbols in terms of crossed bones and, in some cases, also skulls (Figure 2.4b). The damaged memorial to … h McCilkry (d.1744) has a central cherub but crossed long bones on one side; what matched these is unknown (Figure 2.4c). However, the mortality symbols can also be paralleled on some memorials in Pennsylvania Dutch burial grounds, and on the other two the inspiration could have been derived from either tradition. The complexity of headstone profiles here and at Chestnut Level suggests innovation rather than remembrance of tradition, and the other motifs suggest a wide range of influences of which Ulster may be only one, and not in a form distinctive enough to be strongly signalling identity or that of cultural memory. At Derry and Donegal Springs, symbolism is rare on the *c*.200 memorials in these burial grounds, but some headstone profiles have parallels in the homelands. The remembering at these locales is subtle at best, and more likely to be a product of subconscious aesthetic choices matching mental templates of appropriate monument forms than an explicitly remembered evocation of homelands. Clearly, the desire to remember the Ulster Scots identity was not equally strong across all communities, though it may be that the carvers available to the Chestnut Level bereaved had a background that was not sympathetic to or knowledgeable of those Ulster forms and motifs, even if the clients' families came from that area.

Patterson has made comparisons with some memorials in Larne, County Down, which have some stylistic similarities to the Bigham stones, including those at Great Conewago.[50] These can certainly be seen, but that is in part because of similar geology leading to the same type of shallow relief carving and incised fine detail, which is only possible in fine-grained and hard slate-type rocks. Many of the features on the Pennsylvania stones are found more widely in Ulster, though manifested in other areas with more deeply carved styles appropriate to the local

Figure 2.4 Pennsylvania memorials with crowns and mortality symbols: a Margrate MaGinley (d.1771), crowns, Lower Marsh Creek; b John Clark (d.1776), skull and crossed bones, Chestnut Level; c McCilroy (d.1744), cherub and crossed long bones, Chestnut Level. (Photos: Harold Mytum)

sandstones and limestones which were used for all memorials at those sites. The Pennsylvania stones only exceptionally repeat the overall composition of Ulster ledgers and, even then, the use of motifs such as the thistle are not derived from those prototypes. The headstones at Great Conewago, Lower Marsh Creek, and even more so at Chestnut Level, Derry and Donegal Springs, reveal the extent of forgetting and, where there is remembering, it is both selective in terms of motifs and forms which are themselves used in new ways. A weak thread can be traced, but only on some memorials is the remembering strong and capably articulated materially. The understandable focus on these exceptions hides the culturally more important and widespread forgetting as the Ulster Scots settlers adjusted to, and embraced, the new continent and its opportunities and freedoms.

NINETEENTH- AND EARLY-TWENTIETH-CENTURY NEW SOUTH WALES

The settlement of Australia by Ulster Scots was particularly heavy in several areas during the middle and later nineteenth century, though in all cases they were not the majority population.[51] Graveyard data was collected at three burial grounds in an area south of Sydney that had been particularly densely settled by migrants from Ulster (Kiama, Jamberoo, Gerringong, total 400 excluding Roman Catholic memorials)[52] and in the Presbyterian section of Rookwood Cemetery, Sydney. Together, these provide a sufficient sample to consider Ulster migration and the ways in which the migrants chose to commemorate their heritage.

The rural sites around Kiama, in the southern coastal region of New South Wales, offered rolling countryside with mixed farming opportunities that were, despite the different climate, more familiar to Ulster settlers than many other regions. Indeed, two parts of Ireland provided most migrants to Australia, including Clare, Tipperary and Limerick, and the south Ulster counties of Fermanagh, Cavan and Armagh.[53] A system of government subsidy enabled many to migrate to the colony, organised by each state. The New South Wales remittance system commenced in 1848 and lasted until 1886, allowing money from existing residents to be paid towards passage on vessels chartered by the Colonial Land and Emigration Commission.[54] The Presbyterian minister Revd J. D. Lang toured Ulster promoting Australian colonisation in 1848,[55] and it is notable that the Ulster migration had an over-representation of the proportion of Protestants over Catholics. The Kiama region was a stronghold of Protestantism – both Anglican and Presbyterian – and of Orangeism, due to influential landowners in the area encouraging migration from the relevant communities in Ulster to work on their estates; a rare memorial with Orange Order symbolism to William Clark (died 1894), originally of County Fermanagh, still stands in Kiama Cemetery.[56] There is no doubt that a form of chain migration explains the Kiama region's Ulster influx, where family, friends and neighbours follow those they know in a pattern of migration to regions about which they have heard and to stay initially with people who could support them in the period of transition to an alien environment.[57]

The Kiama region sites produced valuable data, and this demonstrates how in this region places of origin are frequently mentioned on migrants' memorials in a variety of styles, but no iconography exists (Figures 2.5a and 2.5b). Rookwood is instead the main focus of discussion here as consideration of the Ulster Scots in the context of commemoration alongside Scottish emigrants provides a particularly valuable insight into remembering and forgetting. Rookwood Cemetery is the largest cemetery in Australia, opening in 1867, and had provision for delivery of coffins and funeral parties to the site by train, with its own mortuary station stop.[58] The cemetery, as was common in Britain and the colonies at this time, was divided into denominational sections, one of which was Presbyterian,[59] and this is where the field survey took place.

The symbolic representation of origins was extracted from the sample of 280 photographically recorded monuments, but the inscribed transcriptions for the whole of the Presbyterian section of 2,150 first-named individuals on memorials provides a robust sample from the late nineteenth and early twentieth centuries. Given the context of large numbers of Roman Catholic migrants (both convicts and free) to Australia,[60] the Ulster Scots were, as they had been in Ulster, keen to differentiate themselves from this group. The Catholic Irish were discriminated against by the political authorities and most of the established business interests, and the Ulster Scots affiliated themselves closely with the largely Presbyterian Scots as part of this differentiation.[61] The Rookwood Presbyterian section of the cemetery therefore forms an appropriate arena within which affiliation, remembering and forgetting can be examined.

A great number of the memorials are of forms popular in Scotland and parts of Ulster at this time, the latter due to the continued close contacts between the two. The Rookwood monuments were not imported from the home country, but they were designed in similar styles. While Romanesque and Gothic revival monuments are common (Figures 2.6a and 2.6b), the most common – and most evocative of

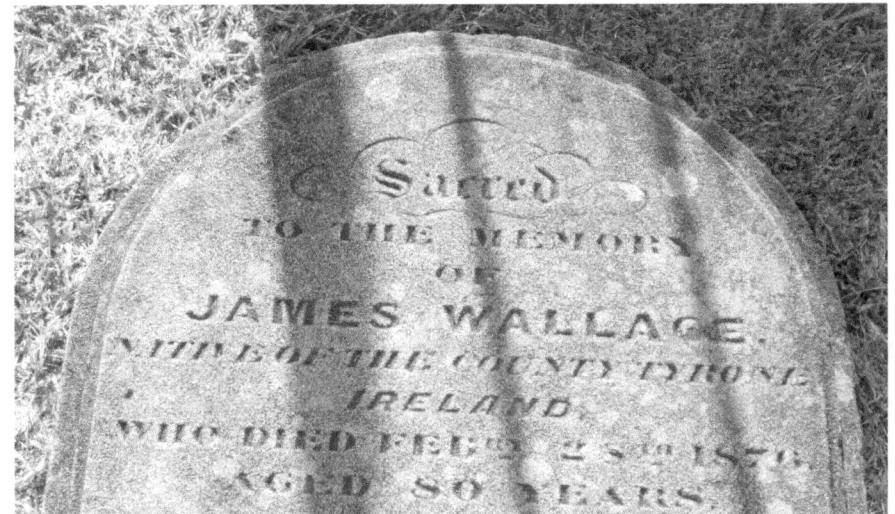

Figure 2.5 Presbyterian Kiama region memorials with Ulster origins stated:
a James Wallace (d.1876), County Tyrone, Jamberoo Presbyterian burial ground;
b Alice Chesters, County Monaghan, Jamberoo Presbyterian burial ground.
(Photos: Harold Mytum)

Figure 2.6 Memorials in the Presbyterian section, Rookwood, Sydney: **a** Isabella Robinson (d.1869) thistle, Newton Stewart, Tyrone; **b** Eliza Thompson (d.1871), Newry County Armagh; **c** Agnes Cleland (d.1884), thistle, Glasgow; **d** Margaret Morton (d.1871), thistle, Lanarkshire. (Photos: Harold Mytum)

c

d

the Scottish repertoire – were the Classical revival headstones set on bases and with minimal foundation elements (Figures 2.6c and 2.6d). It is uncertain to what extent these were being chosen because they explicitly evoked a Scottish mortuary culture, or because they were implicitly selected from the range of alternatives offered by the monumental mason and just seemed 'right'. Also, once the form became well established in the Presbyterian section, it may have been a strategy of new immigrant families that, conforming to existing popular memorial choices, emphasised their inclusion within the group. They could thus demonstrate their conformity within the new community and encourage full acceptance for the next generation as new networks of mutual support were forged in the colonial context far from the old kin-based systems. These headstones have relatively few symbolic or decorative features, as was common both in the homeland at that time and among other memorials in the Presbyterian section, but a minority do display thistles in a variety of arrangements (Figures 2.6a, 2.6c and 2.6d), a design absent from nineteenth-century memorials in Scotland. Just as the thistle was evoked in Pennsylvania, the same occurs in Rookwood. Most thistle motifs are on memorials erected to Scots, but one is to an Ulster migrant (Figure 2.6a), and this motif also occurs in the Ulster Scots rural New South Wales sample. No hands of Ulster were used, and no Ulster motifs appear, even on the one individual identified by his Orange Lodge title.

The main method of explicitly remembering was through the inscription, where the place of origin was often placed in italics in a slightly smaller font than the name, and directly between it and the date of death and age (Figure 2.6). An impressionistic assessment of these memorials indicates that many of the Catholic Irish were content to attribute origin to county (unless it was a large settlement such as Cork or Limerick), whereas the Protestant tendency was more often to emphasise the town (though the county could also be mentioned), perhaps because migrants had urban associations. The Presbyterian section data demonstrates the dominance of Scottish origins, with a small minority from Ulster (Figure 2.7). There were no mentions of Ulster as a location term, even though Scotland was often referenced. Intriguingly, some inscriptions state 'NB' (North Britain), emphasising not a Scottish but a North British identity. It is clear that the explicitly Ulster aspects of identity were not being revealed in an environment where Irish associations were seen as negative for any plans for social and economic advantage, and affiliation with things Scottish took priority. Even the Scottish heritage was no longer emphasised after one generation as it was only the initial migrants

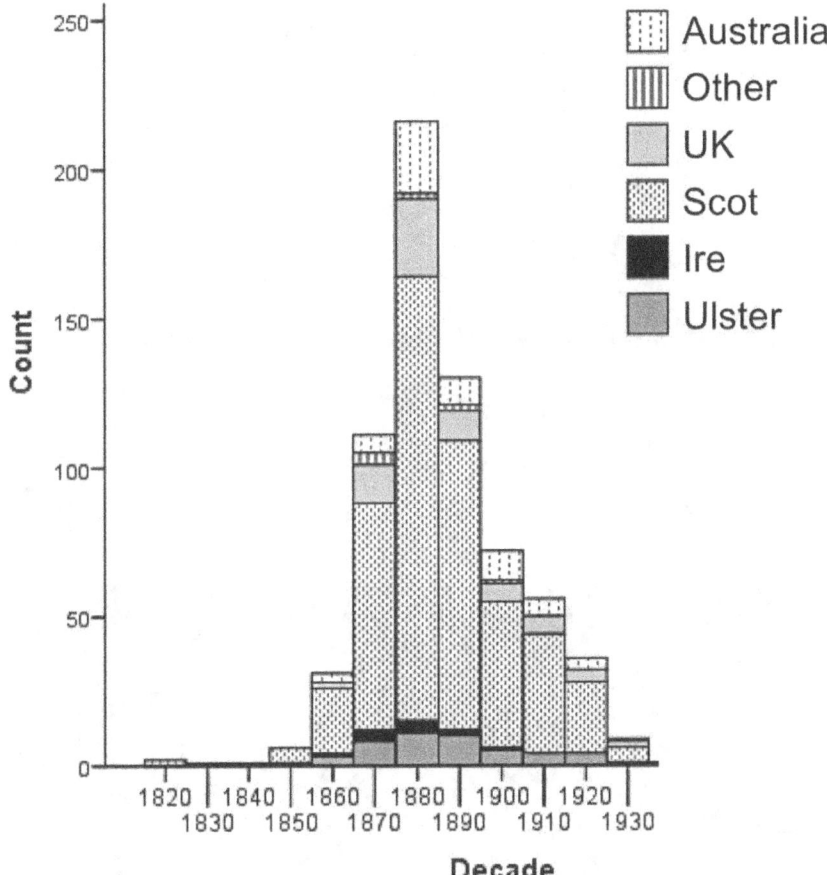

Figure 2.7 Bar graph of stated places of origin by country, Presbyterian section memorials, Rookwood, Sydney. The sample consists of those first mentioned on the memorials. (Data: Harold Mytum)

who signalled their places of origin; two thirds of the memorials in the Presbyterian section had no place of origin stated. Some Australian birthplaces were mentioned, but some of the first-generation and most of the second-generation population did not consider this information worth publicly displaying.

The forgetting of origins is notable in Australia, partly because ethnic or nationalist symbols retained by the Catholics, including shamrocks and harps (Figures 2.8a and 2.8b) do not have popular Protestant equivalents. Statements of place of birth necessarily no longer show Ulster ancestry after the first generation of migrants, but Irish Catholic affiliation – despite or perhaps because of discrimination in the wider

Figure 2.8 Irish symbols on Roman Catholic memorials: a John Collins (d.1901) harp and shamrocks, Jamberoo Roman Catholic burial ground; b Johanna Bourke (d.1886) shamrocks, Gerringong. (Photos: Harold Mytum)

society and economy – lasted longer. Joining the dominant Protestant colonial discourse was more important for Ulster settlers than remembering their heritage, though the Orange Order may have provided one set of social networks that did remain active, and could allow integration with the more numerous Scottish Presbyterian community. The thin thread of remembrance in Pennsylvania can be seen as even more slender in New South Wales. The Protestant–Catholic divisions remained as active as before, but were part of a dynamic within Australia that was dominated by the English and where the Ulster migrants sought allegiance with the Scots. That this reflected part of their Ulster heritage may not have been unrecognised and is seen in the occasional use of the thistle on the Rookwood monuments.

CONCLUSIONS

The choices made by the carver and bereaved together led to the creation of culturally meaningful and socially active artefacts of remembering which stood in the publicly accessible burial ground. Embedded with numerous subconscious norms of endemic practice and belief, conscious choices were made in terms of text and symbol on a memorial of a deliberately chosen form. In Scotland it was family and occupation that were the priority for remembering, as these identifiers were the principal dimensions for social definition which were to be emphasised in the funerary context. Memorials did not generally have long expository texts extolling skills and virtues of the deceased (though a few elite monuments did display such texts, though often with their own remarkably standardised tropes). Therefore, most aspects of the deceased persona, and most of their familial and wider social roles and identities, let alone their character and achievements, were not recorded, and so unavailable to subsequently prompt remembrance.

The Scots settling in Ireland retained the family as a key identifier, but place of residence became a frequent addition. In a newly claimed land, where fluidity in ownership and occupation was far greater and more uncertain than in the homeland, statement of place was both a sign of the present but a marker for the future. Religious affiliation that had been unconsciously taken for granted in the homeland was now an explicit identifier in the presence of the 'other'. Both Catholic and Protestant Scottish planter families indicated their loyalties, and at times this expanded to political affiliation. The need to state, reinforce, remember and perpetuate these beliefs was necessary as the Protestant minority created a material world distinctive from that of the Catholics who used the same graveyards and selected their own symbolic repertoire to the same ends from their perspective.

Pennsylvania saw Ulster Scots create new identities that largely did not rely on material culture replicating with that remembered from across the Atlantic. For a minority, aspects of their commemorative traditions (such as the Great Conewago ledgers with their heraldry, and some of the headstone shapes at Derry and Donegal) were either unconsciously or deliberately retained, and some traditional symbols of identity were newly conscripted to signal identity in ways that they had not been so used in Ulster (including decontextualised heraldic elements). However, elements derived from other migrant groups, such as the tulips and the waisted headstone profiles, were also incorporated, and new motifs such as the dove, and the crown which was so popular at Lower Marsh Upper, indicate innovation. Some of the mortality symbols as seen at Chestnut Level may have resonated with a traditional Ulster Scots mentality, but they were as much derived from another tradition seen in some of the neighbouring Lutheran burial grounds.

The evidence from New South Wales comes from a period when most Protestant memorials – in the British Isles and in Australia – had less complex iconography and texts that emphasised sentimental feelings between family members rather than wider social identities. Nevertheless, it is notable that Presbyterian Ulster migrants were less likely to reveal their origins than those from Scotland through symbols, though in many cases migrants may be remembered with reference to their place of birth. The survival over several generations of elements of Ulster mortuary practices, is, however, completely absent in Australia. The second generation indicates through memorial choices that it is fully integrated with Australian society and its cultural practices and preferences. Some aspects of funerary culture still replicate some features from Britain, but this is because of ongoing distribution of trade items (including coffin fittings and probably trade catalogues) within a colonial context rather than deliberate signalling of origins.

Identities are socially constructed, fluid and contingent. This can be seen in the three different geographical arenas of Ulster, Pennsylvania and New South Wales where individuals made particular choices about how they or their deceased relatives should be defined. Scotland, then Ulster, followed by either North America or Australia, form chains of interlinked contexts each with their own individual internal dynamics that affected how identities were constructed and claimed, but with some shared traits that can be identified. A comparative approach can identify how individual agency of both producer and commissioner can create memorials which allow the modern researcher access to the processes of cultural change that were in operation in these different locales. Aspects of past identities are retained or even revived in new contexts, as also new identities and associative symbols are acquired.

Much is forgotten along the migratory way, but some cultural traits and indicators of identity are retained, albeit rarely for long.[62] This combination of deliberate remembering and passing on or of forgetting can be a by-product of transient lifestyles, early deaths of migrants and problems in establishing traditional carver repertoires in frontier contexts. The creation of new histories must, however, be seen as the most powerful reason for forgetting. These new social and physical landscapes where details of family history could not be corroborated are clean slates for many escaping the challenges and frustrations of their homelands. The great interest in genealogy and ancestry linking back to distant homelands is a recent phenomenon that is enacted by those at a certain level of affluence, and with well-established socio-economic networks.[63] Some of the narratives created within these emergent nostalgic identities have been contested, but they remain popular and are culturally significant today.[64] It was often neither relevant nor advisable to look backwards in an emerging colonial context where the present and the future were more relevant and where the creation of affiliations in the new environment were more urgent than harking back to identities forged thousands of miles away.

The memorials of the Scottish and then Ulster Scots diaspora tell us valuable stories, and no less so for what is forgotten, remembered and created along the way. We, in our time and place, now choose to create new interpretations of these memorials, another stage in the creation and recreation of knowledge, here with academic actors providing a different dynamic and perspective on this complex past.

Acknowledgements

Finbar McCormick kindly advised on suitable west Ulster sites to survey when I commenced fieldwork, and work on the Ulster burial grounds has been supervised by Robert Evans and Kate Chapman as part of annual international archaeological field schools. Some of the data used in this chapter was collected during field research carried out with a grant from the Arts and Humanities Research Council.

NOTES

1. Julia Creet and Andreas Kitzmann (eds), *Memory and Migration: Multidisciplinary Approaches to Memory Studies* (Toronto: University of Toronto Press, 2014); Vijay Agnew (ed.), *Diaspora, Memory and Identity: A Search for Home* (Toronto: University of Toronto Press, 2005); Thomas Lacroix and Elena Fiddian-Qasmiyeh. 'Refugee and diaspora memories: The politics of remembering and forgetting', *Journal of Intercultural Studies*, 34:6 (2013), pp. 684–96.
2. John R. Young and William P. Kelly, *Scotland and the Ulster Plantations: Explorations in the British Settlement of Stuart Ireland* (Dublin: Four Courts Press, 2009); Jonathan Bardon, *A History of Ulster* (Belfast: Blackstaff Press, 1992).
3. Carl Knappett (ed.), *Network Analysis in Archaeology: New Approaches to Regional Interaction* (Oxford: Oxford University Press, 2013); Pedro Paulo Funari, Andrés Zarankin, and Emily Stovel (eds), *Global Archaeological Theory: Contextual Voices and Contemporary Thoughts* (New York: Springer Science and Business Media, 2005).
4. Paul A Shackel, and Barbara J. Little, 'Post-processual approaches to meanings and uses of material culture in historical archaeology', *Historical Archaeology*, 26:3 (1992), pp. 5–11; Ian Hodder (ed.), *Archaeological Theory Today* (Cambridge: Polity Press, 2012).
5. Paul Connerton, *How Societies Remember* (Cambridge: Cambridge University Press, 1989).
6. Susannah Radstone, 'Nostalgia: Home-comings and departures', *Memory Studies*, 3:3 (2010), pp. 187–91.
7. Jeffrey C. Alexander, 'Toward a theory of cultural trauma', in Jeffrey C. Alexander, Ron Eyerman, Bernard Giesen, Neil J. Smelser and Piotr Sztompka (eds), *Cultural Trauma and Collective Identity* (Berkeley: University of California Press, 2004), pp. 620–39.
8. Paul Connerton, 'Seven types of forgetting', *Memory Studies*, 1:1 (2008), pp. 59–71.
9. 'First Australian piano comes home to UK after 231 years', *The Guardian*, 31 March 2019, <https://www.theguardian.com/australia-news/2019/mar/31/first-australian-piano-comes-home-to-uk-after-231-years> (accessed 3 July 2019).
10. Kevin Kenny, *The American Irish: A History* (London: Longman, 2000); Celeste Ray, *Highland Heritage: Scottish Americans in the American South* (Chapel Hill: University of North Carolina Press, 2015); Christina Wilson, 'Illegible ethnicity and the invention of Scots-Irish narratives on the stages of Belfast and Appalachia', *Irish Studies Review*, 23:2 (2015), pp. 194–208.
11. Harold Mytum, *Mortuary Monuments and Burial Grounds of the Historic Period* (New York: Kluwer Academic/Plenum Publishers, 2004); Harold Mytum, 'Popular attitudes to memory, the body, and social identity: The

rise of external commemoration in Britain, Ireland, and New England', *Post-Medieval Archaeology*, 40:1 (2006), pp. 96–110; Sarah Tarlow, 'Romancing the stones: The graveyard boom of the later 18th century', in M. Cox (ed.), *Grave Concerns: Death and Burial in England 1700 to 1850* (York: Council for British Archaeology Research Report, 113, 1998), pp. 33–43.

12. Mytum, *Mortuary Monuments*; Betty Willsher, *Understanding Scottish Graveyards. An Interpretative Approach* (Edinburgh: Council for British Archaeology Scotland, 1985); Peter Benes, *The Masks of Orthodoxy: Folk Gravestone Carving in Plymouth County, Massachusetts, 1689–1805* (Amhurst: University of Massachusetts Press, 1977); Sherene Baugher and Richard F. Veit, *The Archaeology of American Cemeteries and Gravemarkers* (Gainesville: University Press of Florida, 2014).
13. Mytum, *Mortuary Monuments*; Baugher and Veit, *Archaeology of American Cemeteries*.
14. Baugher and Veit, *Archaeology of American Cemeteries*.
15. Mytum, *Mortuary Monuments*; Tarlow, 'Romancing the stones'.
16. Mytum, *Mortuary Monuments*.
17. Sean J. Connolly, *Religion, Law and Power: The Making of Protestant Ireland 1660–1760* (Oxford: Clarendon Press, 1992); Patrick Griffin, *The People with No Name: Ireland's Ulster Scots, America's Scots Irish, and the Creation of the British Atlantic World, 1689–1876* (Princeton, NJ: Princeton University Press, 2001); Michael A Poole, 'In search of ethnicity in Ireland', in Brian Graham (ed.), *In Search of Ireland: A Cultural Geography* (London: Routledge, 1997), pp. 128–47; Benjamin Bankhurst, *Ulster Presbyterians and the Scots Irish Diaspora, 1750–1764* (Basingstoke: Palgrave Macmillan, 2013).
18. V. Gordon Childe, *Piecing Together the Past: The Interpretation of Archaeological Data* (London: Routledge & Kegan Paul, 1956).
19. James R. Sackett, 'Style and ethnicity in archaeology: The case for isochrestism', in M. W. Conkey and C. A. Hastorf (eds), *The Uses of Style in Archaeology* (Cambridge: Cambridge University Press, 1991), pp. 32–43.
20. Sian Jones, *The Archaeology of Ethnicity: Constructing Identities in the Past and the Present* (London: Routledge, 1997).
21. Kerby A. Miller, Arnold Schrier, Bruce D. Boling, and David N. Miller (eds), *Irish Immigrants in the Land of Canaan: Letters and Memoirs from Colonial and Revolutionary America, 1675–1815* (Oxford: Oxford University Press, 2003); Griffin, *The People with No Name*; Robert J. Dickson, *Ulster Emigration to Colonial America 1718–1775* (London: Routledge, 1966); Warren R. Hofstra (ed.), *Ulster to America: The Scots-Irish Migration Experience, 1680–1830* (Knoxville: University of Tennessee Press, 2011).
22. Eoin Grogan, 'Eighteenth-century headstones and the stone mason tradition in County Wicklow: The work of Dennis Cullen of Monaseed', *Wicklow Archaeology and History*, 1 (1998), pp. 41–63.

23. Mytum, *Mortuary Monuments*; Baugher and Veit, *American Cemeteries Gravemarkers*; E. Eckert, 'From Moravia to Texas: Immigrant acculturation at the Cemetery', *Markers*, 19 (2002), pp. 174–211; Richard E. Meyer (ed.), *Cemeteries and Gravemarkers: Voices of American Culture* (Ann Arbor: UMI Research Press, 1989); Richard E. Meyer (ed.), *Ethnicity and the American Cemetery* (Bowling Green: Bowling Green State University Popular Press, 1993); Mytum, *Mortuary Monuments*; Baugher and Veit, *American Cemeteries Gravemarkers*.
24. Harold Mytum, 'Mortality symbols in action: Protestant and Catholic early-eighteenth-century West Ulster,' *Historical Archaeology*, 42:1 (2009), pp. 160–82; Harold Mytum, 'Archaeological perspectives on external mortuary monuments of plantation Ireland', in J. Lyttleton and C. Rynne (eds), *Plantation Ireland: Settlement and Material Culture, 1550–1650* (Dublin: Four Courts Press, 2009), pp. 165–81.
25. Edward W. Clark, 'The Bigham carvers of the Carolina Piedmont: Stone images of an emerging sense of American identity', in R. E. Meyer (ed.), *Cemeteries and Gravemarkers: Voices of American Culture* (Ann Arbor: UMI Research Press, 1989), pp. 31–59; David H. Watters, 'Fencing ye tables: Scotch-Irish ethnicity and the gravestones of John Wright', *Markers*, 16 (1999), pp. 175–209; Harold Mytum, 'Scotland, Ireland, America: The construction of identities through mortuary monuments by Ulster Scots in the seventeenth and eighteenth centuries', in A. Horning and N. Brannon (eds), *Ireland and Britain in the Atlantic World* (Dublin: Wordwell and Irish Post-Medieval Archaeology Group, 2009), pp. 235–52.
26. Daniel W. Patterson, *The True Image: Gravestone Art and the Culture of Scotch Irish Settlers in the Pennsylvania and Carolina Backcountry* (Chapel Hill: University of North Carolina Press, 2012).
27. James A. Slater, 'Principles and methods for the study of the work of individual carvers', in P. Benes (ed.), *Puritan Gravestone Art*, The Dublin Seminar for New England Folklife, Annual Proceedings (Boston: Boston University Press, 1976), pp. 9–13; Peter Benes (ed.), *Puritan Gravestone Art II*, The Dublin Seminar for New England Folklife 3 (Boston: Boston University Press, 1978); Ralph L. Tucker, 'The Mullicken family gravestone carvers of Bradford, Massachusetts, 1663–1768', *Markers*, 9 (1992), pp. 23–57; Vincent F. Luti, *Mallet and Chisel: Gravestone Carvers of Newport, Rhode Island, in the 18th Century* (Boston: New England Historic Genealogical Society, 2002).
28. Patterson, *The True Image*.
29. Betty Willsher and Doreen Hunter, *Stones: Eighteenth-Century Scottish Gravestones* (Edinburgh: Canongate Books, 1978), p. 2
30. David Christison, 'The carvings and inscriptions on the Kirkyard monuments of the Scottish Lowlands', *Proceedings of the Society of Antiquaries of Scotland*, 36 (1902), pp. 280–457; Angus Graham, 'Headstones in

Post-Reformation Scotland', *Proceedings of the Society of Antiquaries of Scotland*, 91 (1958), pp. 1–9.
31. Willsher and Hunter, *Stones*, p. 7.
32. Sarah Tarlow, *Bereavement and Commemoration: An Archaeology of Mortality* (Oxford: Blackwell, 1999).
33. Willsher and Hunter, *Stones*, p. 62.
34. Theodore Chase and Laurel K. Gabel, 'Headstones, hatchments and heraldry, 1650–1850', in Theodore Chase and Laurel K. Gabel, *Gravestone Chronicles II* (Boston: New England Historic Genealogical Society, 1997), pp. 496–604; Patterson, *The True Image*, pp. 134–49.
35. Harold Mytum, 'Local traditions in early eighteenth-century commemoration: The headstone memorials from Balrothery, Co. Dublin and their place in the evolution of Irish and British commemorative practice', *Proceedings of the Royal Irish Academy*, 104C (2004), pp. 1–35; Grogan, 'Dennis Cullen of Monaseed'.
36. Mytum, 'Mortality symbols in action'.
37. Ibid.
38. Ibid.
39. Stefan Burmeister, Marc Andresen, David W. Anthony, Catherine M. Cameron, John Chapman, Manfred K. H. Eggert and Heinrich Härke, 'Archaeology and migration: Approaches to an archaeological proof of migration', *Current Anthropology*, 41:4 (2000), pp. 539–67.
40. Harold Mytum, 'Folk art in context of time and space', in G. Moloney (ed.), *Inscribed Histories: Burial Grounds, Folk Art and Archaeology* (Monaghan: Monaghan County Council Heritage Office, 2009), pp. 62–73; Mytum, 'Mortality symbols in action'; Eóin W. Parkinson and Eileen M. Murphy, 'Memorialisation, settlement and identity in post-Plantation Ulster: Ardess Old Graveyard, County Fermanagh', *Familia*, 33 (2017), pp. 103–47.
41. Dickson, *Ulster Emigration to Colonial America*; Kerby A. Miller, *Ireland and Irish America: Culture, Class, and Transatlantic Migration* (Dublin: Field Day Publications, 2008); Marion Casey and J. J. Lee (eds), *Making the Irish American: History and Heritage of the Irish in the United States* (New York: New York University Press, 2007).
42. Patterson, *True Image*.
43. See numerous studies of New England carvers in the journal *Markers*; Theodore Chase and Laurel K. Gabel, 'The Park family carvers of Groton, Massachusetts', in Chase and Gabel, *Gravestone Chronicles II* (Boston: New England Historic Genealogical Society, 1997), pp. 286–353.
44. Dickson, *Ulster Emigration to Colonial America*; Estyn Evans, 'The Scotch-Irish in the new world: An Atlantic heritage,' *The Journal of the Royal Society of Antiquaries of Ireland* 95, 1/2 (1965), pp. 39–49; James G. Leyburn, *The Scotch-Irish: A Social History* (Chapel Hill: University of North Carolina Press, 1962); Kenny, *The American Irish*.
45. James A. Slater, Ralph L. Tucker and Daniel Farber, 'The colonial gravestone

carvings of John Hartshorne', in Benes (ed.), *Puritan Gravestone Art II*, pp. 79–146.
46. Harold Mytum, 'The dating of graveyard memorials: The evidence from the stones', *Post-Medieval Archaeology*, 36 (2001), pp. 1–38.
47. Clark, 'Bigham carvers'; Patterson, *The True Image*.
48. Patterson, *The True Image*.
49. Patterson, *The True Image*, pp. 172–6; Andrew R. Holmes, *The Shaping of Ulster Presbyterian Belief and Practice, 1770–1840* (Oxford: Oxford University Press, 2006).
50. Patterson, *The True Image*, pp. 119–25.
51. Dianne Hall, 'Defending the faith: Orangeism and Ulster Protestant identities in colonial New South Wales', *Journal of Religious History*, 38:2 (2014), pp. 207–23; Patrick R. Ireland, 'Irish Protestant migration and politics in the USA, Canada, and Australia: A debated legacy', *Irish Studies Review*, 20:3 (2012), pp. 263–81.
52. Hall, 'Defending the faith'; Lindsay Proudfoot and Dianne Hall, 'Points of departure: Remittance emigration from South-West Ulster to New South Wales in the later nineteenth century', *International Review of Social History*, 50:2 (2005), pp. 241–77.
53. David Fitzpatrick, *Oceans of Consolation: Personal Accounts of Irish Migration to Australia* (New York: Cornell University Press, 1994), p. 13.
54. Proudfoot and Hall, 'Points of departure', p. 248.
55. Ibid., p. 255.
56. Ibid., Fig. 6.
57. David Fitzpatrick, 'Irish emigration in the later nineteenth century', *Irish Historical Studies* 22:86 (1980), pp. 126–43.
58. Susan K. Martin, 'Monuments in the garden: The garden cemetery in Australia', *Postcolonial Studies*, 7:3 (2004), pp. 333–52; David A. Weston (ed.), *The Sleeping City: The Story of Rookwood Necropolis* (Sydney: Society of Australian Genealogists in conjunction with Hale and Iremonger, 1989); Harold Mytum, 'Death and remembrance in the colonial context', in S. Lawrence (ed.), *Archaeologies of the British: Explorations of Identity in Great Britain and Its Colonies 1600–1945* (London: Routledge, 2003), pp. 156–73.
59. Weston, *The Sleeping City*; Lisa Murray, '"Modern innovations?" Ideal vs. reality in colonial cemeteries of nineteenth-century New South Wales', *Mortality*, 8:2 (2003), pp. 129–43; Lisa Murray, 'Remembered/Forgotten? Cemetery landscapes in the nineteenth and twentieth centuries', *Historic Environment*, 17:1 (2003), pp. 49–53.
60. David Fitzpatrick, 'Irish emigration'; Patrick O'Farrell, *The Irish in Australia* (Sydney: UNSW Press, 1993); Lindsay J. Proudfoot and Dianne P. Hall, *Imperial Spaces: Placing the Irish and Scots in Colonial Australia* (Manchester: Manchester University Press, 2013).
61. O'Farrell, *Irish in Australia*; Ireland, 'Irish Protestant migration'.

62. Brian Walker, '"The lost tribes of Ireland": Diversity, identity and loss among the Irish diaspora', *Irish Studies Review*, 15:3 (2007), pp. 267–82.
63. This is seen in the frequent identification of many North Americans as, for example, Italian-American, Ukrainian-American, Mexican-American. These are discussed in terms of mortuary monuments in Meyer, *Ethnicity and the American Cemetery*.
64. Ireland, 'Irish Protestant migration'.

3

Imposing Identity: Death Markers to 'English' People in Barbados, 1627–1838

Nicholas J. Evans

English overseas settlement from the beginning of the seventeenth century not only expanded economic and political influence over new parts of the Atlantic world, but also introduced to the Caribbean new methods of burying and remembering the dead. Eschewing any reference to memorialisation rituals of earlier Amerindian and Portuguese settlers on the island, the death of English (and to a lesser extent Scottish, Welsh and Irish) traders, administrators, and members of the armed forces and their families ensured cultural practices associated with death in England were transplanted abroad from the middle of the seventeenth century.[1] Though the earliest evidence of English death culture in continental North American concerned the failed settlement at Jamestown in Virginia, it was the longevity of settlement on the Caribbean island of Barbados that ensured the tiny colony left the richest seam of archaeological evidence of 'English' death culture during the seventeenth and eighteenth centuries.[2] Most of the surviving memorials remember, in stone, marble and even local coral, members of the plantocracy, those whom Matthew Parker described as 'the Sugar Barons'.[3] They largely cover the period of the island's history between 1627, when the English first arrived, and 1838, when slavery ended. The production of so many memorials and epitaphs marked an important part of the cultural colonisation of island life and memorialisation practices introduced by the British reinforced the widely discussed Anglicisation of the island.[4]

The memorials, like that shown in Figure 3.1 to William Arnold, one of the earliest settlers to the island, imposed a cultural tradition of remembrance throughout the island's nine parishes that survived decolonisation. Though they ignore both the enslaved African workers and poor white indentured workers, who represented the majority of people toiling on the island, the chest tablets, sepulchre, gravestones, headstones and later epitaphs collectively present an important insight into how the English memorialised their dead in diaspora.[5] As early as 1875, Captain J. H. Lawrence-Archer had gathered the corpus of inscriptions of key death markers erected across the Caribbean for those buried before 1750. They featured in his *Monumental Inscriptions of the British West Indies*, which included a chapter about memorial inscriptions found on Barbados.[6] Subsequent published volumes focused on just Barbados. The first to do so, in 1915, was Vere Langford Oliver's *The Monumental Inscriptions in the Churches and Churchyards of the Island of Barbados, British West Indies*.[7] The second, in 1956, was Eustace Shilstone's *Monumental Inscriptions in the Burial Ground of the Jewish Synagogue at Bridgetown, Barbados*.[8] All three colonial-era volumes helped draw English-speaking visitors' attention to select memorials erected in the island's Christian and Jewish burial sites.[9] These publications, coupled with fieldwork on the island by the author in 2015, form the basis of evidence analysed here.

With the absence of a public museum on the island until 1934, and the island's solitary surviving public statue to Lord Nelson erected in 1813, the death markers became an accessible mnemonic tool that demonstrated the island's economic importance and its part in Britain's imperial story.[10] Though the memorials erected on Barbados were not uniform in design, as demonstrated in Figures 3.1 to 3.6, they introduced into the heart of the island's nine parishes a mixture of death culture from most of England's rural shires. They documented both the changing notions of English identity in death between the seventeenth and nineteenth centuries and how the form of memorialisation ritual changed in diaspora. What happened on Barbados was important, for it was replicated not only in other parts of the British Caribbean, but also in neighbouring colonial North America, as the British formulated strategies for overcoming the distance from the homeland in their remembrance strategies.

Attention here focuses upon how memorialisation became a tool for demonstrating the Anglicisation of the island during the age of slavery. The chapter begins by considering the cultural 'power' of the white dead in slave society, expanding upon what Vincent Brown has described as life in the Reaper's Garden, and problematising what Harold Mytum called 'national cultural traditions in memorialisation' with regards to the British abroad.[11] Despite the significance of slavery to the island's fortunes, it was never mentioned or symbolically alluded to in any of the slavery-era erected memorials on the island. Anglicisation and not creolisation therefore became the dominant way of marking death and

Figure 3.1 The chest tomb to William Arnold. As a later accompanying memorial notes, he was one of the first English settlers on Barbados. His imposing grave, close to the entrance of All Saints' Church in the Saint Peter Parish, reminded all visitors of the deceased's role in establishing a remote English colony. (Photo: Nicholas J. Evans)

reinforcing Andrew O'Shaughnessy's ideas that the island was dominated by 'British sojourners' and that death provided a way of displaying that loyalty.[12] Secondly, the chapter considers how stones suggest 'Englishness' was a fluid term during this period, not only including how people identified as English on the death markers, but also denoting various identities or activities associated with Britishness. It builds upon ideas advocated by Edward Harwood that landscapes, including those to the dead, reveal much about personal identity in the eighteenth century.[13] Islander loyalism to Britain in peace and war is documented in gravestones and epitaphs and affirms O'Shaughnessy's argument that 'the strength of the social and cultural ties with Britain restrained the development of nationalistic Creole consciousness among whites and was a contributory factor in the failure of the British Caribbean to support the American Revolution'.[14] Thirdly, the chapter examines how Jewish settlers used memorials to demonstrate assimilation with their gravestones, thereby documenting how 'outsiders' became 'English' during the Georgian period, confirming David Malkiel's suggestion that Jewish stones 'speak' to those reading them.[15] Collectively, the chapter contributes to the rapidly expanding analysis of diaspora gravestones by exploring memorialisation on England's first tropical island nearly four centuries after the first settlers from Europe arrived and the notion that the island was seen as a remote extension of the rural English countryside.[16]

THE CULTURAL 'POWER' OF THE DEAD

Following a revolution in agriculture in the first half of the seventeenth century, Barbados quickly became home to many remote English settlers. For more than three centuries of British rule, between 1627 and 1960, these white colonials represented only a tiny proportion of the island's overall population. Until 1838, the majority of those forced to toil the island's plantations were enslaved Africans who helped the island grow to become one of the world's leading sugar economies.[17] When the wealthy died, remembrance reflected neither the memorial practices of the island's indigenous Carib peoples, nor those of the Africans who comprised the greatest proportion of islanders, but instead followed cultural practices associated with death in remote England.

The privileging of this white memory remains problematic, as it diverts attention from the fact that the white islanders represented a declining proportion of the population. As Patricia Molen has noted, in 1655 the 23,000 white residents represented 53.5 per cent of the estimated population on the island, compared with 20,000 enslaved Africans.[18] By 1768, the white population had decreased to 16,139 or just 19.5 per cent of the population, while the enslaved African population grew to 66,827 (or 80.5 per cent of the population).[19] Death markers in England before the seventeenth century were largely erected to preserve the memory of aristocrats and leading landowners. By contrast, those concerning the 'English' dying on Barbados between 1627 and 1838 documented largely self-made white elites. It can be argued, therefore, that had it not been for the risks associated with relocating to this remote colony they would not have been deemed worthwhile lives to record in stone. Movement elevated their fortunes as surviving headstones on the island document.

Unlike their counterparts who permanently settled colonial America from 1620, and had simple grave markers largely in the churchyard, the opportunities afforded on Barbados were firmly secular, especially pecuniary, and the memorials displayed less piety and more bragging. While all English settlers were nominally Anglican, the state church of the mother country, just like the Jacobean England they emanated from, forms of religious practice varied. The religious practice of white settlers ranged from those who happily followed the James I Bible published in 1611, to Anglicans still heavily influenced by Catholicism, as well as non-Anglicans including Jews and Nonconformists. Yet the religiosity of most planters needs to be questioned for, as Larry Gragg observes, 'assertions that the parish churches were "well frequented" and that the sacraments were "celebrated every Sunday" clashed with claims that only the aged worshipped, that only a few received the sacraments, or that ministers spoke to virtually empty buildings'.[20]

While belief was unimportant for what can at best be described as a motley crew of heathens, the island was generally shaped by English rural life.[21] The apparatus of the state church framed everyday life because there was little else to do. In what became characteristic of European imperialism, the small island was divided into nine parishes, named after saints associated with Britain.[22] Each parish in turn had, as its centre, a place of worship. The church remained one of the few public buildings and because of this drew in the white owners of nearby plantations for, at best, weekly services. Entry to the churchyard was strictly reserved and while even some white Barbadians were buried on their own plantations, death culture was segregated with Catholics, Nonconformists and non-religious people buried separately to the Anglicans.

The choice of death marker, including white stone, marble or coral, anchored and protected the deceased planter. Stone, often imported marble, introduced new materials with which to mark a grave on the island.[23] For people who had shown little religious zeal, it enabled artisans and the lower gentry class to occupy burial spaces that 'back home' in their native England would have been reserved for aristocrats. Death markers denoted both social advancement of the 'elect' and the social death of those they ruled.[24] To ensure they remained undisturbed, the wealthiest commissioned heavy marble slabs to sit above their bodies to prevent both grave robbers and the reuse of the burial spot.

Remembrance practices, visible at the island's cathedral of St Michael's in Bridgetown, maintained a degree of hierarchy. Those who had played a crucial role in financing the erection of early stone churches – including governors and merchants – were afforded protection under the central nave of the church. Thus, numerous members of the Willoughby family, governors of the island from 1650 to 1651 and 1663 to 1672, were provided with numerous memorial spots for which they made premium payments.[25] Those who followed cherry-picked select sites surrounding the church's exterior. Not just satisfied with the size and prime location of their family memorials and vaults, the aristocratic pretensions of the plantocracy were further demonstrated by the use of heraldic devices to ensure the onlooker knew of the 'ancient' credentials of the deceased.[26] Memorials thereby masked the newcomer status of the deceased.

DOCUMENTING 'ENGLISH' IDENTITY IN STONE

Though the shape and form of memorials in their rural parishes in England had shown a degree of conformity, the form of the memorialisation in diaspora varied enormously as each settler transplanted rural folkways associated with their native England. Those with the most power or wealth adopted architectural forms in marble, from sepulchre to flat slabs, headstones to memorial tablets. Memorial ritual was thereby translocated and examples included mounded earth with stones (mirroring burial ritual in East Anglia), grave markers made from stone (mirroring Lancashire and Yorkshire gravestone tradition), and headstones made of slate (like those in Derbyshire and South Wales). Written in the English language, few displayed links to Catholicism through use of Catholic symbolism (ISN) or using Latin; instead, the memorials were diverse, yet more secularised than in England. Collectively, they removed any traces of earlier indigenous settlement on the island and elevated the death rites associated with the burying and remembrance of Europeans compared with their enslaved counterparts.[27]

Identity recorded on the diverse range of memorials often noted the importance of ancestral origins, rather than the place of settlement on the island. In England, memorials generally noted where a parishioner resided, often to show off their societal position in village life, but on Barbados the significance of the island dwelling was initially of lesser importance than that of familial place of origin. Origin did not mean an estate or parish nearby, but instead was a reminder of the superiority of the deceased because they had been born, educated, lived or worked in England. While a small number of settlers had come from Wales, Scotland and even Ireland, it was the primacy of an English rural birth that most frequently appeared on memorials, showcasing the county or town of the deceased's origins. As a recent doctoral study demonstrates, memorials erected on the island between 1627 and 1960 revealed geographic origins in at least thirty-seven counties of England, Scotland and Wales.[28] The counties mentioned on gravestones include Northumberland, Kent, Shropshire, Hertfordshire, Dorset, Cumbria, Derbyshire, Surrey, Lancashire (shown in Figure 3.2), Gloucestershire, Devon, Somerset and Middlesex.[29] Yet other places of origin mentioned included estates, villages, streets, boroughs and towns. Crucially, the spatial breadth of memorial references both challenge ideas by David Hackett Fischer that early colonial settlement, like at Virginia, was solely by English people from the Home Counties and the south-west of England and suggest remembrance to English regions was more commonplace than ties to the nation state.[30]

Over time, as some families established an intergenerational permanence on the island, the importance of place changed. By the beginning of the nineteenth century, they also remembered their 'home' on the island. The importance of the name of an estate had grown from being a mere plantation to a building affording status to the deceased, something to flaunt.

Not all memorials, however, marked the place of permanent residence. Some also record those who, presumably ill, died in transit back to England. For example, Frances Orderson's memorial tablet observed: 'on her Passage to England (her native Country) / *DIED AT SEA* / and whose Body, during an awful Calm was / committed to the unfathomable deep.'[31] The reverse was also documented where a former islander was remembered upon their permanent return to England. Lucy Crichlow's memorial from 1801 noted she died in England: 'Sacred to the Memory of Lucy Crichlow daughter of / John Cobham Esq. & Wife of Henry Crichlow Esqr of this Island / Who died in the City of Bath in the Kingdom of England / on the 7th and was buried in the Abbey Church of that City'.[32]

Such references to the country of origin changed over time, closely

Figure 3.2 The gravestone of John Smith of Liverpool. As well as revealing the town of origin, this memorial erected in 1822 identifies to readers that the port was in the English county of Lancashire. That only the deceased's ashes were interred here suggests that he died of disease and his body was cremated to prevent it spreading. (Photo: Nicholas J. Evans)

following political changes to the United Kingdom. Thus, a memorial to Nicholas Crisp, a London merchant, in 1678 noted: 'Here lyeth ye body of / Mr Edward Crisp Marcht: of this / place. Ye eldest sonn of Nicho: / Crisp Marcht in Bred Street in / London in ye Kingdom of England / Hee departed this life ye 14th of / Ienvary 1678 Aged 50 Years[.]'[33] Three years after the Act of Union in 1707, which united England and Scotland, merchant William Godman was described as being of Great Britain and not England: 'Here lyes interr'd the body of / Mr William Godman Mercht / Son of the Revd Mr Henry Godman / of the Kingdom of great Brittain / who departed this life the first / day of August 1710 Aged 37 years / and Resident in this / Island 22 years.'[34] National identities were fluid. As late as 1801, Mrs Laetitia Austin was noted as being from England and not Great Britain.[35] Scots appear to be less likely to attest to a British origin. For instance, merchant Michael Cavan's gravestone proudly observed, 'Sacred to the memory of / Michael Cavan Esquire / who died the 6th June 1832 / Aged 53 years / A native of Scotland and for / thirty years a merchant of this Island'.[36] Following Britain's union with Ireland in 1801, to establish the United Kingdom of Great Britain and Ireland, the number of Irish people acknowledging their origins in death also grew – despite being small in number – and included people from Killala, Drogheda, Dublin, Tandragee, Aghanloo (Londonderry), Tulley (County Donegal), and Galway.[37] Only one memorial, from the seventeenth century, noted the deceased was from the 'Kingdom of Ireland'.[38]

Not all 'English' people originated in the mother country. Other identities acknowledged on memorials revealed that people had come from near and far, but largely within the Anglophone parts of the British Empire. Some, upon arrival from England, had settled in other Caribbean Islands, such as Alexander Enright who died in Barbados en route to visiting his grandfather on Jamaica:

> Sacred
> to the memory of
> Mr Alexander Hunter Enright
> of Kentish Town, near London
> who died on the 16th
> of September 1836, in the
> twenty fifth year of his age
> he expired only four days after
> landing in this Island being too
> ill to proceed to Jamaica where he
> was going to visit his Grandfather Alexander Aikman Senr Esqre.
> of Prospect Pen near Kingston
> in that island.[39]

Other identities reveal the intra-continental connections between Barbados and colonial America, largely driven by the slave economy in both regions.[40] These included both those of English origin as well as families who, though born in diaspora, retained strong commercial, political and cultural ties to England and were thus considered 'English'.[41]

They included Colonel William Wanton, who was described as 'Of Newport on Road Island'.[42] Meanwhile, fellow Anglo-American George Badcock, dying in 1714, was described as being from Boston: 'Here lyes ye body / of George Badcock / of Boston in / New England'.[43] Other Anglo-Americans, such as Peleg Almy, noted residence in England and New England, being the son of 'Job Almy of Tivertown in ye / County of Bristol & Province / of ye Massachusetts Bay in / New-England'.[44] Meanwhile, merchant David McClenahan came from colonial Virginia: 'Here lieth the Body of / David M.Clenahan Merchant / in Princess Ann County in Virginia / Aged about 38 Years who departed / this Life 30th day of October 1735 / the Son of Nathaniel M.Clenahan / Merchant in Virginia / this Stone is [? was] order'd here by his / Loving Mother / Elizabeth M.Clenahan.'[45]

After the American War of Independence ended in 1783, references to settler ties with this former part of the British Empire diminished. Conversely, other parts of the expanding British Empire began to feature more prominently, such as that to Alfred Bartrum, Esq. who was noted as passing away in 1826, sixteen years after the British acquired the Indian Ocean island of Mauritius: 'Sacred / to the Memory of / Alfred Bartrum, Esq. of the Island of Mauritius'.[46] People being memorialised increasingly tended to come from Britain's surviving North American colonies. They included 'Maria Sophia / wife of John Leander Start* / . . . daughter of John Ratchfor* / . . . arrousborough Nova Scoti[a].'[47] The origins of settlers noted in death markers therefore document various 'English' people as well as those deemed 'British' as having worked, lived or traded within the broader Anglophone world.

Affiliations to England can also be discerned through references to professional or scholarly identities. John Ellis's memorial noted his degree and affiliation to the Society of Arts: 'In memory of / John Ellis Esqr / M.A. F.S.A. / *Barrister at Law* / Late of the / Middle Temple / London / Born 19th Jany 1791 / Died 24th May 1825.'[48] Meanwhile, Alexander Bruce's grave noted: 'Alexander Bruce / Doctor in Physick / Died Novr' 3 / Anno Domr 1768 AEtatis37 / *Peculiar Blessings bear y' shortest Date!*'[49] Though the memorials inevitably show what the mourners instructed monumental masons to erect, the agency of fellow comrades are discernible. An early settler noted he was a goldsmith and citizen of London, amongst many other parts of his identity: 'Here lieth the Body of / John Felton Citizen / and Goldsmith of / London who Departed / this life the 14th of May / 1694 Aged 62 / years 9 Months.'[50]

Others remembered noted multiple identities, exemplified by the memorial tablet to Henry Noble Shipton, which recorded his contribution to society in England and overseas:

> Sacred to the Memory of HENRY NOBLE SHIPTON,
> Senior Ensign of the Fourth or King's Own Regiment of Foot,
> and youngest Son of the Reverend JOHN SHIPTON,
> Doctor in Divinity, Rector of Portishead near Bristol, Vicar of
> Stanton Bury, in the County of Buckingham, and one of His Majesty's
> Justices of the Peace for the County of Somerset, in England.
> He was an active and valued Officer,
> as well as a singularly amiable and excellent young Man:
> who, escaping the dangers especially incident to his Profession,
> particularly those of the siege of New Orleans,
> and the ever memorable Battle of Waterloo, was cut off, when on the Eve
>   of Promotion, by the yellow Fever,
> after only five days illness, whilst stationed with his Regiment
> in this Island, on the fifth day of December 1821,
> in the 26th year of his age,
> to the very deep regret of his afflicted Parents,
> who have caused this Tablet to be erected as a Token of
> their affection for their beloved Son.[51]

Others, revealing the agency of the donor, identified membership of fraternal groups, including the Freemasons. Founding Freemasons recalled:

> To the Memory of
> ALEXANDER IRVINE Gent
> The Founder of Free Masonry
> in Barbados
> who lived Beloved and died
> Lamented by all who knew him
> the Brethren of Saint Michaels Lodge
> of which he was the First Master
> have placed upon his Remains this Stone
> to be a Monument of his Merit
> and their Gratitude
> He departed this life the 13th
> day of November 1743
> in the 49th year of his Age.[52]

Meanwhile, other memorials to Freemasons recalled their 'brother'. In 1840, the memorial to John Alleyne Beckles noted, 'Sacred to the memory of / The Honorable John Alleyne Beckles, / for many years President of this Island; / Judge of the Court of Vice Admiralty, / And Provincial Grand-Master / of the Free and Accepted Masons of

Barbados.'[53] Identities displayed on monuments reveal a layering of cultural ties – familial, social and fraternal. Whether the deceased pre-directed what their memorials would include we cannot say, but the agency of fellow Freemasons suggests nineteenth-century social networks were of central importance in life and death.

During the middle of the eighteenth century, as life on the island became more established and thereby stratified, so the memorialisation spread to include epitaphs that told the story of an individual buried remotely from the place of internment. This mirrored the growth of widespread memorialisation in English churches after 1715, with memorials beginning to 'gather' remote kith and kin on a single epitaph. Rather than above the corpse, island elites increasingly provided detailed portraits of dynasties on the walls inside the church.[54] Expensive memorials imported from England increasingly adorned the island's churches and might well have been the only thing that the parishioners viewed while in church.[55] Perhaps replicating the popularity of wall tablets in Georgian churches in England, those on the island mirrored the most elaborate of their English counterparts. Crucially, a local stonemason was no longer de rigueur. Instead, elaborate works by sculptures were commissioned in Bristol and London, before being shipped out to Barbados and erected indoors; they then dominated places of worship for centuries to come.

The memorials varied in size, shape and detail. By far the most elegant was the rococo relief portrait to Thomas Withers, now displayed in the Barbados Museum and Historical Society and shown in Figures 3.3a and 3.3b. Commissioned by his son Daniel Moore, it displayed not only the bonds of family but also friendship. His memorial shipped from England read:

> To the Memory of THOMAS WITHERS Mercht. who Died Aug. 30th 1750, Aged 68 Years. A Man of fair Character in his Profession And unaffected Piety in his Life. In the Dispatch of Business punctual and exact. In his Friendships hearty and sincere, In his Conversation affable and free. Charity which actually extended itself to man[y,] [A]nd readiness with a Benevolence that reached Al[l.] This monument was erected by his Son ... Daniel Moore.[56]

As Joan Coutu has identified, the monument mirrors one by Robert Taylor to John Andrews in Trinity Hall, Cambridge, and the sculptor based his relief portraits 'on painted portraits or miniatures sent to him by the people who commissioned the monuments'.[57] Yet the time and money entailed in the remote commissioning of a marble portrait, and its production in Bath, followed by transhipment via Bristol to

a

Figures 3.3a and b The memorial tablet to Thomas Withers, now redisplayed at Barbados Museum and Historical Society. This elaborate tablet demonstrates the deceased's friendships as well as family relationships. Kith and kin were all erectors of memorials; their agency was important in framing the memory of English colonialists. The rococo-style memorial was created in Bath, before being shipped via Bristol to Barbados, and shows how death in diaspora was augmented by a memorial imported from England. (Photo: Nicholas J. Evans)

Barbados, shows the lengths many remote Englishmen went to in order to have an English-crafted memorial to preserve their memory. While Withers' heirs clearly had substantial wealth to erect such a memorial, by the beginning of the nineteenth century, as Georgian London became a retail emporium for death, a number of suppliers of English monumental masons were recorded on the island's marble death markers. They included T. Gaffin of Regent Street, London; Caton of 491 Oxford Street, London; and Bedford of 256 Oxford Street, London.[58] Having a bit of England transported to Barbados furthered the associations between the deceased and England. The justification in expending so much money on these memorials was perhaps explained by their central position within viewing distance of congregants during weekly services. It was a wise investment for they were a tool for maintaining status, rather than just to aid mourning. In bringing memorialisation back into the church, these remote Britons were once more securing their place in the heart of island life.

The memorials celebrated only snapshots of the individual's, or the family's, wider story. Alongside their origins and family relationships, military encounters were also displayed; they retold to readers the islander's defence of Britain's imperial possessions and strong loyalty to England as the mother country both before and after the American War of Independence. Proclaiming Christian heroism, such martial ties were apparent even when the deceased was the progeny of a soldier or sailor, as evident with Ann Sansum's memorial:

> Here lie the Remains of
> Mrs ANN SANSUM,
> Daughter of Lt Coll John Morris,
> late of the Provincials in
> North-America,
> (where he bravely supported the Royal Cause,
> and was an active and faithful Officer
> during the whole of the Revolution in that Country)
> and SARAH his Wife
> descended of the
> Noble House of Montrose,
> and wife of Samuel Sansun
> of the Kingdom of England,
> but late of the City of New-York,
> Merchant,
> She departed this Life,
> (in pure Christian Faith and Hope)
> in the night

of the 14th of September 1803,
Aged 22 Years & 9 Months.[59]

Yet of all involvement in imperial military campaigns, it was the Battle of Waterloo in 1815 that featured most frequently in memorials.[60]

Despite the large number of planters and colonial elites living on the island between 1627 and 1838, in total only a small proportion of islanders' lives were remembered. Victorian antiquarians no doubt posited through their data gathering a propagandist view of valorising the importance of the British in civilising and cultivating the island.[61] But the memorialisation practices for the plantocracy demonstrate that difference rather than conformity was the norm on Barbados. Though earlier scholars have observed the dominant influence of a single grave marker in colonial America, or the transmission of burial tradition from Britain or Ireland to continental North America, diversity was the key on Barbados.[62] Without doubt, memorialisation practices evident before 1838 demonstrate that England was foremost in the minds of the mourners, if not the deceased. In the case of one long-forgotten colonial-era Barbadian, shown in Figure 3.4, even before death England was so much in his mind that he commissioned a marble relief of King's Lynn in Norfolk. Originally displayed in the home of English-born governor of Barbados, Sir Jonathan Atkins (and now in the Barbados Museum), it was erected not to mourn anyone but to serve as a mnemonic device to remember England.[63] Yet in the tropical conditions of Barbados, marble was a durable form for displaying identity. In the absence of an art gallery, such memorials, like the death markers displayed inside and around churches, were the harbinger of colonial identities. Like art, what they portrayed was very selective.

BECOMING 'ENGLISH': ASSIMILATION IN STONE

One of the most unusual features of the surviving death markers on Barbados is that the largest set were to Jewish residents. Antiquarians Lawrence-Archer and Langford Oliver were clearly unable to translate the non-English-language epitaphs when they gathered memorials on Barbados for their published lists of epitaphs in 1875 and 1915. However, the founder of the National Trust for Barbados, Eustace Shilstone, persevered with the gravestones at the island's largest synagogue for his book of Jewish monumental inscriptions, published to mark the tercentenary of the readmission of Jews to England in 1956.

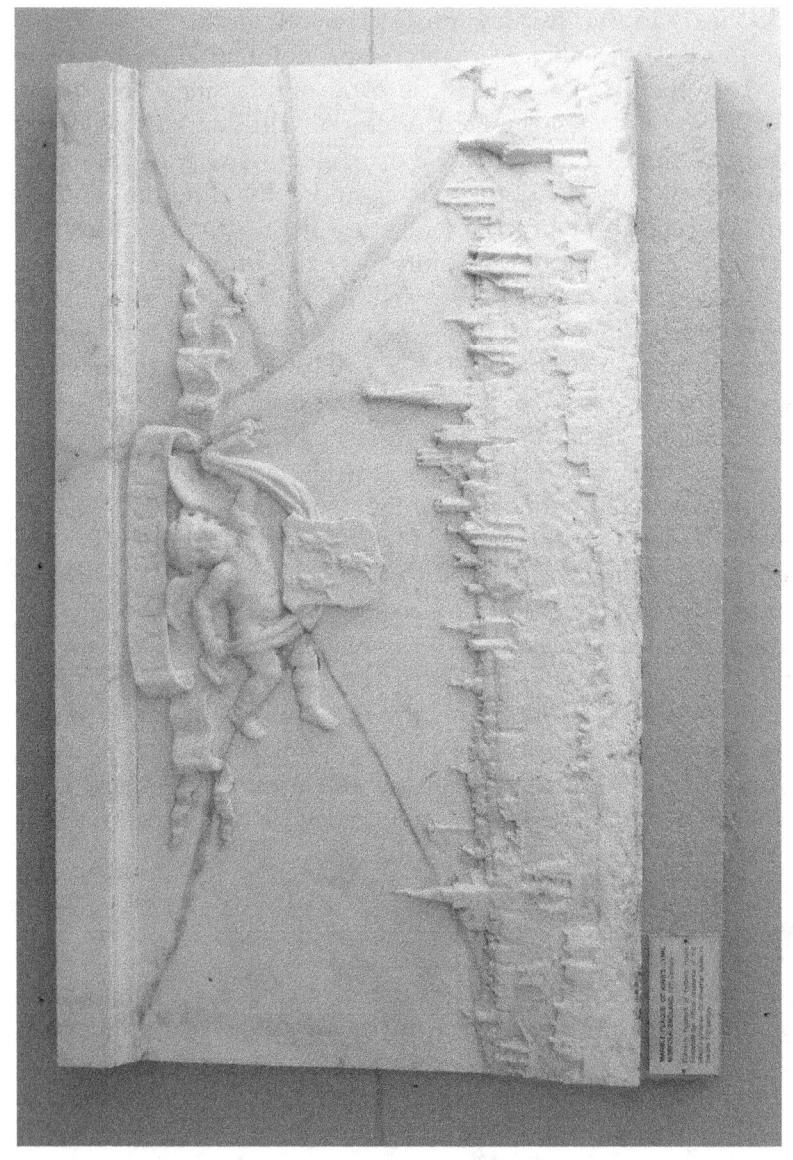

Figure 3.4 A marble relief plaque of King's Lynn. Originally displayed in the home of English-born governor of Barbados, Sir Jonathan Atkins (now displayed in the Barbados Museum), it was erected not to mourn anyone but to serve as a mnemonic device to remember England. (Photo: Nicholas J. Evans)

His work carefully included the Hebrew, Portuguese and English memorials of the Sephardic community.[64]

Because Jewish Law forbids multiple grave occupancy, the walled cemetery adjoining the island's largest surviving synagogue at Bridgetown provides ample evidence of the oldest English Jewish community after the readmission of Jews to England and her colonies by Oliver Cromwell in 1656.[65] That Jewish settlement at Barbados predated the readmission on the British mainland is important.[66] The prime urban location of the cemetery was central and sizeable. While evidence of other non-Jewish headstones has long vanished, the stones off Swann Street (also shown on some Georgian maps as Jews Street) are especially useful for they reveal many themes not present on the death markers of other contemporaneous settlers.[67]

Although the Anglicans had settled the island and introduced the culture of the state church, Sephardic Jews were encouraged to settle on Barbados because of their displacement from the Portuguese Empire in 1654.[68] Originally from Portugal, the Alhambra Decree of 1492 had forced practising Jews to flee Europe 162 years earlier.[69] They had first settled in Recife, in Latin America, where they introduced and developed an expertise in the cultivation of sugar, a skill originating in Africa.[70] When the Portuguese reasserted their control over Recife in 1654, these Portuguese diaspora Jews were forced once more into exile, this time dispersing to Dutch, British and French Caribbean colonies.[71] Their expertise in sugar cultivation enabled the Sephardic Jews to be assured the right to worship their religion in Barbados, ahead of readmission to England, because they were economically useful. One of the central expressions of that toleration was to create a synagogue and to have a burial space. The graves of Jews at Barbados were therefore among the earliest readmission of English Jews, with the earliest dating from 1660.[72] Though granted the rights to live and work on the island, they remained taxed as non-Anglicans in special Jew taxes, were forbidden from employing Christians and were prevented from running plantations.

Overcoming persecution, their right to have a burial plot and memorial presented the opportunity to display their burial culture in Barbados, as earlier Dutch Jews had done at Surinam.[73] The form was alien in three ways. Firstly, the monuments were in stone – typically marble – something at that stage which was unusual for island remembrance. Secondly, as shown in Figure 3.5, the style of the earliest graves differed from other Jewish graves, displaying 'a sepulchral culture of their own. In terms of its sepulchral language and art, it differs from the

Judeo-Spanish sepulchral culture and the one that was practised by the Jews who emigrated from Spain to North Africa, to the Ottoman Empire or Italy', as well as to Germany and the Netherlands.[74] Thirdly, as with most Jewish graves in diaspora, they had memorials in two languages: the secular language (Portuguese) and then the language of their religion (Hebrew).

For several generations, c.1654 to 1726, the language of gravestones remained Portuguese and Hebrew.[75] Yet from the mid-eighteenth century the language deployed changed, initially to three languages (Portuguese and Hebrew surrounded by a short reference in English), and then around 1770 to English and Hebrew. Finally, as revealed through graves in a rediscovered smaller section of the cemetery in 2015, some stones by the late eighteenth century were entirely in English.[76] The stones thereby reflect the assimilation of this outsider group to become 'English Jews'.

The most noticeable difference from non-Jewish graves is that for the first one hundred years of the community's existence, often detailed memorials never referred to their country of origin, either ancestral origins in Portugal or diasporic connections to Recife. Unlike other 'English' graves on the island that remembered homeland origins in the first generation, perhaps this absence can be explained due to the persecution they had faced in their previous lives. Alternatively, it could suggest the first generation of Jews chose to hide their foreign birth to avoid further anti-alienism. Regardless, over time Jewish memorialisation tradition showed signs of changing. By the mid-eighteenth century, the gravestones of Jews began to mirror their 'English' counterparts by revealing origins. Luna, widow of Moderechay Burgus, who died in 1756, was listed, in Portuguese as 'Luze en la Empireo' ('long in the Empire').[77] Isaac Hisquiau, dying in 1739, was described, in Portuguese, as 'de Londres' ('of London'), revealing that by this stage Sephardic Jews were relocating to Barbados from London.[78] Merchant Samuel Hart, dying in 1773, was described in Portuguese, as 'dela Ciuda de New York' ('from New York City').[79] Meanwhile, more epitaphs on gravestones were increasingly written in English. So when Rabbi Ralph Haim Isaac Carigal died in 1777, he was described as formerly of New York on his Hebrew- and English-language gravestone.[80] Meanwhile Jacob Montefiore, dying in 1801, was described entirely in English as 'Of London, Merchant'.[81]

The community diminished by the late eighteenth century, completely dying out in the years following the abolition of slavery in 1838.[82] The increased use of the English-language memorials may therefore be suggestive that the community was dwindling, and felt the need to display

Figure 3.5 A replica marble gravestone in Bridgetown Jewish Cemetery to David Raphael De Mercado, who died 14 August 1685. The style was similar to Jewish graves in the Mediterranean. By the end of the eighteenth century, Jewish gravestones on the island mirrored their non-Jewish counterparts, sometimes even abandoning the use of Hebrew entirely. (Photo: Nicholas J. Evans)

their memorials in a secular language. Alternatively, fears concerning the Napoleonic Wars may account for why one stone, shown in Figure 3.6, had text entirely in English.[83] Yet the stones demonstrate how non-Christian white elites displayed aspects of their identity in memorials in diaspora.

As with other Jewish graveyards in Europe, certain features of the death culture were very different from the Christian burial spaces. Barbadian Jews buried their children in separate rows to adults with graves of smaller memorials filling the space between rows of larger adult graves. All graves lay flat, again mirroring their Iberian Sephardic origins.[84] Many also contained the initialism SBAGDG – translated from *Sua Bendita Alma Goze De Gloria* ('as may his/her soul delight in glory') – on their gravestones.[85] Religious symbols associated with Jewish death culture were also displayed on gravestones and tombstones. These include: a broken or cut-down tree to represent a life cut short; two hands, with four fingers each divided into two sets of two fingers, the symbol of a priestly blessing – signifying the priest was a Kohen, a descendant of the biblical high priest Aaron; and the inclusion of a Menorah candelabra to signify the deceased was a woman – and would have lit the Menorah candles at the start of each sabbath. The gravestone to Hazan Meher-Acohen Belifante includes multiple visual symbols pertaining to his religious duties including carvings showing: '1. A Man's figure, in knee-length skirted coat blowing a shofar, 2. [A] hand holding a quill pen, symbolic of his being scribe, and 3. [A b]ottle, spatula, scissors, forceps, needle and other marks of the Mohel's art'.[86]

The memorials to the Jewish islanders typically contained a select number of references. First, they had a religious message, demonstrating the importance of faith and the deceased's religiosity. Second, they exhibited a personal story, including family relations. Third, the stones showed their occupation of the deceased and their perceived importance to island life. Fourth, the memorials highlighted broader contributions to either the Jewish community or the broader Barbadian society. It was the latter point that often appeared in English surrounding a Portuguese and Hebrew memorial, perhaps suggesting Jews knew that, in the words of many scholars, 'Stones Speak' and that the host society would read the loyalty of these 'English' Jews when visiting the graveyard.[87]

Crucially, as all men and women were buried in separate single graves, the gravestones reveal contemporary attitudes to female remembrance on the island. The English portion of the gravestone to Mrs Angel de Piza recorded her strong morality:

Figure 3.6 Marble gravestone in a smaller Jewish cemetery at Bridgetown. Building work to the site adjoining the Jewish cemetery in Bridgetown in 2015 revealed twelve long-forgotten Jewish gravestones. The one shown here reveals the degree of assimilation on some of the late-eighteenth-century Jewish gravestones, as the memorial appeared entirely in the English language. (Photo: Nicholas J. Evans)

> Here lies the remains of Mrs. Angel de Piza Wife of Emanuel de Piza Mercht. Who departed this life on Thursday the 20th Adar 5555, A; M, corresponding to the 12th March 1795. Aged 48 years. Regretted by all who Knew her as she Possessed every amiable endowment and estimable Quality as a tender Wife – an Affectionate Parent & a Sincere friend her habits of life were conducted with unexampled moral rectitude & all whom had the happiness of her acquaintance received from the pleasures of her society & engaging manners every enjoyment and gratification that the heart of Benevolence can desire. *Scared to Virtue is the Record here, Reader bestow the tribute of a tear; Respect the worth that claims your friendly sigh, Live thus like her: and as lamented Die.*[88]

Though her grave does not note a relationship to place, the language and sentiment of respectability were sure signs she was as English as someone in Regency London.

The Jewish memorials are therefore an important contribution to the death culture evident on the island, and broaden our understanding of Jewishness and Englishness in the Anglophone world before 1838.[89] Although there were many differences, especially that Jews did not follow the Anglican tradition of erecting memorial tablets to their life story in the nearby synagogue, the grave markers augmented the cultural range of symbols and text representing death on Barbados. Denied full equality to their non-Jewish counterparts in life, the memorials demonstrate that both Jews and non-Jews engaged with all death culture on the island. Messages were important and reinforced the significant economic and societal contribution of Jews to the island, and broader imperial, economy.[90] They were also important in terms of documenting the degree of pluralism on the island, even if it was not complete toleration. Examination of the cultural deathways on the island, however, evidences that during the age of slavery any signs of creolisation were removed gradually, and Anglicisation gained a dominant influence over Jewish memorialisation as it had always done for non-Jewish white elites.

CONCLUSION

The diverse form and texts displayed on over a thousand headstones and memorial tablets located across the nine parishes on the island of Barbados reveal the deep attachment to Englishness that merchants, mariners and traders had throughout the era of slavery between 1627 and 1838. England was not simply the economic glue that united the remote island and the mother country, it remained of crucial cultural influence to remembrance practices. The death culture of white settlers on Barbados for over three centuries would continue to influence remembrance after the end of slavery in 1838. Death markers should not be seen in isolation; instead, they were an extension of ecclesiastical and secular architecture that had a purpose in helping to subjugate colonial society. While some other chapters in this volume focus upon the symbolism on graves, after what Julie Rugg has detailed as the birth of the cemetery burial around 1820, identity in the earlier period discussed here was both fluid and represented inside or outside the main religious buildings in each parish. Englishness could be inferred by the architectural style, textual evidence, or suggested connections through occupation, status or even membership of organisations such as the Freemasons. Identity varied over time, but was important enough to be included on most memorials in diaspora, something that has been under-explored by scholars of British imperialism and death studies.

Acknowledgments

I am grateful to Professor Angela McCarthy, Professor Emeritus Aubrey Newman and Professor Trevor Burnard for helpful comments on earlier drafts of this chapter.

NOTES

1. Sullivan describes the lack of a living indigenous population on the island in 1627. See Myles Sullivan, 'Sacred Grounds and Profane Plantations: The Spiritual Landscapes of Barbados', *Undergraduate Honors Theses*, Paper 945 (2016), p. 5. Available at <https://scholarworks.wm.edu/cgi/viewcontent.cgi?article=1930&context=honorstheses> (accessed 8 February 2020).
2. Samir Patel, 'Jamestown's VIPs', *Archaeology*, January/February 2016, <https://www.archaeology.org/issues/200–1601/features/3959-jamestown-colonial-america-burials> (accessed 1 September 2019).
3. Matthew Parker, *Sugar Barons: Family, Corruption, Empire and War* (London: Windmill, 2012).
4. Author's observations during fieldwork in 2015. The latter was part of the AHRC 'Remember Me: The Changing Face of Memorialisation' project based at the University of Hull. It included fieldwork at the following sites: The Cathedral Church of St Michael and All Angels, Bridgetown; St Mary's Church, Bridgetown; The Jewish Cemetery in Bridgetown, The Garrison Military Cemetery, St Michael; St James Parish Church, Holetown; St Matthias Anglican Church, Hastings; Christchurch Parish Church, Oistins; St Matthew's Anglican Church, Jackmans; and All Saints' Church, Saint Peter.

5. Jerry Handler has documented the death culture of the enslaved population on the island. On the elision of the enslaved more generally see, for example: Ross W. Jamieson, 'Material culture and social death: African-American burial practices', *Historical Archaeology*, 29:4 (1995), pp. 39–58; Orlando Patterson, *Slavery and Social Death: A Comparative Study* (Cambridge, MA: Harvard University Press, 1982). Regarding the seventeenth century see Hilary Beckles, *White Servitude and Black Slavery in Barbados, 1627–1715* (Knoxville: University of Tennessee Press, 1989).
6. Captain J. H. Lawrence-Archer, *Monumental Inscriptions of the British West Indies* (London: Chatto & Windus, 1875).
7. Vere Langford Oliver, *The Monumental Inscriptions in the Churches and Churchyards of the Island of Barbados, British West Indies* (London: Mitchell, Hughes and Clark, 1915).
8. Eustace M. Shilstone, *Monumental Inscriptions in the Burial Ground of the Jewish Synagogue at Bridgetown, Barbados* (New York: American Jewish Historical Society, 1956).
9. This was augmented by the recent publication by Mary Gleadall of the memorials at the island's military cemetery. See Mary E. Gleadall, *Monumental Inscriptions in the Barbados Military Cemetery* (St Michael: Barbados Military Cemetery Association, 2000).
10. David C. Devenish, 'The Barbados Museum', *Museums and Contested Histories*, 38:1 (1985), p. 15; David Lambert, '"Part of the blood and dream": Surrogation, memory and the national hero in the postcolonial Caribbean', *Patterns of Prejudice*, 41:3–4 (2007), p. 346.
11. Vincent Brown, *The Reaper's Garden: Death and Power in the World of Atlantic Slavery* (Cambridge, MA: Harvard University Press, 2008); Harold Mytum, *Recording and Analysing Graveyards* (York: Council for British Archaeology, 2000), p. 61.
12. The 'Britishness' of Barbados is discussed in numerous works. See David Lambert, *White Creole Culture, Politics and Identity During the Age of Abolition* (Cambridge: Cambridge University Press, 2005), Karl Watson, *The Civilised Island: Barbados: A Social History 1750–1816* (Ellerton, Barbados: Caribbean Graphic Production Limited, 1979), and Larry Cragg, *Englishmen Transplanted: The English Colonization of Barbados, 1627–1660* (Oxford: Oxford University Press, 2003).
13. Edward S. Harwood, 'Personal identity and the eighteenth-century English landscape garden', *The Journal of Garden History*, 13:1–2 (1990), pp. 36–48.
14. Andrew O'Shaughnessy, *Empire Divided: The American Revolution and the British Caribbean* (Philadelphia: University of Pennsylvania Press, 2000), p. 4.
15. David Malkiel, *Stones Speak: Hebrew Tombstones from Padua, 1529–1862* (Leiden: Brill, 2013).
16. For example: Stephen Deed, *Unearthly Landscapes: New Zealand's Early*

Churchyards, Cemeteries and Urupā (Dunedin: Otago University Press, 2015); Thomas W. Laqueur, *The Work of the Dead: A Cultural History of Mortal Remains* (Princeton, NJ: Princeton University Press, 2015); Harold Mytum, 'Scotland, Ireland and America: The construction of identities through mortuary monuments by Ulster Scots in the Seventeenth and Eighteenth Centuries', in Audrey J. Horning, Nick Brannon, Peter Edward Pope (eds), *Ireland and Britain in the Atlantic World* (Dublin: Wordwell, 2009), pp. 35–252; Elizabeth Buettner, 'Cemeteries, public memory and Raj nostalgia in postcolonial Britain and India', *History and Memory*, 18:1 (2006), pp. 5–42.
17. The economic significance of the island has been discussed widely. See, for example: Hilary Beckles, *The First Black Slave Society: Britain's 'Barbarity Time' in Barbados, 1636–1876* (Kingston, Jamaica: The University of the West Indies Press, 2016); Simon D. Smith, *Slavery, Family, and Gentry Capitalism in the British Atlantic: The World of the Lascelles, 1648–1834* (Cambridge: Cambridge University Press, 2006).
18. Patricia A. Molen, 'Population and social patterns in Barbados in the early eighteenth century', *The William and Mary Quarterly*, 28:2 (1971), p. 289.
19. Ibid.
20. Larry D. Gragg, *Englishmen Transplanted: The English Colonization of Barbados, 1627–1660* (Oxford: Oxford University Press, 2003), p. 72.
21. Expanding the British folkways described by David Hackett Fischer in *Albion's Seed: Four British Folkways in America* (New York: Oxford University Press, 1989).
22. Christ Church, St James, St Lucy, St Michael, St Peter, St Thomas, St Andrew, St George, St John, St Joseph, and St Philip.
23. Mytum, *Recording and Analysing Graveyards*, pp. 98–103, notes how British gravestones were typically made from locally sourced materials until recently, with new materials being sourced from South Africa and India.
24. Patterson, *Slavery and Social Death*.
25. On the Willoughbys' influence in the establishment of Barbados see Justin Roberts, 'Surrendering Surinam: The Barbadian diaspora and the expansion of the English sugar frontier, 1650–75', *The William and Mary Quarterly*, 73:2 (2016), pp. 225–6.
26. Lawrence-Archer, *Monumental Inscriptions of the British West Indies*, pp. 359, 361–3, 366–7, 373–9, 385–7, 390, 394–5, 399–400.
27. No gravestones for enslaved Africans remain on the island. On death rites associated with burial see Watson, *The Civilised Island*, pp. 89–90.
28. Katherine R. Cook, 'New World Memory: Identity, Commemoration, and Family in Transatlantic Communities' (PhD, University of York, 2015), p. 53.
29. Langford Oliver, *The Monumental Inscriptions*.
30. Hackett Fischer, *Albion's Seed*, pp. 237–9.
31. Langford Oliver, *The Monumental Inscriptions*, p. 11.

32. Ibid., p. 13.
33. Ibid., p. 4. Spelling errors appear in the published transcription.
34. Ibid., p. 3. Spelling errors appear in the published transcription.
35. Ibid., p. 19.
36. Ibid., p. 79.
37. Ibid., pp. 18, 58, 61, 73, 103, 127, 150.
38. Ibid., p. 157.
39. Ibid., p. 75.
40. Watson, The *Civilised Island*, pp. 11–25; Jack P. Greene, 'Colonial South Carolina and the Caribbean connection', *The South Carolina Historical Magazine*, 88:4 (October 1987), pp. 192–210; Gregory E. O'Malley, 'Beyond the middle passage: Slave migration from the Caribbean to North America, 1619–1807', *The William and Mary Quarterly*, 66:1 (2009), pp. 125–72.
41. The best example on Barbados is the Lascelles family. See Smith, *Slavery, Family, and Gentry Capitalism*.
42. Langford Oliver, *The Monumental Inscriptions*, p. 28. Original spelling retained for Rhode Island.
43. Ibid., p. 38.
44. Ibid., p. 40.
45. Ibid., p. 46.
46. Ibid., p. 16.
47. Ibid., p. 42.
48. Ibid., p. 15.
49. Ibid., p. 122.
50. Ibid., p. 27.
51. Ibid., p. 16.
52. Ibid., p. 46.
53. Ibid., p. 20.
54. As landscape historian Joan Coutu observed, the planters were not above commissioning a statue of themselves. In 1756, Henry Grenville 'encouraged the Barbadian House of Assembly to commission a statue of himself'. Joan Coutu, *Persuasion and Propaganda: Monuments and the Eighteenth-Century British Empire* (Montreal and Ithaca: McGill-Queen's University Press, 2006), p. 10.
55. Ibid., p. 10.
56. Barbados Museum and Historical Society, Memorial to Thomas Withers.
57. Coutu, *Persuasion and Propaganda*, pp. 96–8.
58. Langford Oliver, *The Monumental Inscriptions*, pp. 13, 22, 114.
59. Ibid., p. 52.
60. Ibid., p. 16.
61. Jack P. Green, *Imperatives, Behaviors, and Identities: Essays in Early American Cultural History* (Charlottesville and London: University Press of Virginia, 1992), pp. 13–68.

62. Ron Romano, *Early Gravestones in Southern Maine: The Genius of Bartlett Adams* (Charleston, SC: The History Press, 2016).
63. Peter Hoare, 'Sir Jonathan Atkins – Holborn House, Barbados – The marble relief of King's Lynn, Norfolk (1687): A puzzling link?', *Norfolk Archaeology*, 46 (2010), pp. 48–62.
64. Shilstone did not include the graves to Ashkenazi Jewish refugees who were buried on the island after 1933, probably out of respect.
65. Harry A. Ezratty, *500 Years in the Jewish Caribbean: The Spanish and Portuguese in the West Indies* (Baltimore, Md.: Omni Arts, 2002), p. 59.
66. Salo W. Baron, in the preface to Shilstone, *Monumental Inscriptions*, p. ii.
67. Barbados Museum, 'A topographicall description and admeasurement of the Ysland of Barbados in the West Indyaes with the Mys. Names of the Severall plantacions' [spelling taken from the original document].
68. Ezratty, *500 Years in the Jewish Caribbean*, p. 59.
69. Ibid., pp. 2–5.
70. Ibid., pp. 59–60.
71. Ibid., p. 14.
72. Shilstone, *Monumental Inscriptions*, p. xx.
73. Aviva Ben-Ur and Rachel Frankel, *Remnant Stones: The Jewish Cemeteries of Suriname: Epitaphs* (Cincinnati, OH: Hebrew Union College Press, 2009).
74. Agnes Seemann, 'The Jewish cemetery of Altona Königstrasse: Justification of outstanding universal value' (Hamburg: Freie und Hansestadt Hamburg / Kulturbehörde, 2012), <http://www.jüdischer-friedhof-altona.de/img/Welt kulturerbe/tentativlistentext_juedischer_friedhof_altona.pdf> (accessed 1 November 2019).
75. Shilstone, *Monumental Inscriptions*, p. 16.
76. Ibid., p. xx, shows knowledge of the smaller cemetery in 1956. He suggests that one explanation for the separation of the smaller cemetery was that it could have been used for those who committed suicide.
77. Ibid., p. 54
78. Ibid., pp. 66–7.
79. Ibid., pp. 117–18.
80. Ibid., p. 100.
81. Ibid., pp. 157–8.
82. Ezratty, *500 Years in the Jewish Caribbean*, pp. 60–1.
83. The European wars during the long eighteenth century were heavily disruptive to both island life and trade. See, for example, Richard Pares, *War and Trade in the West Indies, 1739–1763* (London: Frank Cass & Co., 1963).
84. With the frequent environmental catastrophes facing the Caribbean, this strategy also helped to preserve the memorials over time.
85. Ezratty, *500 Years in the Jewish Caribbean*, p. 67.
86. Shilstone, *Monumental Inscriptions*, p. 142.
87. Malkiel, *Stones Speak*.

88. Extension to the Barbados Jewish Cemetery. Thanks to the Barbados Jewish Museum for permission to access what were then newly discovered graves.
89. David Feldman, *Englishmen and Jews: Social Elations and Political Culture, 1840–1914* (New Haven and London: Yale University Press 1994).
90. See Eli Faber, *Jews, Slaves, and the Slave Trade: Setting the Record Straight* (New York: New York University Press, 1998) and Jonathan Schorsch, *Jews and Blacks in the Early Modern World* (Cambridge: Cambridge University Press 2014).

4

Looking for Thistles in Stone Gardens: The Cemeteries of Nova Scotia's Scottish Immigrants[1]

Laurie Stanley-Blackwell and Michael Linkletter

During the early nineteenth century, John the Hunter MacDonald, who emigrated from the Braes of Lochaber to Cape Breton in 1834, poured heart and soul into his poetic musings about Inverness-shire's historic graveyard of Cille Choirill.

Cille Choraill, Cill' as bòidhche
Air 'n d'chuir mi eòlas riamh; . . .
'S an robh mo sheòrs' bho chian;
'S truagh, a Rìgh, gun mi 's a' chòmhlan
Mar bu deòn le m' mhiann.

At St Cairrail's churchyard, the most beautiful cemetery
That I ever knew; . . .
Where those of my kind have lain for years,
alas, Lord, that I am not among them
as I ardently long to be.[2]

There is much more to this poem than immigrant nostalgia and homesickness, and the poignancy of separation. It gives insight into the physical and psychic claims that the Scots made on their cemeteries, a relationship shaped by a strong allegiance, affective bonds, and a sense of an ongoing continuum between the living and the dead. For diasporic Scots, the creation of new burial sites and modified deathways was central to their transition from homeland to hostland. In fact, it was part of the 'broader adaptation' of immigrant Scots to their new environments.[3] As they put down roots and evolved beyond strangers and sojourners, they continued to look at the cemetery as the place of the ultimate homecoming with its 'metaphorical embrace' of kin and community.[4]

Although Scottish immigrants marked their new landscapes in death as well as life, their headstones, as a vital expression of material culture, are an underutilised source of historical evidence. This situation is particularly striking in regions such as Nova Scotia where many of the cemeteries of the province's pioneer Scots have outlived almost all other material remnants of their pioneer landscape. It is in the cemetery that one is able to find a common ground, where group identities and individual lives intersected, and the forces of homogenisation and particularisation interacted. Operating on the assumption that cemeteries are not 'refuges from history' but places 'where history ends up', this chapter explores the untapped potential of cemeteries in Northeastern Nova Scotia for studying 'necroethnicity' and determining whether they represent a convincing portrait of an immigrant community kept alive culturally through death as well as life.[5] In short, what do their buried voices tell us and can these cemeteries be read productively as manifestations of Scottish immigrant cultural identity?

There is an abundant wealth of stories which confirm the cultural significance of the cemetery to Nova Scotia's immigrant Scots who populated many parts of Northeastern Nova Scotia and Cape Breton. One memorable example of how they rallied to honour and bury their dead involves Father Alexander MacDonald, a native of Glen Spean, near Lochaber, Scotland, who served as 'the first regular and permanent Catholic priest in Eastern Nova Scotia'.[6] In April 1816, he had the misfortune of dying in Halifax, some distance from Arisaig, the centre of his vast Nova Scotian mission, which stretched from Merigomish to Margaree Harbour. Determined to repatriate the remains of their much beloved priest, three sturdy Highlanders refused to let him be handled by strangers and transported him through the snow, a distance of almost 125 miles, carrying his coffin part of the way on their shoulders. As the trio pressed on, past New Glasgow, they were met by 'nearly all the male parishioners of Arisaig – all on foot'.[7] Clearly, the resolve to bury MacDonald in Arisaig, Nova Scotia, a place where their roots were still relatively shallow, was driven by a stronger imperative than respect. A burial site signified *dùthchas* and identity, one's attachment and belonging to a specific place and people.[8] Being buried among kindred, although far from one's ancestral homeland, possessed the reassuring certainty of keeping communal bonds intact.

This perception was hardly limited to MacDonald's loyal flock. The famous Nova Scotian Gaelic bard, Alexander the Ridge MacDonald, born on the Ridge in Mabou, Cape Breton, saw death not as a sorrowful termination to life's uncertain path, but as a passport to an eternal community reunion. In his iconic poem, '*Cumha Cheap Breatuinn*' ('Lament for Cape Breton'), he ruminated: '*Nis bho 'n tha mi air bheag stath, Leam a b' aill, nuair nach beo, Mi bhi comhla ri m' chairdean, Am Mabou fo 'n fhoid*' ('Now that I am so useless, I would love when I die, To be joined with my kindred, In Mabou at rest').[9] For MacDonald, life experiences were not structured exclusively in the present. Moreover, his perception of the intermingling of the living and the dead was far more literal than imagined. Writing in 1913, W. D. Cameron of Dunmore, Antigonish County, also testified to the emotional hold of the dead over their descendants among Nova Scotia's immigrant Scots:

> Apart altogether from lineal connections, the fact that they were from the 'Old Country' made them like brothers and sisters, in love and friendship. – Did one of them die, in any of the settlements from Upper South River to Cape George, a messenger was sent forthwith, on foot of course, to give the tidings, so that each family would be represented at the funeral. This was regarded as a sacred duty to be strictly observed and without fail.[10]

In addition to a strong identification with Scotland, other constitutive elements of individual and group identities, such as religion, homeplace and kinship were integral to the deathways of Nova Scotia's Scottish immigrants. One prime example was the heated controversy generated by the burial of Angus MacDonald, a Protestant convert to Catholicism, who was initially banned from the local cemeteries of his fellow Catholic and Presbyterian Scots on the grounds of being either a lapsed convert or an apostate. In the end, holy water proved thicker than blood, as ethnic bonds unravelled into 'a fist fight between the opposing factions'.[11] The Catholic side stood firm and 'the remains of the poor *Tuathach* (the Northerner)' were finally laid to rest in *Cladh nan Leòdhasach*, the Lewis people's Protestant cemetery near Washabuck, Cape Breton.[12] The location of Mary MacGillivary Robertson's final resting place was also based on religion- and kin-centred factors. In September 1857, the body of this Roman Catholic from Dunmaglass, who had married a Protestant from Barney's River, was at the centre of a local fracas. In the full light of day, some of MacGillivary's Roman Catholic kinfolk disinterred her remains from the Protestant cemetery in Barney's River and transported them to Arisaig so that she could be buried 'among her relations in a Catholic Church yard'.[13] In the case of the McDougalls of South West Branch of the Margaree River, Cape Breton, attachments to kinship and locale took precedence in matters related to death. The descendants of John McDougall of South West Branch of the Margaree River, even as they scattered across the continent with outmigration, displayed a singular homing instinct when it came to burial. By the 1920s, between 'fifty and sixty' of this family resided in the same cemetery, St Mary's S. W. Margaree, known locally as *Cladh nan Dughallach* or McDougall's Cemetery.[14]

The main geographical focus of this chapter, Antigonish and Pictou Counties, were heartlands of early Scottish settlement in Nova Scotia, where Scots constituted a large proportion of the local population. This region contains in excess of 200 cemeteries. The two counties represent fascinating foils in terms of the contrasting demographic and denominational backgrounds of their settlers. During the late eighteenth and early nineteenth centuries, Pictou County was peopled largely by Presbyterians from Sutherlandshire, Ross-shire, Eastern Inverness-shire, and Perthshire. There was also a goodly mix of Lowlanders, especially from Dumfriesshire. In vivid contrast, Antigonish County's Scottish-Catholic character was shaped over this same period of time by immigrants from Inverness-shire, most notably from the islands of Barra, South Uist and Eigg, as well as the mainland areas of Strathglass, Lochaber, Moidart, Arisaig, Knoydart and Morar.[15] The imported placenames in both counties demonstrate how extensively Scottish immigrants asserted their physical presence by engaging in what has been termed 'transferences' and 'cross-domain mapping'.[16] Such placenames as Gairloch, Lanark, Glengarry, Loch Broom, Arisaig, Knoydart, Moidart, and Lochaber all have their counterparts in Scotland.

A study of this nature comes with caveats. Most notably, one must be wary of being trapped by surviving evidence. For example, a substantial number of early headstones, especially in Antigonish County, are no longer extant, for reasons unknown. In the Old Pioneer Cemetery in St Andrew's, only 70 of the original 200 headstones have survived. In Arisaig, the 'old-timers' remember the hillside of St Margaret's Cemetery being heavily 'dotted with stones when they were young.'[17] This, sadly, is no longer the case. Furthermore, many of the early headstones, reflecting the custom in the Western Isles, were simply rough pieces of fieldstone that offer minimal historical information, although they do attest to the power of memorialising among Scottish immigrants. In researching local cemeteries, one must be mindful of the fact that not every Scottish immigrant, either because of poverty or a shortage of carvers, had a headstone, or even a 'proper' burial. For example, it is alleged that the legendary Revd James MacGregor of Pictou County once buried a man whose last resting place was a hollowed-out tree trunk, there being no boards to make his coffin.

In researching this topic, one would wish for a larger critical mass of textual evidence to cast into sharp relief the relationship between

Scottish immigrants and their cemeteries. For example, how did the Scots negotiate for burial space in Nova Scotia, especially in those areas where they lived in close proximity to Indigenous people or the original settlements of the Acadians? One wonders how Donald McGregor of Big Island, Pictou County, mentally processed his discovery of human bones, stone axes and flint arrowheads which surfaced as he ploughed his field. And why did he continue to farm this ancient cemetery site, which, by 1874, was so 'thoroughly dug over' that the bones were in disarray and the burial goods removed?[18] Or how did Hugh Fraser of Middle River reconcile himself to disturbing a gravesite with a human skeleton and removing a sword, which he repurposed for knives to cut mackerel?[19]

Fortunately, fragments of information, derived from archival sources as well as oral tradition, offer some tantalising glimpses into the burial customs of Scottish immigrants in Eastern Nova Scotia. For example, diocesan records indicate that the Scottish priests in Antigonish County registered disapproval of the dispersed locations of early local cemeteries. Clerical correspondence highlighted the need to consolidate cemeteries, 'so that there may not be too many burial places', to situate them closer to the chapel and priest's house, and to enclose them with fences.[20] In short, this regulation checked to some degree the immigrants' instincts to create more individualised burial sites, and resulted in the cemetery becoming a site where orthodoxy, both in terms of beliefs and behaviour, could be enforced. Equally revealing is the story of Archibald 'The Big Bachelor' MacKinnon, who, in 1820, migrated to Nova Scotia from the Isle of Muck, and signalled before his death a determination to dictate how his passing would be marked. Years in advance of this event, he ordered and installed in MacKinnon's cemetery (on his brother's property) a magnificent sandstone headstone, encrusted with such images as a stag, lion's head, archer's arms with bow and arrow, and boar's head with the shank bone of a deer, the latter a central symbol on the MacKinnon crest. Furthermore, against the wishes of his clergyman, he left precise instructions about the distribution of five gallons of liquor at his funeral, to refresh the mourners as they wound their way from his home, to the gate of Neil 'Mór' MacDonald's farm, and to his graveside.[21] Equally explicit were the instructions of Mrs Allan Livingston, who directed Antigonish merchant John MacMillan to obtain for her deceased husband in October 1855 a headstone for five pounds, with an inscription spelling out his accomplishments as an 'elder of the Presbyterian Congregation Cape George' and 'native of Lochaber, Scotland'.[22] This example further reinforces the probability that Scottish immigrants, under the guiding hand of clergy, had some input into the plans for their funerals, as well as the design of their headstones in a way that reflected their own cultural needs and expectations.

In a cemetery, headstone inscriptions are abbreviated snapshots which distil the deceased's life into as few characters as possible. They epitomise a personalised and public declaration of individual and group identities. As if staking territory and establishing legitimacy, some of Pictou County's early headstone inscriptions evince little modesty. There was no hiding of lights under bushels, especially if the deceased enjoyed the distinction of being one of the County's earliest Scottish settlers.[23] These first-comer claims possess what historian David Lowenthal has called 'a primordial resonance', for they bespoke a sense of entitlement and precedence, and trumped potential rivals.[24] Even more historically illustrious for Pictonians was the arrival of the *Hector* in 1773. As the ultimate bragging right in Pictou County, *Hector* connections bestowed status on the original passengers and their descendants, enjoyed enormous cultural capital in Pictou County and were given visual prominence and permanence on their headstones. Sometimes, details about links to the *Hector* were added to a headstone at a later date, a remedial decision spurred by ancestral pride to redress what was regarded as a serious oversight.[25] The scions of the *Hector* passengers shared in their collective glory, claiming a lineage and a family legacy which aggrandised group prestige and secured immortality in their headstone inscriptions. Similarly, an association with Pictou County's historic Pictou Academy possessed the lustre of celebrity, and this fact was deemed sufficiently significant to record for posterity, for both the living and the dead.[26]

In Antigonish County, headstone inscriptions present a different narrative of personal achievement. There, the chief metric for measuring social standing was proximity to the hierarchy of the Catholic Church, especially to eminent local clerics. This represented the most prestigious and laudable of pedigrees. In Antigonish's Old Catholic Cemetery, the headstone inscriptions of Jane Chisholm (d.1850) and Jessie Fraser (d.1871) certified familial ties to the much beloved Bishop Fraser as a significant status marker.[27] Similarly, the headstone inscription for Mrs Janet Chisholm vaunted her sibling bond with the Revd Colin Grant, an early priest who helped turn Northeastern Nova Scotia into 'a bastion of Roman Catholicism'.[28]

In Pictou County, there are other specimens of inscriptions which offer insights into the self-identification of some of the region's early Scottish immigrants. Some examples seem to substantiate the contention of Canadian historian Phillip Buckner that 'for many of the Scots', especially Lowland Scots, as well as their descendants, 'a sense of possessing a distinctive ethnic identity' was subsumed by an awareness of citizenship in a larger British community.[29] As a case in point, the headstone of the Lowlander, Renfrewshire-born Squire Robert Patterson, reads: 'one of the first English Settlers in Pictou'. Patterson was a prominent local merchant who was plugged into the Scottish merchantocracy, which played a pivotal role in the North Atlantic trade. This 'far-sighted businessman', who died in Pictou in 1808, construed his identity in strategic terms, undoubtedly perceiving 'the opportunities for profitable trade if the colony remained in Britain's good graces'.[30] A similar impulse may also explain why the Ayrshire and County Donegal roots of Thomas Harris were substantially downplayed by the time he died in Pictou in 1809. His now vanished monument proclaimed him to be 'the first descendant of an Englishman born in Pictou'.[31]

The most common hallmark of early Pictou County Scottish headstone inscriptions is stated place of origin. A significant number of Scottish immigrants used their grave markers to reaffirm connections between the old world and the new, by identifying the deceased's place of origin and forever linking them with their original home. Inscription data from Australian cemeteries shows similarly high frequency of specified origins on the headstones of Scottish immigrants.[32] There are several possible explanations for this phenomenon. Some historians suggest that noting birthplace on a headstone expresses 'alienation from the present and attachment to a faraway past' but equally credible is the theory that it exemplifies how individuals 'crystallizing' a new community 'identify themselves for themselves and for each other'.[33]

In many instances, headstone inscriptions, as demonstrated by Alexander McLeod's 1840 cemetery marker in Alma Cemetery, Pictou County, specified parish and county affiliations but not national origin.[34] Equally commonplace was the practice of delineating a three-part hierarchy of relationships, local, county and national, indicative of multiple senses of self-identity. This scale of identifiers echoes the findings of historian Leigh Straw, whose analysis of migrant headstones in colonial Tasmania demonstrates that Scottish identity was communicated 'in a variety of ways, including national, regional, and personal'.[35] The widespread use of the term 'Native of', instead of 'born' or 'of', is also telling for it asserted visually and self-consciously the indissoluble ties with the homeland. The 1859 headstone inscription for Agnes McIntosh, buried in Laurel Hill Cemetery, contains some instructive insights, particularly its use of the abbreviation 'N.B.' for North Britain, and the fact that birthplace was integral to her self-definition, although she had spent fifty-six of her seventy-one years as a resident of Pictou County.[36] In New Glasgow's Pioneer Cemetery, with headstones dating from 1793 to 1880, at least one-tenth of the markers use the term North Britain rather than Scotland, while simultaneously disclosing parish or county origins. A visit to Pictou County's cemeteries attests to the normative usage of 'North Britain', as well as 'Scotland' (although seldom concurrently) during the first half of the nineteenth century.

In contrast with Pictou County, the practice of stating place of origin was negligible in Antigonish County's Scottish Catholic cemeteries, although a meagre number of examples do exist. Inscription evidence for that county shows that the inhabitants seldom identified Scotland as their homeland and they steered completely clear of the term North Britain. In St Ninian's Old Catholic Cemetery in Antigonish, only five out of forty-eight extant headstones, many of them ledger stones dating from the mid-nineteenth century, specify place of origin, and only three of these actually identify Scotland. On the other hand, representing the exception rather than the norm, members of the Chisholm clan of Heatherton, Antigonish County, showed a marked predisposition for attesting to their Strathglass origins on their headstones.

In Antigonish County cemeteries, Scottish Catholic identity was framed almost exclusively in religious symbols rather than in stated birthplace origins. Many of the headstones in Antigonish County's early-nineteenth-century cemeteries can be classified as overt statements of Roman Catholic doctrine. Carvers did not shy away from displaying religious affiliation, despite the long years of penal repression which had left many of Scotland's Roman Catholics a small and often persecuted minority. It is said that Highland Catholicism flourished in Nova Scotia, particularly in Antigonish County, in 'a coherence not found elsewhere in Canada'.[37] Perhaps Antigonish Catholics were emboldened by their majority position, as well as the potent alliance of church and community, for in the early nineteenth century, 90 per cent of the coastline along the Northumberland Strait, stretching from the Pictou County–Antigonish County boundary to Margaree, Cape Breton, was Gaelic-speaking Catholic.[38] Catherine McLeod's 1832 headstone in Antigonish County's Paddy's Hollow Cemetery boldly declares her Catholicism with a crucifix and two descending doves, and a large pommee cross and christogram sculpted on the reverse side. The 1845 marker for 75-year-old Ann MacDonald in St Margaret's Cemetery, Arisaig, speaks of a lifetime of faith, displaying a centrally positioned cross, candlesticks and the Latin initialism, INRI, signifying Jesus of Nazareth, the King of the Jews. Ann Chisholm's faith and religious allegiance were plain for all to see on her St Andrew's Old Cemetery headstone, dated 1851, which gives central prominence to an altar-like ledge, four candlesticks, a crucifix, and the portal to heaven (Figure 4.1). The marker for the 21-year-old John McLelland, who died in a tragic drowning accident in 1857, also provides tangible expression of his Catholic affiliation. Situated in Antigonish's Old Catholic Cemetery, this stone incorporates the popular hand motif, clasping not another hand (which was the nineteenth-century convention), but rather a blessing cross encircled in vines, a common visual trope for Christ and the church.

The headstones of Antigonish County's early- to mid-nineteenth-century Scottish Catholics clearly lent themselves admirably to the display of religious orthodoxy. As simplified pictorial summaries of Catholic doctrine, many of these headstones feature such images as sculpted chalices and ciboria, crosses, and doves, all proxies for Christ. Crucifixion scenes were also incorporated into the tympana of some of the more elaborate early headstones in early Antigonish County. Inspired by liturgical art, these carved reliefs frequently featured realistic renditions of Christ, some of which were more skilfully executed than others. A cross-section of crucifixion scene types can be identified, including the depictions of Christ in human form, flanked by angels in the devotional postures of kneeling and praying.[39] The most striking permutation of the crucifixion scene, which has surfaced in several clusters throughout Antigonish County, features the two Marys, namely the Virgin Mary and Mary Magdalene. Their bodies, now sadly worn, are shown as virtually shrouded in full-length veils, the folds of which stream like hair, further accentuating their mournful poses.

Regrettably, it is nearly impossible to retrace the path these headstones followed on their journey from the carver's workshop to the cemetery. Were they carved locally, or regionally, or imported? At this stage of our research, we can only conclude that the carvers who produced Antigonish County's early headstones were conversant with Christian iconography, especially the pictorial language of the crucifixion. Furthermore, it is worth noting that, despite superficial similarities with Irish graveyards, Antigonish County's Scottish Catholic cemeteries seldom exhibited the emblems of the Passion. Folklorist Gerald Pocius discounts any parallels with Newfoundland's early Catholic cemeteries, which are noticeably devoid of such motifs as hand-held crosses and crucifixions.[40]

Given its visibility as a cultural reference point and as a cross-generational space, the Scottish immigrant cemetery would have been a perfect place to record and perpetuate the Gaelic language in Nova Scotia's

Figure 4.1 Catholic symbols on Ann Chisholm's headstone. (Credit: John D. Blackwell)

Scottish immigrant communities. Thus far in our research in Eastern Nova Scotia and Cape Breton, we have encountered sixty-six nineteenth-century and early-twentieth-century headstones with Gaelic inscriptions. This number may sound modest, but it is interesting to speculate about the large cohort of Nova Scotian Scots who did not articulate their cultural identity through Gaelic headstone inscriptions. For example, why is Gaelic text so conspicuously absent on the grave marker for the Revd D. B. Blair, who ministered to Nova Scotia's Free Church congregations of the Garden of Eden, Blue Mountain and Barney's River for almost forty years and distinguished himself as one of the foremost Gaelic scholars and poets of the nineteenth century? Similarly, why did William Cameron, a West River carpenter, leave explicit instructions in his 1893 will about the disposition of his cherished Gaelic bible but nothing about a Gaelic headstone inscription? Or why was there no Gaelic memorial language for the Caithness-born Alexander Forbes, also of West River, Pictou County, whose 'last words' were uttered in his mother tongue: '*Cha'n eagail duit's, tha Dia làidir*' ('Fear not, God is strong')?[41]

The oldest example in our inventory of Gaelic headstone inscriptions dates from 1829.[42] It can be found on the headstone in St Margaret's Cemetery, Arisaig, erected to commemorate Mary MacDonald, wife of John McLeod, who relocated to Antigonish County from Parrsboro, Nova Scotia, in 1801. One late-nineteenth-century example, dating from 1895, exists in St Andrew's Old Cemetery, Antigonish County for 83-year-old unmarried Christy Chisholm, who emigrated from Strathglass with her parents in 1818. She went to her grave with a somewhat generic Gaelic sendoff, '*SITH DHIA* [sic] *DHA H-ANAM*' ('The peace of God to her soul'), as well as a more particularised identification as '*NI'N IAN DUINN*' ('the daughter of brown-haired John'). One of the most striking examples of a Gaelic inscription can be found on the headstone of the Gaelic-speaking tradition bearer and bard, John MacLean, which enjoys an almost shrine-like status in Antigonish County's Glen Bard Cemetery. His inscription offers a novel twist on the age-old entreaty, 'Stop, passerby'. Rather than inviting reflection on human mortality, MacLean's inscription is an impassioned directive: '*Cùm a' Ghàidhlig suas ri d' bheò*' ('Keep up the Gaelic as long as you live') (Figure 4.2). Nearby is a constellation of grave markers, also adorned with Gaelic inscriptions, for MacLean's four children, his grandson and great grandson.

The dearth of Gaelic inscriptions in our sampling raises questions about the attrition of Gaelic and the perceived prestige of English as

Figure 4.2 Gaelic inscriptions on Bard John MacLean's headstone. (Credit: Michael Linkletter)

the language of the educated and literate, even among homogeneous Scottish populations. Why was Gaelic, the so-called language of the Garden of Eden, not the language of the cemetery? One is tempted to hypothesise whether English usage on so many headstones was an attempt at both status-marking and integration. This discussion closely intersects with the issue of why death became a catalyst for conformist expression among so many Scottish immigrants and why they opted for a pictorial rather than a linguistic signifier of identity.

It is axiomatic that the thistle is universally recognised as the national symbol of Scotland. The correlation between Scottishness and thistles dates back to the mid- to late fifteenth century.[43] According to J. H. Dickson and Agnes Walker, visual renditions of thistle heads and leaves became increasingly 'conventionalised' from the sixteenth century onward, as this emblem gained visibility in coinage, architecture and portraiture.[44] John Cameron's *The Gaelic Names of Plants*, published originally in 1883, offers a more religious shading to the thistle's meaning, noting that Mary's thistle (*fothannan beannuichte*) derived its name from folk beliefs linking the mottled leaves to the 'Virgin Mary's milk'.[45] Although imbued with secular and religious significance, thistles were also burdened with a stigma as a formidable menace to farmers in many of the colonies impacted by the Scottish diaspora.[46] In Nova Scotia, the flower was targeted in early-nineteenth-century county statutes as a noxious weed whose 'growth and increase' should be stamped out.[47] Despite this negative reputation, the colony of Nova Scotia issued a penny and halfpenny between 1823 and 1856, which featured a stylised thistle, symbolising the link between old and new Scotland.[48] One of the earliest headstones in our study, which dates from 1829, displays two thistles near its base. Presented in roundel form, they echo the shape of Nova Scotia's early-nineteenth-century thistled coinage.

Although thistle motifs enjoyed popularity in Pictou County cemeteries, they were not all-pervasive. In the New Glasgow Pioneer Cemetery, the resting place of many of Pictou County's early Scots, there is only one headstone out of seventy-one which is decorated with a thistle motif. It marks the burial site of John Weir, the sixteen-month-old son of Jonathan Weir of Paisley, Scotland, and Pictou County-born Agnes Park. A nineteenth-century stylistic preference for rosettes, as well as a variety of other neoclassical adornments, clearly predominates in this locale. In other Pictou County cemeteries, thistle motifs have a patterned incidence, which points to personal preferences through family groups as a deciding factor. In Pictou's Seaview Cemetery, the imposing markers of Robert McLeod (d.1865) and Hugh McLeod (d.1866) stand out, with sculpted thistles prominently displayed. In *Cladh MhicChoinnich* / MacKenzie Cemetery, situated near the Pictou County–Colchester County boundary, the headstones of husband and wife, Robert (d.1862) and Mary Murray (d.1852), exhibit thistle motifs, as if symbolising their ethnic solidarity in facing eternity. Catherine Ross McKay (d.1846) and Donald McKay (d.1857), buried in adjacent plots in the nearby Earltown Village Cemetery, also present a common front with their thistled grave markers (Figure 4.3).

The thistle enjoyed its greatest prominence in Pictou County cemeteries during the 1850s to 1870s, and appears to have commanded near equal popularity among the Scottish-born and Nova Scotia-born. Carvers in Pictou County showed a willingness to adapt the thistle symbol, so that it could be accommodated within the popular bedhead outline. They also demonstrated remarkable ingenuity and variation as the roundel variation morphed into different stylised thistle permutations, ranging from climbing thistles to sorrowful thistles, limply suggestive of death and mourning. The carvers also seamlessly integrated the thistle into a pre-existing repertoire of motifs, juxtaposing the wild flower (with stem, head and leaves) alongside laurels, bibles, urns, birds and hands (Figure 4.4). Sprigs of thistles were incorporated into the Victorian iconography of flowers, in combination with roses and lilies and even matching nosegays of forget-me-nots. Over time, the thistle began to look increasingly graceful and benign, an anaemic surrogate for its prickly and hardy antecedent.

Although the thistle enjoyed some measure of popularity throughout Pictou County cemeteries, its incidence in Antigonish County during the first half of the nineteenth century was comparatively limited. As noted earlier, we have identified in this region of Eastern Nova Scotia an early example dating back to 1829. Two striking variants of the roundel-style thistle, dating from the 1840s and 1850s, have been located respectively in cemeteries in St Joseph's and Heatherton. Two other mid-nineteenth-century examples in South River Cemetery capture the thistle's duality as a Scottish emblem and as a religious symbol, denoting earthly sorrow and sin, and closely identified with the Passion of Christ. In one instance, the spiky thistle leaves (without the thistle head) partially encircle a cross like a fiery crown of thorns, whereas in the other case, the cross is seemingly cradled by the stems of two flowering thistles (Figure 4.5). Both versions epitomise fittingly the conjoining of religion and ethnicity, which formed the core identity of Antigonish County's Scottish Catholics.

There was a discernible partiality among Nova Scotia's Scottish

Figure 4.3 Thistle motifs on the headstones of Catherine Ross McKay and Donald McKay. (Credit: John D. Blackwell)

Figure 4.4 Thistle, scroll, rosette, bible and hand motifs on David McIntosh's headstone. (Credit: John D. Blackwell)

immigrants in their spontaneous affection for specific plant species. For example, one suspects that many Gaels shared the sentiments of Mrs Mackintosh quoted in Patrick Campbell's *Travels in the Interior Inhabited Parts of North America* (1793): 'This is an ugly country that has no heather; I never yet saw any good or pleasant place without it.'[49] Certainly, Pictou County's Revd D. B. Blair was apologetic to his future wife about heather's absence in an otherwise 'large and splendid country' (*'Tìr ro ghreadhnach fharsainn'*).[50] Among the MacDonalds, the plant provoked special recognition and resonance as a clan emblem. John Campbell, a contemporary of the bard Allan the Ridge MacDonald, used the metaphorically striking image of heather when recounting the arrival of the MacDonalds in Mabou, Cape Breton, writing, *''S nuair a thig am brig ùr, bi smuid ri Geancaich / Bi Màbu fo fhraoch le laoich Abrach'* ('When the new ship arrives, the Yankees will be turfed out and the heather will take over in Mabou as the Lochaber warriors move in.').[51] Despite heather's symbolic connections to 'Old Scotland', thistles won out in Nova Scotia's cemeteries as the outward and official signifier of Scottishness, sanctioned by the state in the form of thistle coinage, and long-time usage.[52] As part of a metonymic code of images signifying Scottish ethnicity, the thistle's chief asset as a motif was its instant readability. It is also possible that the Scottish immigrants felt an affinity for the plant's distinctive qualities, which although often maligned and misunderstood, contributed to its hardiness and resilience. The Revd John Hugh Gillis (1910–2006) of MacKinnon Harbour and St Francis Xavier University recalled his father's more homespun explanation of the thistle's appeal as 'the one flower you cannot wipe your arse with'![53]

One of the most frustrating gaps in our research is the story of the carvers themselves. Unfortunately, there is little information to be found about them. Still, it seems reasonable to speculate that, when presented with new pressures and possibilities, the carvers' instinct for the familiar was tempered by a willingness to experiment as they derived impetus from the present as well as the past. This tendency is reflected in the housing traditions of the Scottish immigrants in Northeastern Nova Scotia, so it would logically also apply to their cemeteries.[54] In Eastern Nova Scotia, especially with its ties to oceanic trade and the expanding impact of contemporary British American consumer society, there was bound to be cross-fertilisation of visual imagery with other groups. The stone carvers, like the merchants and the clergy, worked with a varied clientele. Indeed, some crossed religious boundaries in terms of patronage, and probably acted as cultural brokers, bridging diverse cultures and visual traditions.

Figure 4.5 Cross and thistle motifs on Hugh Cameron's headstone. (Credit: John D. Blackwell)

Perhaps it is below ground that the historian will find some additional clues about the role that cemeteries played as repositories of identity in the lives of Nova Scotia's Scottish immigrants. In this regard, we are referring specifically to the recent discovery on the base of a local headstone, dated 1859, of the outline of a grinning semi-human face.[55] What is one to make of this singular and cryptic piece of work (see Figure 4.6)? It certainly does not fit into Antigonish County's vocabulary of mortuary motifs, such as flaming hearts, soul effigies and resurrection scenes. Although its full meaning is lost to us today, its location, underneath the groundline, removed from public gaze, suggests something unsanctioned by local Catholic clergy – an image that was figuratively and literally underground. It reminds one of the importance of supernatural folk beliefs among Eastern Nova Scotia's Scottish immigrants during the early nineteenth century, many of whom brought from Western Scotland an omen-reading tradition, an arsenal of practices serving as good-luck charms and numerous stories about fairies, ghosts, witches and the 'evil eye'.[56] Despite official church orthodoxy on death and burial, folklore, as was the case in the Highlands and Islands of Scotland, remained an integral part of early Scottish immigrant deathways in Eastern Nova Scotia. Although the headstones of the early immigrants represented an important strand of official theological expression among Antigonish County's nineteenth-century Scottish Catholics, the cemetery could have also functioned as a 'place of slippage between orthodoxy and "folk" Christianity'.[57] This headstone, and admittedly we know of only one of its kind, points to the possibility that other factors related to self-identity – based on the people's timeless lore – were also contained within the cemetery.

Cemeteries are but one aspect of the Scottish immigrant experience, albeit an important one. Just as there is no homogeneous narrative of Highland migration, there is no uniform reading of their cemeteries, which can be collapsed into a single theory. They were varied and complex places. In short, the cemeteries of immigrant Scots were fields of tension, where Scottishness was negotiated, new meanings of belonging forged, and religious differences spatially enforced. Although Scottish Presbyterians and Scottish Catholics in Pictou and Antigonish counties shared some iconography, they asserted strong religious perspectives and denominational boundary maintenance in their cemeteries, manifesting self-identity through physically segregated spaces and divergent religious symbolism. Early Pictou County's Presbyterian headstones, for example, seldom display human figures, either face or full body, utilising instead such decorative elements as rosettes, urns, bibles, and clasped and

Figure 4.6 Folk image on base of Mary McPherson's headstone. (Credit: Ann Macquarrie, Antigonish Heritage Museum)

pointing hands. Antigonish County's early-nineteenth-century Catholic cemeteries present a very different deathscape, one graced with images of doves, crosses, chalices, crucifixion scenes, and angel-like soul effigies.

The variability of inscriptional language in these two counties also offers useful insights to the historian. It demonstrates that the identities of diasporic Scots were woven and rewoven from multiple strands, fashioned from what historian Richard J. Finlay describes as 'a great many varieties of Scottishness and Britishness'.[58] Finlay provides a further key to unlocking the meaning of inscriptions with his statement that 'facets of regional and religious identity were probably more significant in the everyday lives of most Scots than the abstract notion of national identity.'[59] Still, one wonders what the abbreviation 'N.B.' meant to those Scottish immigrants who used it on their headstones? Was it an alternative vision of Scottishness or just a convenient shorthand for a carver faced with space constraints? Scholars have cautioned against the temptation to interpret a North British identity as an assimilated one. Historian T. C. Smout has argued persuasively that Scottish identity encompassed concentric loyalties, which permitted the Scots to reconcile fidelity to their history, culture and community, and fealty to the British monarchy, British constitution and British Empire.[60] However, it is also likely that the use of the term North Britain on a headstone was a status marker, involving to some degree a distancing from (not disowning of) the past, in order to announce one's membership in an expanding British Empire and carve out a role in the nineteenth-century's master narrative of progress. The socially aspirant nature of inscriptions also explains the near absence of Gaelic on headstones in both Pictou and Antigonish counties. Clearly, many Scottish immigrants, both Catholic and Presbyterian, did not want 'their personal stories inaccessible to outsiders'.[61] The cemetery was a public stage, not unlike the Pictou Academy and St Francis Xavier University, which became tools of an 'emerging culture of aspiration', masterminded by clerical leaders determined to elevate the social standing of their flocks.[62] As the language of instruction, English, not Gaelic, was the centrepiece of the agenda for these educational institutions.[63] Similarly, the cemeteries mirrored the larger societal pressures on Scottish immigrants to conform to the dominant mainstream language and culture, to mute expressions of exceptionalism, and to maximise their acceptance and opportunities.

Equally striking is the fact that Scots in Eastern Nova Scotia were not overly wedded to an exclusive set of Scottish symbols in their cemeteries. Headstones, such as John Maclean's, were far from typical, with its bold pairing of Gaelic and a thistle, a fitting juxtaposition for the bard who defended Highland honour during Pictou County's 1830 election with his rousing battle call for 'ethnic solidarity': *'Nuair 'dh'àrdaichear an cluarain'* ('When their thistles are raised high') and *'cuimhnichibh na Gàidheil'* ('remember the Gaels').[64] Admittedly, there were other expatriate Scots, both Catholic and Presbyterian alike, who adopted the thistle as an identifiably Scottish motif on their headstones. But what did this gesture signify to them? Did the thistle symbolise a meaningful ornamentation as an articulation of Scottishness or just a fashionable embellishment? Although there is no definitive answer to this question, it is clear that Antigonish County's Scottish Catholics assigned to the thistle a meaning that aligned with their theology and reflected their separate religious identity. In Pictou County, in particular, the stylised thistle, as a culturally relevant symbol, joined a broad transnational iconography of commemoration and was grafted onto obelisks, columns and urns, which flooded the cemeteries of nineteenth-century North America.[65] This process epitomised one of the many realities of the Scottish diaspora and serves as a metaphor for their experience – that many of the Scottish immigrants who came to Eastern Nova Scotia felt compelled to adapt successfully to the growing challenges of a modern transatlantic world. The act of relocating themselves geographically, socially and culturally necessitated that the old make concessions to the new, at least partially, as the price for belonging and the opportunity to get ahead. In sum, cultural tradition found ways to come to terms with the exigencies of everyday life. It is in the last resting places of Nova Scotia's Scottish immigrants that one sees so vividly displayed the dual forces of change and continuity, tradition and innovation, retention and adjustment, which reshaped their lives and deaths as immigrants.

NOTES

1. The authors gratefully acknowledge the financial support of the Social Sciences and Humanities Research Council of Canada (SSHRC). The authors also acknowledge their indebtedness to Dr Bernard Liengme who designed their database and to Steven Stamatopoulos, Natalie Chicoine, Hannah Krebs and Ryan MacDonald for their data entry. The support and assistance of the following people and organisations are also noted: Antigonish Heritage Museum, John D. Blackwell, Cape Breton Genealogy and Historical Association, Marleen Hubley-MacDonald, Ann Macquarrie, John Marshall, New Glasgow Public Library, Pictou County Roots Society, Dr Margaret Mackay, McCulloch House Museum & Genealogy Centre, Effie Rankin, and Bob Spurgeon.

2. Excerpt from *'Oran do dh'America'* ('Song for America'), translated by Sr Margaret MacDonell. M. MacDonell, *The Emigrant Experience: Songs of Highland Emigrants in North America* (Toronto: University of Toronto Press, 1982), pp. 86–7. Such is the esteem that many among Nova Scotia's Scottish community still have for this site that they helped finance its refurbishment in 1932 after the church had been without a roof for many years. It is also an important destination for many Scottish descendants getting in touch with their roots on visits to the 'Old Country'.
3. Leigh Straw, 'Landscapes of the Scottish dead: Headstones and identity in colonial Tasmania', *Journal of Australian Colonial History*, 14 (2012), p. 94.
4. Shamus MacDonald, '"*Dh'fheumadh iad àit' a dhèanamh*" (They would have to make a place): Land and belonging in Gaelic Nova Scotia' (PhD dissertation, Memorial University, 2019), p. 184.
5. Bill Bryson, *At Home: A Short History of Private Life* (Toronto: Doubleday Canada, 2013), p. 5; Richard E. Meyer (ed.), *Ethnicity and the American Cemetery* (Bowling Green: Bowling Green State University Popular Press, 1993), pp. 222–37. The term 'necroethnicity' was popularised in Meyer's monograph and pertains to the intersectional relationship between ethnicity and memorial practices, for example, funerary markers.
6. J. L. MacDougall, *History of Inverness County, Nova Scotia* (Belleville: Mika Publishing Company, 1976; reprint of original 1922 edition), p. 37.
7. Ibid., p. 38.
8. The concept of *dùthchas* is explored in James Hunter and Hugh Cheape, *Fonn's Duthchas / Land and Legacy* (Edinburgh: NMS Enterprises Limited Publishing, 2006), p. vi. In the foreword, the term is defined as 'a hereditary right to the place of your birth'. This term has multiple dimensions. In the context of this chapter, we are emphasising how a connection to a specific place helps to define the identity of its residents.
9. Donald A. Fergusson (ed.), *Fad Air Falbh as Innse Gall Leis Comhchruinneachadh Cheap Breatuinn / Beyond the Hebrides including the Cape Breton Collection* (Halifax: Lawson Graphics Atlantic Limited, 1977), p. 60.
10. Drummer on Foot (W. D. Cameron), 'Boyd's settlement', *The Casket*, 31 July 1913, in D. MacFarlane and R. A. MacLean (eds), *Drummer on Foot* (Antigonish: The Casket Printing & Publishing Company, 1999), p. 17.
11. Vincent W. MacLean, *These Were My People, Washabuck: An Anecdotal History* (Sydney: Cape Breton University Press, 2014), p. 172.
12. Ibid.
13. 'Letter to the editor', *The Casket*, 24 September 1857.
14. MacDougall, *History of Inverness County, Nova Scotia*, p. 408.
15. D. Campbell and R. A. MacLean, *Beyond the Atlantic Roar: A Study of the Nova Scotia Scots* (Toronto: McClelland and Stewart Limited, 1974), pp. 35–65.

16. D. M. R. Bentley, 'Simile, metaphor, and the making and perception of Canada', *Studies in Canadian Literature*, 1:42 (2017), pp. 66–83.
17. Marleen Hubley-MacDonald, 'Introduction: St. Margaret of Scotland, Arisaig', in *Antigonish Area Catholic Cemeteries*, DVD (no date, no pagination).
18. George Patterson, *A History of the County of Pictou, Nova Scotia* (Montreal: Dawson Brothers, 1877), p. 30.
19. Ibid., p. 40.
20. A. A. Johnston, *A History of the Catholic Church*, 1 (Antigonish: St Francis Xavier University Press, 1960), p. 320.
21. MacDougall, *History of Inverness County Nova Scotia*, p. 516.
22. Antigonish Heritage Museum, Antigonish, MS. Collection of John McMillan, St Andrews, 22 October 1855.
23. In New Glasgow's Pioneer Cemetery (also known as MacGregor Cemetery or Founders Cemetery), the inscription for William McKay (d.1814) reads: 'Among the first settlers in this districk'. This cemetery also includes the following inscription for Alexander Fraser (d.1829): 'The First man child Born of European Parents on the East River of Pictou'. Similarly, Alma Cemetery includes headstones for Alex Fraser (d.1803), described as 'the first settler upon the Middle river' and John Crocket (d.1790) and his spouse, Margaret Young (d.1817), characterised as 'of the First inhabitants of Pictou'.
24. David Lowenthal, *The Heritage Crusade and the Spoils of History* (Cambridge: Cambridge University Press, 1998), p. 173.
25. For example, the New Glasgow Pioneer Cemetery headstone inscription for Colin McKay (d.1804) and his son, Colin (d.1850), reads: 'BOTH ARRIVED PICTOU 1773 ON FIRST TRIP OF BRIG HECTOR'. This distinction, rendered in capitals in a plainer, more modern script, clearly postdates the original hand-carved inscription for the father.
26. David Fraser's (d.1827) connection to the Pictou Academy was immortalised in the following headstone inscription, which can be found in Union Centre Pioneer Cemetery: 'He was one of the first Divinity Students taught in the Pictou Academy.'
27. Their headstone inscriptions read as follows: 'The deceased was the mother of the late Rt. Rev. William Fraser, Bishop of Arichat' and 'Only sister of the late Bishop Fraser.'
28. R. A. MacLean, 'Colin P. Grant', in *Dictionary of Canadian Biography*, VII (Toronto: University of Toronto Press, 1988), p. 355. Her headstone states that she was 'Rev. Colin Grant's sister'.
29. Phillip Buckner, 'The transformation of the Maritimes, 1815–1860', *The London Journal of Canadian Studies*, 9 (1993), p. 26.
30. A. A. MacKenzie, 'Robert Patterson', in *Dictionary of Canadian Biography*, V (Toronto: University of Toronto Press, 1983), p. 660.
31. Patterson, *A History of the County of Pictou*, p. 57.
32. Benjamin Wilkie, 'Space, commemoration, and iconography: Scottish

memorials in Australia', in Fred Cahir, Anne Beggs Sunter and Alison Inglis (eds), *Scots under the Southern Cross: Scottish Impressions of Colonial Australia* (Ballarat: Ballarat Heritage Services, 2015), pp. 157–65; Straw, 'Landscapes of the Scottish dead', pp. 89–106.

33. Frances Swyripa, 'Ancestors, the land, ethno-religious identity on the Canadian prairies: Comparing the Mennonite and Ukrainian legacies', *Journal of Mennonite Studies*, 21 (2003), pp. 49–50.
34. For example, McLeod's headstone inscription reads: 'A native of the Parish of Tongue Sutherland Shire'.
35. Straw, 'Landscapes of the Scottish dead', p. 95.
36. McIntosh's inscription reads: 'The deceased was a native of Edinburgh N.B. and for 56 years an Inhabitant of Pictou'.
37. Dan MacInnes, 'The legacy of Highland "heather" priests in Eastern Canada', in Daniel MacLeod and Stuart Macdonald (eds), *Keeping the Kirk: Scottish Religion at Home and in the Diaspora* (Guelph: Guelph Series in Scottish Studies, 2014), pp. 89–90.
38. Ibid., p. 105.
39. For a more detailed description of these crucifixion headstone motifs, see Laurie Stanley-Blackwell, '"What lies beneath": The Green Man in Eastern Nova Scotia and Scottish folk beliefs' *Markers*, 32 (2016), pp. 45–8.
40. Personal communication, e-mail from Gerald Pocius to Laurie Stanley-Blackwell, 2 October 2016.
41. McCulloch House Museum & Genealogy Centre, Pictou, Diary of Alexander Forbes Jr. 1883 (unpublished typescript), File 92–22.
42. For a more detailed overview of Gaelic headstone inscriptions in Nova Scotian cemeteries, see Laurie Stanley-Blackwell and Michael Linkletter, 'Inscribing ethnicity: A preliminary analysis of Gaelic headstone inscriptions in Eastern Nova Scotia and Cape Breton', *Genealogy*, 2:3 (2018) <https://www.mdpi.com/2313-5778/2/3/29> (accessed 1 June 2019).
43. J. H. Dickson and Agnes Walker, 'What is the Scottish thistle?', *The Glasgow Naturalist*, 20:2 (1981), p. 102.
44. Ibid., p. 118.
45. John Cameron, *The Gaelic Names of Plants (Scottish, Irish, and Manx)* (Glasgow: John MacKay Celtic Monthly Office, 1900), p. 53.
46. Clint Evans, 'The 1865 *Canada Thistle* Act of Upper Canada as an expression of a common culture of weeds in Canada and the Northern United States', in Donald H. Akenson (ed.), *Canadian Papers in Rural History*, 10 (Gananoque, Ontario: Langdale Press, 1996), pp. 127–48.
47. *The Revised Statutes of Nova-Scotia* (Halifax: Richard Nugent Publisher, 1851), p. 504.
48. D. A. K., 'The coinage of Nova Scotia', *The Canadian Stamp and Coin Journal*, 1:1 (July 1888), p. 6.

49. Patrick Campbell, *Travels in the Interior Inhabited Parts of North America* (Edinburgh: John Guthrie, 1793), p. 57.
50. John A. Macpherson and Michael Linkletter (eds), *Fògradh, Fàisneachd, Filidheachd / Parting, Prophesy, Poetry* (Sydney: Cape Breton University Press, 2013), pp. 226–7.
51. Effie Rankin, *As a 'Bhràighe / Beyond the Braes: The Gaelic Songs of Allan the Ridge MacDonald, 1794–1868* (Sydney: University College of Cape Breton Press, 2004), p. 19.
52. Suzanne Zeller, 'George Dawson, Victorian botany, the origin of species and the case of Nova Scotian heather', in Paul A. Bogaard (ed.), *Profiles of Science and Society in the Maritimes Prior to 1914* (Fredericton: Acadiensis Press, 1990) pp. 51–62.
53. MacLean, *These Were My People*, p. 127.
54. During the early nineteenth century, the tradition-based practices of builders and carvers alike were affected by the growing profusion of published pattern books. According to Daniel Maudlin, despite their fierce loyalty to their language, literature, music and dance, Scottish Gaelic immigrants to Nova Scotia were not inflexible in their attachment to their own vernacular building traditions, which were quickly subsumed by 'contemporary colonial British American architectural standards'. In short, they adopted the classically styled and proportioned timber-framed houses of the northeastern seaboard with 'near total uniformity', closely replicating them in terms of 'form, plan and elevation, architectural ornament, building materials and construction methods'. See Maudlin, 'Architecture and identity on the edge of empire: The early domestic architecture of Scottish settlers in Nova Scotia, Canada, 1800–1850', *Architectural History*, 50 (2007), p. 100.
55. For a more detailed analysis of this remarkable headstone, see Stanley-Blackwell, '"What lies beneath"', pp. 40–63.
56. Charles W. Dunn, *Highland Settler: A Portrait of the Scottish Gael in Cape Breton and Eastern Nova Scotia* (Wreck Cove, Cape Breton: Breton Books, 1991, reprint of original 1953 edition), p. 47.
57. Elizabeth Ritchie, '"A palmful of water for your years": Babies, religion and gender among crofting families in Scotland, 1800–1850', in Jodi A. Campbell, Elizabeth Ewan and Heather Parker (eds), *The Shaping of Scottish Identities: Family, Nation, and the Worlds Beyond* (Guelph: Centre for Scottish Studies, 2011), p. 66.
58. Richard J. Finlay, 'Caledonia or North Britain? Scottish identity in the eighteenth century', in Dauvit Broun, R. J. Finlay and Michael Lynch (eds), *Image and Identity, The Making and Re-making of Scotland through the Ages* (Edinburgh: John Donald Publishers Ltd, 1998), p. 143.
59. Ibid., p. 144.
60. T. C. Smout, 'Perspectives on the Scottish identity', *Scottish Affairs*, 6 (Winter 1994), pp. 101–13. This concept is explored in Michael Newton,

'Scotland's two solitudes abroad: Immigrant identity in North America', in Campbell et al. (eds), *The Shaping of Scottish Identities*, pp. 215–33.
61. Swyripa, 'Ancestors, the land, ethno-religious identity on the Canadian Prairies', p. 49.
62. James D. Cameron, '"Erasing forever the brand of social inferiority": Saint Francis Xavier University and the Highland Catholics of Eastern Nova Scotia', CCHA, *Historical Studies*, 59 (1992), p. 57. As noted in Cameron's article, this concept and terminology are adapted from David O. Levine's *The American College and the Culture of Aspiration, 1915–1940* (Ithaca and London: Cornell University Press, 1986).
63. Gaelic language courses were offered at St Francis Xavier University by 1890–1, but English remained the primary language of instruction. See Michael Linkletter, '*Gàidhlig aig Oilthigh Naoimh Fransaidh Xavier agus an t-Urramach Alasdair MacIlleathain Sinclair* / Gaelic at St Francis Xavier University and the Rev. Alexander Maclean Sinclair', in Kenneth E. Nilsen (ed.) *Rannsachadh Na Gàidhlig 5: Fifth Scottish Gaelic Research Conference* (St Francis Xavier University, Antigonish, Nova Scotia, 21–4 July 2008) (Sydney: Cape Breton University Press, 2010), pp. 134–48.
64. Sheila M. Kidd, '*A Thaghdairean Gaedhealach* / Early Gaelic electioneering', in Kenneth E. Nilsen (ed.), *Rannsachadh Na Gàidhlig 5: Fifth Scottish Gaelic Research Conference* (St Francis Xavier University, Antigonish, Nova Scotia, 21–4 July 2008) (Sydney: Cape Breton University Press, 2010), p. 117; Robert Dunbar, 'The secular poetry of John MacLean, "Bàrd Thighearna Chola", "Am Bàrd MacGilleain"' (PhD dissertation, University of Edinburgh, 2006), pp. 564–5. This excerpt comes from the poem, 'Don Phàrlamaid Ùir' ('To the New Parliament'), which opens with the line: 'A Toast to the People of the Plaids'. It was first published in A. Maclean Sinclair, *Clarsach na Coille* (Glasgow: Archibald Sinclair and R. McGregor & Co., 1881), pp. 142–5, where it is entitled 'Brosnachadh Roghnachaidh' ('The Election Incitement').
65. The following article explores how the figural monument of Mary Sutherland Morrison in Pictou County's Garden of Eden Cemetery partially exemplifies the inroads of North American trends and tastes into the County's late-nineteenth-century cemeteries. See Laurie Stanley-Blackwell and Brenda Appleby, 'Romancing the stone: Female figural monuments in late-nineteenth-century Nova Scotian cemeteries' *Markers*, 29 (2014), pp. 16–53.

5

Scottish Gravestones in Ceylon in Comparative Perspective

Angela McCarthy

In May 1892, Scotsman James Taylor, renowned as the 'father of the Ceylon tea enterprise', died in disgrace after his dismissal from Loolecondera, the plantation he had managed for forty years. This termination took place despite his fellow planters publicly recognising his achievements the previous year. In acknowledging Taylor's accomplishments, they had subscribed funds that enabled him to receive a silver tea service and a sum of money. Following his death, his friends and fellow planters took to the press to hotly dispute accusations from his employer that Taylor was lethargic.[1] Instead, they declared vigorously that Taylor 'spoke too plainly about the interference of the Managing Director in the management of Loolecondura ... It is indeed a sad reflection that this respected and honoured old planter, just after receiving a spontaneous testimonial from the whole body of Ceylon planters, should have been dismissed by a body of London Directors on whose board there is neither a practical planter nor a Ceylon man.'[2]

That press coverage further documents developments surrounding Taylor's burial and memorialisation. On Tuesday 3 May 1892, a day after his death, Taylor was taken from the Loolecondera estate where he lived and worked for burial at the Mahaiyawa Cemetery near Kandy. Two gangs of twelve estate workers reputedly carried Taylor's body (said to have weighed 246 pounds) to his final resting place, alternating every four miles during the eighteen-mile journey.[3] Among friends who attended the committal were several neighbouring planters and others who had subscribed to the fund for Taylor's silver tea service. The Revd Watt conducted the funeral service.[4]

Such was the esteem with which Taylor was held among the Ceylon planting community that fellow planter W. H. Walters, of the neighbouring Gonavy estate, recommended the erection of a granite slab and headstone on Taylor's grave together with an inscription recognising his contributions to both the tea and cinchona enterprises in Ceylon.[5] E. Hamlin of the Oriental Bank Estates Company, Taylor's employers, similarly wrote to the press stating his intention to provide funds for the erection of a headstone and recommending that a memorial tablet 'be placed in the church at Kandy'.[6] A memorial fund for a headstone was established and among the fifty-two contributors were Taylor's sister Margaret Nairn in Scotland and Sir Thomas Lipton (another Scotsman whose name is most famously linked to Ceylon tea). Of a total sum of 1,135 rupees and 86 cents, Margaret donated the largest amount (one third, or 410 rupees and 26 cents). This was likely due to her being a beneficiary of Taylor's will as well as a recipient over the years of substantial remittances from her brother. The memorial fund was used to obtain a tombstone (costing £44 1s 0d) and ship it from the UK, pay landing charges, rail, cart and 'coolie' hire, erect the headstone at the cemetery, acquire chains and pillars to place around the grave and build the foundations, and provide photographs of Taylor and his grave along with postage to send the images to Scotland.[7] Walters, who managed the nearby Gonavy estate, sent the press a photograph of the tombstone and described how 'At one end of the marble-enclosed grave, rises a tasteful pedestal surmounted by a granite and flower-carved cross' (Figure 5.1).[8]

The headstone's grey granite construction reflects Taylor's origins in the north-east of Scotland[9] while the vegetation depicts the passion flower, not only symbolising the passion of Jesus Christ, but being in full bloom represented Taylor as being in the prime of his life, possibly an act of defiance against his employers. At the centre of the cross is engraved 'IHS', also redolent of Christ. Absent, however, is any explicit reference to Taylor's origins in Scotland, either through an inscription or symbolism. Instead, his contribution to Ceylon's economy is to the fore. In part, this is likely due to the role of the male planting community rather than his immediate kin connections proposing the text on his headstone and organising his funeral. Crucially, however, his gravestone did not simply illustrate secular respectability and the affection of friends but had important Christian connotations.[10]

In 1997, 105 years after Taylor's death, a group of Japanese tea dignitaries added an additional plaque to the gravesite to commemorate the 130th anniversary of Taylor's first cultivation of Ceylon tea. It was presumably on this visit that the delegation is said to have cracked open a miniature bottle of whisky on the grave. More recently, tea trees have been planted beside the grave in recognition of Taylor's importance to the country's tea economy. Such additions showcase the ongoing social

Figure 5.1 The headstone of James Taylor, 'father of the Ceylon tea enterprise'. (Copyright: Angela McCarthy)

relevance and significance of organised British burial spaces overseas and the role of headstones in the tourism industry.[11]

As well as his gravesite, James Taylor is commemorated in Sri Lanka in diverse ways including tea tins, sculptures and exhibits at the Ceylon Tea Museum. Perhaps most striking of all is a sixteen-foot-high bust of Taylor which stands at the entrance to the Mlesna tea castle at Talawakelle, a mock Scottish baronial castle, made of Sri Lankan granite, which opened in 2008, a tribute to the Scot from Anselm Perera of Mlesna tea.

In 2017 and 2019 smaller replica busts of Taylor, also funded by Perera, were unveiled and placed on display in Taylor's home area of the Mearns in Scotland, at the Laurencekirk Academy and at Auchenblae. Yet unlike his memorialisation at the Mahaiyawa Cemetery, James Taylor is not commemorated in the Presbyterian church cemetery at Auchenblae, Kincardineshire, in north-east Scotland where he originated and where his father and mother are buried. This is puzzling as when Taylor's sister Margaret erected a plaque to their parents, Michael and Margaret Taylor, in 1896, her brother had been dead four years. It is even more perplexing in light of the reference on her stepmother's headstone, in the same cemetery, to their half-brother William's death at Jeypore, India, in 1894.[12] Other references to Scots who died abroad likewise appear on assorted stones in the Auchenblae churchyard, including Joseph Stephen at Jamaica in 1821, William Allan at Demerara in 1831, John Caird at New South Wales in 1878, James Bruce at Calcutta in 1879, George Duncan in New Zealand in 1883, John Bonar at Armalade [?Armadale], Australia in 1888, William Andrew Brown at Colombo in 1895, Charles Keppie at South Africa in 1938, and William John Menzies Keppie at India in 1989.

Analysis of James Taylor's headstone therefore raises an interesting question: with only the Aberdeen granite suggestive of his Scottish origins, were ethnic and national identities unimportant for Scots in Ceylon? If so, does that reflect a disinterest towards ethnic and national origins in the country more broadly? How far do the headstones of British and Irish migrants in Ceylon resemble or differ from their counterparts in other parts of the world in displaying attachment to home? Engaging with such questions is critical in light of debates which explore the retention or abandonment of ethnicity and issues surrounding migrant belonging. For instance, ethnicity is often associated with minority status and victimhood but research on the Scots abroad demonstrate ethnicity emerging from a positive standpoint. Furthermore, ascertaining the presence or absence of Scottish identity on headstones is important as some leading Scottish intellectuals in the early nineteenth century had voiced concerns that Scottish identity was under threat from Anglicisation and that the ancient nation might become 'North Britain', a mere regional appendage of England with Scottish traditions and institutions made invisible and its culture anglicised. What made Scotland distinctive was said to be fast disappearing.[13]

The following analysis draws on evidence from five cemeteries in the central Highland region of Sri Lanka: the Garrisons Cemetery at Kandy (established 1817), and burial yards attached to the Anglican Holy Trinity Church at Nuwara Eliya (established 1852), St Andrews at Haputale (opened 1869), St John's Church at Lindula (consecrated in 1876), and the Anglican Christ Church Warleigh at Dickoya (built 1878). The chronological coverage spans the mid- to late-Victorian period, a time of high imperialism. It moves, however, beyond considering exceptional graves and memorials commemorating renowned individuals often found inside churches. Instead, it focuses on those who lost their lives – often at a young age – without fame or recognition.

While the emphasis in what follows draws largely from fieldwork in Sri Lankan cemeteries, it also utilises written records to extend the analysis further. Important here is J. Penry Lewis's published monumental collection of transcriptions from Ceylon cemeteries. Published in 1913, the volume came about due to the disappearance of many Portuguese inscriptions, partly due to destruction, and the erosion of Dutch inscriptions arising from carelessness. Lewis sought to 'record the monumental inscriptions of historical or local interest in the Island which have survived the ravages of time and the ruthless hands of the utilitarian and the vandal'.[14] Lewis's transcriptions, however, are limited to the words on headstones, thereby missing any depiction of origins through iconography or the type of stone itself, both of which can aid in identifying ethnicity. His collection is also far from comprehensive, failing, for instance, to include the headstones of St Andrew's Haputale and only recording some of the headstones at the other four cemeteries investigated for this chapter. Lewis does, however, provide supplementary genealogical information about those buried in addition to headstone transcriptions, some of which connects the deceased to their place of origin. The entry for James Taylor, for instance, notes that he was part of a cohort of young men from Laurencekirk who went to Ceylon and that he had planted nineteen acres of tea at Loolecondera which formed the oldest tea field in the country. Meanwhile, the entry for his relative David Moir states that he was one of four brothers from Kincardineshire who went to Ceylon.[15] Publications such as that by

Lewis reveal the interest shown in memorials by contemporaries in the early twentieth century.

Further helpful published works include the family history records compiled by Eileen Hewson, founder of the Kabristan Archives. Hewson has reproduced many monumental inscriptions from Sri Lanka, together with baptismal and marriage records. With the first transcripts published online in 2013, as at September 2019, there are almost 85,000 burial records.[16] Similar to Lewis, however, Hewson does not include reference to the symbolism or composition of headstones, aspects that can offer clues about ethnic and national identities.

Much previous scholarly work on gravestones focuses primarily on one burial yard, thereby raising conceptual problems of representativeness that this chapter attempts to address through situating its analysis within a broader British imperial world in order to investigate divergence as well as similarities and borrowings. The promise of comparative analysis among different ethnicities is also evident in other studies of death. For instance, in his study of Symonds Street Cemetery at Auckland, New Zealand, Shaun Higgins points to Presbyterians being more inclined than other denominations to be buried in family plots, with their headstones listing up to twelve others interred in the same grave.[17] Contemporaries also remarked on certain funeral practices as being distinctive. In 1852 John Askew visited Auckland and noted that Catholic burials were free of grass and soil and 'distinguished by a large wooden cross, painted white' while Protestant graves 'were covered with long grass and fern'.[18] Some other chapters in this book similarly seek comparative insights. How far, then, did Scottish headstones in Ceylon mirror or deviate from the stones commemorating other migrants, and how did the situation in Ceylon compare with burials elsewhere in the British World?

SCOTTISH HEADSTONES IN CEYLON

James Taylor made his move to Ceylon within the context of family networks. He travelled there at sixteen years of age in 1851 with his second cousin Henry Stiven to join Peter Moir, another relative who was an agent on coffee estates. All three emerged from the Mearns district of north-east Scotland, an area with a strong educational and agricultural tradition, which made them ideal recruits to develop Ceylon's planting economies. With Ceylon a tropical environment, it is no surprise to find that many planters from Scotland and other parts of Europe were cut down in the prime of their life.[19] Henry Stiven was just thirty-five years of age when he died at Colombo in May 1865. Taylor recorded details of his relative's passing beside a photograph of the two men in one of his surviving albums, noting that Stiven had died at the Galle Face Boarding House in Colombo and was buried the next morning in the city. Stiven's grave in Colombo has not been located, but it may have originally been at the Galle Face Burial Ground, from where surviving headstones were relocated to the Kanatte Cemetery at Borella in Colombo. Stiven's wife, Margaret, had died two years earlier and the surviving children were sent to relatives in Scotland. Margaret's headstone recorded that she was on the 'Soudoogana' [Suduganga] estate but, here again, later transcriptions make errors.[20]

Several years earlier, in 1857, another of Taylor's relatives, David Moir, died at thirty-one years of age from cholera, having spent just five years on the island. Transferred by water, food and bodily fluids and causing symptoms of 'mental depression and internal distress, followed by vomiting, stomach cramps, and acute diarrhea', cholera was a feared killer. Victims became weak and thirsty, cold and clammy, and suffered from cramp. They usually died from dehydration within hours of contracting the disease.[21] Taylor described his relative's death to his father in solemn terms: 'He was seized with it about 8 O'Clock in the morning and died at 4 O'Clock in the afternoon was carried into Kandy that night and buried next day.'[22] All told, around 60 per cent of those who contracted cholera in the nineteenth century were likely to die from the disease.[23] David Moir was laid to rest in the renowned Garrisons Cemetery at Kandy where his headstone, like Taylor's, provides no indication of his Scottish origins and little more than his name, age, date and place of death.

Established in 1817 and closed to new burials in 1873, the Garrisons Cemetery contains the headstones of 195 men, women, and children. Many more graves are unmarked. Originally created to bury military officers and their families, it soon became the final resting place for many civil servants and coffee planters. Among a range of memorials are table tombs, tablets, obelisks, and pillars. The cemetery underwent restoration in 1998 to coincide with Sri Lanka's fiftieth anniversary of independence and Prince Charles' visit to the country; it remains carefully tended by the caretaker, Charles Carmichael.

If David Moir's headstone fails to note his origins, other headstones at the Garrisons Cemetery do testify to the diverse homelands of those buried there. The stone marker erected in 1859 for James McPherson, for instance, notes his origins at 'Kingussie N.B.' [North Britain]. Capital lettering stated that the stone was 'Erected by Highlanders who desire

Figure 5.2 The headstone of James McPherson at Garrisons Cemetery, Kandy. (Copyright: Angela McCarthy)

thus to record the piety integrity and sterling worth of a countryman whose loss they deeply deplore'. As noted earlier, the reference to North Britain reflects a period in which Scotland was seen in regional terms, with fears emerging that the nation was losing its sense of Scottish identity. James Urquhart, meanwhile, 'born in the parish of Marytown, Scotland', died from cholera in 1865 at thirty-two years of age. As with Taylor, Urquhart's headstone was erected by fellow planters, in his case the proprietors of the Hantane estate 'in appreciation of the worth of the deceased, and of the zeal displayed by him for their interest while Manager of that Property'. Charles Burnett, 'born at Fraserburgh' and who died in 1862, was another whose stone 'was erected by his sorrowing friends in Ceylon in remembrance of his amiability and worth'.

Apart from cholera, the headstones at Garrisons Cemetery record other causes of death. John Spottiswoode Robertson 'born in Edinburgh' in 1823 was 'Killed by an Elephant' in 1856, while Archibald Montgomerie of 'North Britain' died in 1821 from 'Jungle Fever'. George Baxter Wilson, 'a native of Aberdeenshire', died in 1865 from 'remittent fever'. In a country where fragile historical documents are subject to deterioration and destruction, the sturdiness of these stones helps provide important insight into Ceylon society. Only rarely, however, do the stones reveal their stonemasons, including J. Taylor from Harrow Road, London, England; Caffin of London; and the Great North of Scotland Granite Company at Peterhead.

All told, of 144 transcriptions available for the Garrisons Cemetery at Kandy, just over one-fifth (n=31) made reference to the British origins of the deceased. Almost half of those stones (n=14) related to Scots with town, county and/or country recorded. Irrespective of the birthplace of the deceased, almost all inscriptions that specified place of origin testified to family relationships, particularly the ranking of birth, for example whether the eldest, second or third son and so on.[24] Statistical analysis of the transcriptions for headstones in other cemeteries has not been undertaken, though the example of Holy Trinity Churchyard at Nuwara Eliya is instructive. There, of 231 transcribed inscriptions compiled by Eileen Hewson, just 12 per cent (n=27) noted migrant origins, with 8 from Scotland, 13 from England and 5 from Ireland. The greater percentage of stones stipulating the origins of those buried at the Garrisons Cemetery is likely due to its earlier establishment.

Consideration of the specific Scottish burials at Trinity Church, Nuwara Eliya, is similarly informative. Buried there were John David Purdie Maclean (d.1908), 'born at Calgary Castle, Isle of Mull' in 1869, John Gordon (d.1916) 'born at Rhynie, Aberdeenshire' in 1845, John

Figure 5.3 The headstone of Archibald MacPhee MacNeill at Trinity Church, Nuwara Eliya. (Copyright: Angela McCarthy)

Arbuthnott Smith (d.1894) 'who was born at Edinburgh' in 1851, and Archibald MacPhee MacNeill (d.1949) born in 1883 on the 'Isle-of-Colonsay, Argyllshire'. MacNeill's headstone does not appear in Hewson's transcripts, which further demonstrates the value of field research. Among English migrants buried in the church grounds were William Clarence Watson of Colworth House, Bedfordshire, who died in 1906, William White who was born at Bath in 1819 and died in 1892 and his wife Eliza from Hampshire (born 1822, died 1897), and Arthur John Hamilton-Harding, born in England in 1868 and his wife Ebba born in 1865 in Sweden. A few stray Irish also appear: the Revd David Tweed, born in Ireland in 1870 and died at Nuwara Eliya in 1939, and George William Lindsay White, born in Limerick and who died in 1922.

A possible explanation for this display of migrant birthplaces at Nuwara Eliya is that the church – an Anglican one – catered to a small community and was open to burials from all denominations and ethnicities, some of whom may have been prompted to demonstrate their ethnic difference. Lindula's difference, meanwhile, apart from being noticeably overgrown, is the greater ethnic diversity of those buried in its grounds. Burials there include not just migrants from Britain and Ireland but those from Drontheim in Norway and Montego Bay in Jamaica.[25]

While national and ethnic origins do appear on gravestones in churchyards in Ceylon, they are not widespread. Part of the reason may have been that friends and family were more likely to want to record the professions or connect migrants to their local areas across Ceylon, especially in the key sphere of economic activity, such as plantations. Among those buried at Trinity Church, Nuwara Eliya, for instance, was Alexander Burnett Oliver (d.1892), 'tea and coffee planter', who, as the stone notes, had worked on the Gowerakellie estate at Badulla. The St Andrew's Church at Haputale is the final resting place of Alfred Scovell (d.1926) of Beauvais estate and Joseph Harper (d.1895) of Craig estate, Bandarawella. Headstones at Lindula also marked occupations including William Wilson Smith (d.1939), 'for 55 years planter in Ceylon', along with assorted medical officers, priests, soldiers, chief superintendent of police in Ceylon, and vice-principal of Trinity College Kandy. Occupation, then, was as likely as place of origin to appear on grave markers, perhaps reflecting the admiration of family and friends who were responsible for selecting such inscriptions. For Scots, the recording of occupations continues a tradition from earlier times when trade symbols were inscribed on headstones across north-eastern Scotland.[26]

If place of birth, occupations and cause of death appear on the headstones of various ethnic groups in Ceylon, English migrants were striking in using memorials to reinforce connections with their families back in the UK. For example, at Trinity Church, Nuwara Eliya, we find William McFerran, the younger son of William McFerran (d.1879) of Grotburn, Kersal, Lancashire. Donald George Maclean Loxdale (d.1912) was commemorated on a Celtic cross as the 'beloved son' of Joseph and Caroline of Saundby Grove, Nottinghamshire, while Otway Hensley Woodhouse (d.1912) features as the second son of Coventry Woodhouse of Mincing Lane, London, and Southmead, Wimbledon Park, the places of work and residence of his father. This striking aspect of family lineage among the English-born is also evident at Christ Church, Warleigh. Here, in a breathtaking setting, are the final resting places of the following: Edith Mary, 'daughter of the late Rev Fitzwilliam Taylor, Rector of Ogwell and Haccombe, Co. Devon'; Ida Daphne (d.1909), the 'beloved daughter' of Hastings Gilbert Hickey and Alice Leila Hickey who came from Reading in Berkshire; Eric William Morris (d.1919), the son of Hugh Stanley and Grace Morris of 'Brownhill, Bursledon, S. Hants'; and James Berick (d.?1893), the son of Major General Heste of Brighton. Parts of the British diaspora, then, catalogued specific individuals at home. In some cases, individuals who returned from Ceylon to Britain then wanted to be repatriated back to Asia. Among them was Trevor Alistair Moy who died in Eastbourne, England, but was buried 'in his beloved Sri Lanka' in 2002.

Why, though, were English migrants more likely to be connected to their family lineages back in England? That they may have had greater resources to cover the cost of such detailed genealogies is one explanation, though without access to probate information such a hypothesis is only tentative. Additionally, the English-born may have been more inclined to have families in Ceylon who could testify to such lineages, thereby distinguishing them from their Scottish counterparts who were frequently single.

EXPLAINING THE ABSENCE OF ETHNICITY

How, then, can we explain the fleeting references to Scottish ethnicity, in words or symbols, on gravestones in Sri Lankan graveyards? Does it reflect a broader disinterest in identity among the various national groups of the British World in Ceylon in the nineteenth and early twentieth centuries? Broader research, at least for the Scots, suggests this explanation is not tenable. Highland Scots controlled the press in Ceylon and routinely published on Scottish activities on the island, including accounts of St Andrew's Day gatherings. Planters often named coffee and tea estates after places back in Britain and Ireland.[27] Certainly, James Taylor was proud of his Scottish identity, as his letters home demonstrate. In 1859 he boasted:

> Really neither the English nor Irish in this part of the world are nearly so good as Scotchmen with few exceptions. Even English proprietors try to get Scotch superintendents as for example Pride my old master and his brother says he thinks them the most useful people in the world and the Messrs Hadden proprietors of the Moirs' places have found scotchmen serves them better than any other manager in the country perhaps of any class would have done. When ever any estate is doing well it is a Scotchman that is on it. If we speak with a Scotchman it is about estate matters and wives if with an Englishman his whole heart and soul is in dogs and horses and I think the few Irish that I know seem generally to give themselves precious little trouble about anything. I see little of the wit they are famed for and terrible little practical sense.[28]

Moreover, when Taylor died, although his headstone does not commemorate his origins, his Scottishness was to the fore. Newspaper tributes connected him to the Mearns area of his birth.

During the nineteenth century, Ceylon also emerged as one of the most Scottish colonies in the world. Although a numerically small cluster, census data shows the Scots-born on the island formed approximately 25 per cent of the total UK-born population, whereas in the UK the Scots-born were only around 10 per cent of the entire UK population. Such was the early penetration and influence of Scots in the island, particularly in the coffee and tea enterprises, that claims arose of it being a 'Scotch colony'.[29] Figure 5.4 shows visually the Scottish influence within the tea economy, which came to replace the coffee industry after it was devastated by blight. The article accompanying the caricature boasted: 'The directors are all Scotch, the chairman is a Scotchman, the secretary – a real live baronet, by the way – is a Scotchman, and the shareholders look Scotch to a man. It is queer to find Scotchmen combining together to vaunt the virtues of tea ... in view of the insult which the fact offers to whisky.'[30] Importantly, this contemporary emphasis on Scotland's influence in Ceylon emerged from other ethnicities and not just from Scots. For example, in 1870, Lancashire-born George Wall, Chairman of the Planter's Association, claimed that 'The prosperity in the island was due ... to Scotch enterprise and Scotch labour.'[31] Such influence, as argued elsewhere, came about from skills that Scots took to Ceylon – including their education and agricultural knowledge – and their networking.[32]

Figure 5.4 Mr David Reid, Sir W. Johnstone and Mr Shand enjoy their tea! (*Tropical Agriculturalist*, 1 April 1892, p. 742, cropped to image. Courtesy of Edinburgh University Library, available under a Creative Commons BY 3.0 licence)

The Scottish influence in Sri Lanka lingers to this day. Several organisations and tourist sites emphasise that heritage, including The Steuart by Citrus hotel in Colombo with hotel bedrooms named after places in Scotland, clan shields on the walls, tartan interiors and Scottish fare featuring in its Scottish-themed pub. Nearby is the St Andrew's Scots Kirk. At Talawakelle, in the heart of Sri Lanka's highland tea country, a mock Scottish baronial castle emerges from the landscape at the entrance to which is a monument to the Scottish tea planter, James Taylor. Promulgating such legacies is, of course, driven by commercial tourist interests, but it also demonstrates early Scottish dominance in Sri Lanka.

What, then, accounts for the relative absence of ethnic markers on Scottish headstones in Ceylon? One explanation is that they had no need to testify to their identity because it was so apparent in other ways, particularly in the press, with major publications controlled by Scottish interests. Such an omission may also be due to planters and their families and friends accumulating little in the way of wealth, a situation in diametric opposition to the wealth obtained among the EIC workers in India and slave plantations in the West Indies. Ceylon's British and Irish workforce were primarily managers rather than plantation owners. They were therefore without the financial means to organise elaborate inscriptions and symbols let alone the construction of a memorial. Examples from cemeteries elsewhere buttress this finding. To take an example from New Zealand, Dunedin's Southern Cemetery contains 23,000 interments but just 3,450 individuals are commemorated on 1,134 memorials.[33] We also need to remember that the inscriptions on stones were made by family or friends and they were the ones making a social statement about the deceased. It was they who could choose to emphasise the occupation of the deceased, rather than origins or ethnicity, and thereby reinforce the powerful role of the British in Ceylon society. The remoteness of the burial sites, in the Highlands of Ceylon, also did not lend themselves to large-scale memorialisation.

It is more likely, however, that the general absence of Scottish ethnic identity on headstones in Ceylon was part of a general tendency throughout the British World to only occasionally document their origins in cemeteries in the late Victorian era. In their study of Stawell in Australia, for instance, Dianne Hall and Lindsay Proudfoot note that Scottish symbols of identity rarely appeared on headstones. Scots in Ceylon, then, may have replicated a predisposition to avoid placing their origins on grave markers. By contrast, 30 per cent of Irish burials at Stawell indicated their origins with place of birth or ethnic symbols such as harps, shamrocks, round towers and Celtic crosses. These expressions of Irishness were especially prominent during the period of the Celtic Revival, that is 1890–1920.[34] Timing, then, may be a further factor in the lack of ethnic identification in Ceylon, for there the peak of European presence was during the nineteenth century.

Similar findings to Ceylon emerges from evidence in other remote British colonies, including the headstones at the Southern Cemetery in Dunedin, New Zealand. Founded in 1858, the cemetery was the final resting place of many different ethnic groups, their burials in sections according to denomination. Primarily a Scottish city, the general section of the cemetery largely features the remains of Presbyterians, while Anglicans, Catholics and Jews all had their own adjacent burial plots. Here, again, Scottish symbols and origins were less prevalent on headstones compared with other ethnicities such as Chinese or Jewish migrants. For instance, 104 of 114 Chinese headstones in the Southern Cemetery contain reference to county of origin, probably in order to one day facilitate the repatriation of Chinese remains to their homeland.[35] Jewish graves, meanwhile, featured the Hebrew language and symbols such as the Star of David. All styles, however, were generally restrained, irrespective of ethnicity.

These comparisons provide us with a further explanation for the lack of ethnicity on Scottish migrant headstones in Ceylon and Dunedin. First, the findings may be due to the Lowland origins of many Scots in these destinations. Studies of Highland Scots, by contrast, reveal a greater tendency towards ethnic markers. In their study in this volume, Laurie Stanley-Blackwell and Michael Linkletter indicate that Highland Presbyterian Scots at Pictou, Nova Scotia, were more likely than their Catholic counterparts at Antigonish to record place of origin. How extensive such recordings were, however, is unknown. A study of headstones at Waipu, north of Auckland in New Zealand, a settlement of Highland Scots who had previously resided in Nova Scotia, would be instructive in this regard. It certainly appears, from a random survey, that headstones there were more likely to commemorate place of birth and feature Scottish symbols.

CONCLUSION

Connecting migrants to their national and ethnic origins was clearly one factor for those commemorating their loved ones on gravestones and was an example of situational ethnicity.[36] In Ceylon during the nineteenth century, such ties on headstones were most frequently evident from references to place of birth or links to family in the homelands, rather than symbolism or the type of stone used. Even though not a widespread practice among Scots in Ceylon or elsewhere, for some individuals the desire to demonstrate ties to place of origin remained an important element of the migration experience. National and ethnic identities, however, were only one aspect of migrant lives, with family and friends also drawing attention on headstones to the occupations and localities of the deceased in the new destination. National and ethnic identities were therefore just one aspect of a migrant's identity in new lands.

NOTES

1. Taylor's life is examined in Angela McCarthy and T. M. Devine, *Tea and Empire: James Taylor in Victorian Ceylon* (Manchester: Manchester University Press, 2017).
2. *Overland Ceylon Observer*, 4 August 1892, p. 821.
3. D. M. Forrest, *A Hundred Years of Ceylon Tea, 1867–1967* (London: Chatto & Windus, 1967), p. 57.
4. *Overland Times of Ceylon*, 4 May 1892, p. 592.
5. *Overland Times of Ceylon*, 23 May 1892, p. 678. The text Walters proposed was: 'To the memory of James Taylor of Loolecondura, the originator of the tea and cinchona enterprise, in Ceylon, who died May 2nd, 1892. This stone is erected by his friends in token of their high respect and esteem'. The final inscription deviated slightly from Walters' proposed text as the photograph of Taylor's grave shows.
6. *Overland Times of Ceylon*, 25 May 1892, p. 694. There is no plaque at the Scots Kirk at Kandy.
7. *Overland Ceylon Observer*, 27 October 1893, p. 1206.
8. *Overland Ceylon Observer*, 25 November 1893, p. 1323.
9. There was a significant granite industry in north-east Scotland. See Jim Fiddes, *The Granite Men: A History of the Granite Industries of Aberdeen and North East Scotland* (Stroud: The History Press, 2009).
10. Julie-Marie Strange, *Death, Grief and Poverty in Britain, 1870–1914* (Cambridge: Cambridge University Press, 2005), pp. 100–1.
11. Harold Mytum, 'Artefact biography as an approach to material culture: Irish gravestones as a material form of genealogy', *Journal of Irish Archaeology*, vols 12/13 (2003–4), p. 124.
12. Ancestry.com lists William Taylor's death at age thirty-nine at Tezpur, Bengal: Ancestry.com, *India, Select Deaths and Burials, 1719–1948* [database online] (accessed 7 January 2020). David Air advises that Taylor was buried at Tezpur Cemetery and that many of the original graves have subsequently been moved to Pertabghur Tea Estate Cemetery. Records for Tezpur Cemetery, initially known as the European and Indian cemetery but named the Christian cemetery since 1974, verify this. The tombstones

were re-sited in 1987 though the physical remains are still at Tezpur. Neither map for Pertabghur or Tezpur shows William Taylor's grave. See the records for Pertabghur and Tezpur in the British Library, Mss Eur 370/61, 66, Archives of the British Association for Cemeteries in South Asia and personal correspondence with Angela McCarthy, 12 March 2015. William Taylor was an engineer who died on board the SS *Cashmere* at Tezpore. The volume of his estate – £233 2s – was granted to his sister Elisabeth. See Ancestry.com, *Scotland National Probate Index (Calendar of Confirmations and Inventories), 1876–1936* [database online] (accessed 7 January 2020), William Taylor, 1895, p. 482.

13. See T. M. Devine, *The Scottish Nation, 1700–2000* (London: Penguin, 1999), p. 286.
14. J. Penry Lewis, *A List of Inscriptions on Tombstones and Monuments in Ceylon, of Historical or Local Interest, with An Obituary of Persons Uncommemorated* (Colombo: H. C. Cottle, 1913), online at <https://archive.org/stream/cu31924007648516#page/n0/mode/2up> (accessed 7 January 2020).
15. Ibid., James Taylor's entry appears on p. 333, while Moir's is on p. 311.
16. The Kabristan Archives, <https://www.kabristan.org.uk> (accessed 7 January 2020).
17. Shaun Higgins, 'Reflections After Life: The Social Dimensions in Colonial Auckland's Symonds Street Cemetery' (MA thesis, University of Auckland, 1998), p. 6, cited in Debra Powell, '"It was hard to die frae hame": Death, Grief and Mourning Among Scottish Migrants to New Zealand, 1840–1890' (MA, University of Waikato, 2007), p. 84.
18. John Askew, *A Voyage to Australia and New Zealand* (Christchurch: Kiwi, 1999), p. 337, cited in Powell, '"It was hard to die frae hame"', p. 82.
19. Philip D. Curtin, *Death by Migration: Europe's Encounter with the Tropical World in the Nineteenth Century* (Cambridge: Cambridge University Press, 1989).
20. Margaret's death on 6 February 1865 is noted in the *Colombo Overland Observer*, 16 February 1865, p. 42. However, the date of February 1867 is given in Eileen Hewson, *Graveyards in Ceylon: Tea Country, Volume III* (Wern: Kabristan Archives, 2009), p. 56.
21. Curtin, *Death by Migration*, p. 71; James S. Duncan, *In the Shadows of the Tropics: Climate, Race and Biopower in Nineteenth-Century Ceylon* (Aldershot: Routledge, 2007), p. 115, citing C. L. Briggs and C. Mantini-Briggs, *Stories in the Time of Cholera: Racial Profiling During a Medical Nightmare* (Berkley: University of California Press, 2003), p. 1.
22. James Taylor (Loolecondera) to his father Michael Taylor (Auchenblae), 17 September 1857, National Library of Scotland (NLS), 15908, Papers of James Taylor, Planter in Ceylon.
23. Duncan, *In the Shadows of the Tropics*, p. 116, fn 72.
24. This statistical assessment was made from the inscriptions found in

Eileen Hewson, *Graveyards in Ceylon, Kandy Region, Volume IV* (Wem: Kabristan Archives, 2009), pp. 1–18.
25. Cecil Palliser of Drontheim, Norway; Alexander Vantosky Renton from Montego Bay, Jamaica. Drontheim is now Port Trondheim.
26. Harold Mytum, 'Scotland, Ireland and America: The construction of identities through mortuary monuments by Ulster Scots in the seventeenth and eighteenth centuries', in Audrey J. Horning, Nick Brannon, Peter Edward Pope (eds), *Ireland and Britain in the Atlantic World* (Dublin: Wordwell, 2009), p. 243.
27. Among other Scottish place names in the nineteenth century were Caledonia, Glen Alpine, Fassifern, Ettrick, Lochnagar, Craigie Lea, Devon, Glencairn, Holyrood, Eildon and Dunsinane.
28. James Taylor (Loolecondera) to his father Michael Taylor (Mosspark), 21 February 1859, NLS, Papers of James Taylor.
29. Angela McCarthy, 'Ceylon: A Scottish colony?', in T. M. Devine and Angela McCarthy (eds), *The Scottish Experience in Asia, c.1700 to the present: Settlers and Sojourners* (Cham: Palgrave Macmillan, 2017), pp. 187–211.
30. 'The Ceylon Plantations Tea Company', *Tropical Agriculturalist*, 1 April 1892, p. 742.
31. *Overland Ceylon Observer*, 3 December 1870, p. 428.
32. Angela McCarthy, 'The importance of Scottish origins in the nineteenth century: James Taylor and Ceylon tea', in Angela McCarthy and John M. MacKenzie (eds), *Global Migrations: The Scottish Diaspora since 1600. A Tribute to Professor Sir Tom Devine* (Edinburgh: Edinburgh University Press, 2016), pp. 117–37.
33. Alexander Trapeznik and Austin Gee, '"Each in his narrow cell for ever laid": Dunedin's Southern Cemetery and its New Zealand counterparts', *Public History Review*, 20 (2013), p. 49.
34. Dianne Hall and Lindsay Proudfoot, 'Memory and identity among Irish migrants in nineteenth-century Stawell', *Australasian Journal of Irish Studies*, 7 (2007/8), p. 77.
35. Stephen Deed, *Unearthly Landscapes: New Zealand's Early Churchyards, Cemeteries and Urupā* (Dunedin: Otago University Press, 2015), p. 182.
36. John Downing and Charles Husband, *Representing 'Race': Racisms, Ethnicities and Media* (London: Sage Publications, 2005), p. 18.

6

Irish Memorialisation in South Australia, 1850–99

Janine McEgan

The Irish left an enduring heritage across the Australian continent. Though Irish immigrants in Australia during the nineteenth century were much fewer in number compared with those who journeyed to Britain and the United States, they were a significant contributor to the southern colonies' population,[1] having comprised about 25 per cent of the nineteenth-century immigrant populace.[2] These outposts of British settlement attempted to attract English and Scottish Protestants to settle but, while these groups were generally reluctant, the Irish were keen to embrace opportunities in the burgeoning colonies that had a high need for unskilled workers.[3] Prior to the Great Irish Famine of the 1840s, Irish Protestants emigrated in large numbers, many becoming notable landholders and professionals, as was the case in southern New South Wales. Such success stemmed from financial 'networks of patronage' or for those already possessing significant capital.[4] With the onset of the Famine, however, the influx of Catholics numbered some 80 per cent of the Irish emigration to Australia, being particularly dominant among assisted migrants,[5] as these people tended to be the poor and most affected by the Famine.

The numbers of Irish settling in South Australia were considerably lower than in the east of the continent, averaging only about 6.5 per cent,[6] making it one of the lesser Irish settlements in Australia.[7] South Australia's Mid-North region became home to many of these newcomers originating from numerous Irish counties. Two means of emigration especially relevant to South Australia were assisted migration, where funds from land sales financed the journeys of poor rural workers, and chain migration, in which the continual arrival of migrants linked by county or, more particularly, family, was practised during the nineteenth century,[8] and most prevalent among the Irish.[9]

According to much historical research, the Irish in South Australia readily adjusted to their new environment among migrants from other nations, resulting in a distribution of their culture.[10] Yet there are debates surrounding their distinctiveness. Eric Richards suggests the Irish avoided developing concentrated areas of kin, and that their mobility and way of living showed little distinction from British migrants, enabling them to assimilate.[11] The 'ordinariness' of the Irish is further considered by Stephanie James to have enabled the Irish to blend into South Australian society.[12] Even so, James's recognition of strong communal bonds between Irish Catholics suggests that the Irish were distinctive in at least some ways, such as endogamous marriage and the settlement patterns based on family or clans, until well into the twentieth century. Indeed, nearly 100 per cent of Irish marriages in Stanley in the 1860s were restricted to those of the same nationality and the same religion. Thus, James inferred restricted levels of communication between denominations and ethnicities in the Mid-North, with some overt political movements developing a distinct Irish network established by the 1870s.[13] Susan Arthure, on the other hand, argues that a tendency to not see the Irish as distinctive is a generalisation of the entire colony and not based on artefactual evidence.[14]

Given the highly symbolic and communicative functions of cemetery material culture, one avenue in which we might expect to find expressions of 'Irishness' is the memorialisation of death and remembrance. The presentation of Irishness and how it may change over time can be examined by the study of gravestones, offering a physical mechanism by which memorialisation practices can be considered.[15] By studying Irishness in more detail, including within individual communities and within individual families, the archaeology of Irish graves has the potential to provide an alternative window into the dominant historical narrative, as gravestones enable ethnic and religious individuality to be expressed.[16]

This chapter explores the degree to which cultural traditions were incorporated in the material culture of Irish graves and gravestones in the period 1850–99, and what this implies for expressions of Irishness in South Australia. The archaeological research of the memorialisation of Irish settlers over the first fifty years of their arrival in South Australia, concentrating on its Mid-North district, is assessed with a comparison of other Australian colonies in the same time period. Considering that the majority of the Irish settlers were of the Catholic faith, it is important to determine what aspects of memorialisation may indicate 'Irishness' as opposed to 'Catholicism' or 'Protestantism'. To that end, graves of both denominations were examined. Areas of comparison and contrast are explored here in three ways: through the use of motifs of affection and grief; motifs related to religious beliefs; and overtly Irish symbols of identity. Before turning to examine these headstones, some context of the South Australia and the Mid-North regions is necessary.

THE IRISH IN SOUTH AUSTRALIA

South Australia was a free-settled, British colony, founded on Edward Gibbon Wakefield's plan of 'systematic colonisation'.[17] Men with capital bought land with the promise of labour and profit,[18] with the revenue being used to pay for or assist with emigrant labourers' passages.[19] The high price of £1 per acre prevented labourers from having the means to buy land for many years after their arrival, thus retaining them as a labour force. This enabled the colony to exist with two levels of society: 'men of capital' and 'labourers with free passage'.[20]

With South Australia being English in its provenance, the Irish were not among the earliest immigrants. In fact, it was a calculated decision by administrators to shun association with Ireland as a source of emigrants.[21] However, the architect of the South Australian colonisation scheme, Wakefield, considered that encouraging Irish migration could assist in alleviating the influx of Irish peasants to England, and suggested creating an emigration fund for that purpose.[22] From 1835, Captain Robert Torrens, a Derry-born Protestant, actively campaigned for Irish emigration.[23] Many of the colony's residents, however, were opposed not only to immigration of the poor but also to the establishment of Catholicism in the province,[24] as occurred in the eastern colonies. As such, the numbers of Catholic Irish were few until the 1840s, but the Protestant Irish were encouraged to emigrate from the beginnings of the colony in 1837 and thus escaped conflict and unrest in Ireland. As the need for labourers increased, Irish Catholics were recruited and upon arrival had the freedom to work for whomever they chose.[25] It was under these conditions that the *William Nichol* brought the first company of free Irish settlers directly from Ireland to South Australia, departing in April 1840, with only three other vessels ever departing directly from Ireland to South Australia.[26] As the emigrants originated from numerous counties, it ensured the colony would be well publicised among the many peasant farmers across Ireland through letters from their emigrant relatives.[27] Systems of free and assisted passages were established by the governing body with prospective migrants recruited by emigration agencies, which not only alleviated the excess of labour in Ireland but facilitated the establishment of the South Australian economy.[28] This enabled those with little or no financial means of migrating the opportunity of an improved life in South Australia and accounted for nearly half of the Irish migrants, with the remainder being self-funded.

THE IRISH IN MID-NORTH SOUTH AUSTRALIA

Initial settlement of Mid-North South Australia occurred in the early 1840s, with three individuals – Edmund B. Gleeson from County Clare in Ireland,[29] Sir Montague Chapman of County Westmeath[30] and Colonel George Wyndham of Sussex, England[31] (all Protestant) – acquiring land under the first special survey; the counties of Stanley and Light were then proclaimed in 1842. Gleeson had arrived in the colony in 1838 from Ireland via military service in India[32] and was one of the first Mid-North settlers in 1840, establishing a homestead and sheep station in the Clare Valley, named after his home county (Figure 6.1).

Chapman purchased land near the area now known as Kapunda, while Wyndham, who possessed substantial land holdings in counties Clare, Tipperary and Limerick in Ireland, invested in land at Hutt River, near the Clare Valley. This allowed him to alleviate the excess of tenant farmers on his Irish estates by assisting them to migrate and work the lands in South Australia, as did Gleeson and Chapman, both of whom brought many Irish people to the colony to labour on their properties. Neither Chapman nor Wyndham ever migrated to South Australia, but had managers to oversee their colonial acreages. Chapman transferred a sizeable proportion of land to his manager, Charles Bagot, in 1851.[33]

Bagot, of Ennis, County Clare, in association with Chapman, also recruited people who had been displaced by evictions and closures to work on Chapman's South Australian holdings,[34] sending more than 200 people from Ireland's southern and eastern provinces of Munster and Leinster to the colony. Bagot travelled as manager of the land purchase, sailing on the *Birman* in 1840 with his family from Cork.[35] Two further emigrant ships sailed from Cork in 1840: the *Mary Dugdale* and the *Brightman*. Some immigrants found work on the properties of John Reid, another Protestant Irishman from County Clare,[36] while others worked for Bagot on Chapman's land at Kapunda and the River Light or for Gleeson in the Clare Valley.[37]

Chapman, Gleeson and Bagot were typical of the earliest Irish settlers to South Australia, who were mainly Protestants, since, according to South Australia's first Catholic priest, William Benson, in 1843 'no Catholic gentlemen of property were allowed to join the founders'.[38]

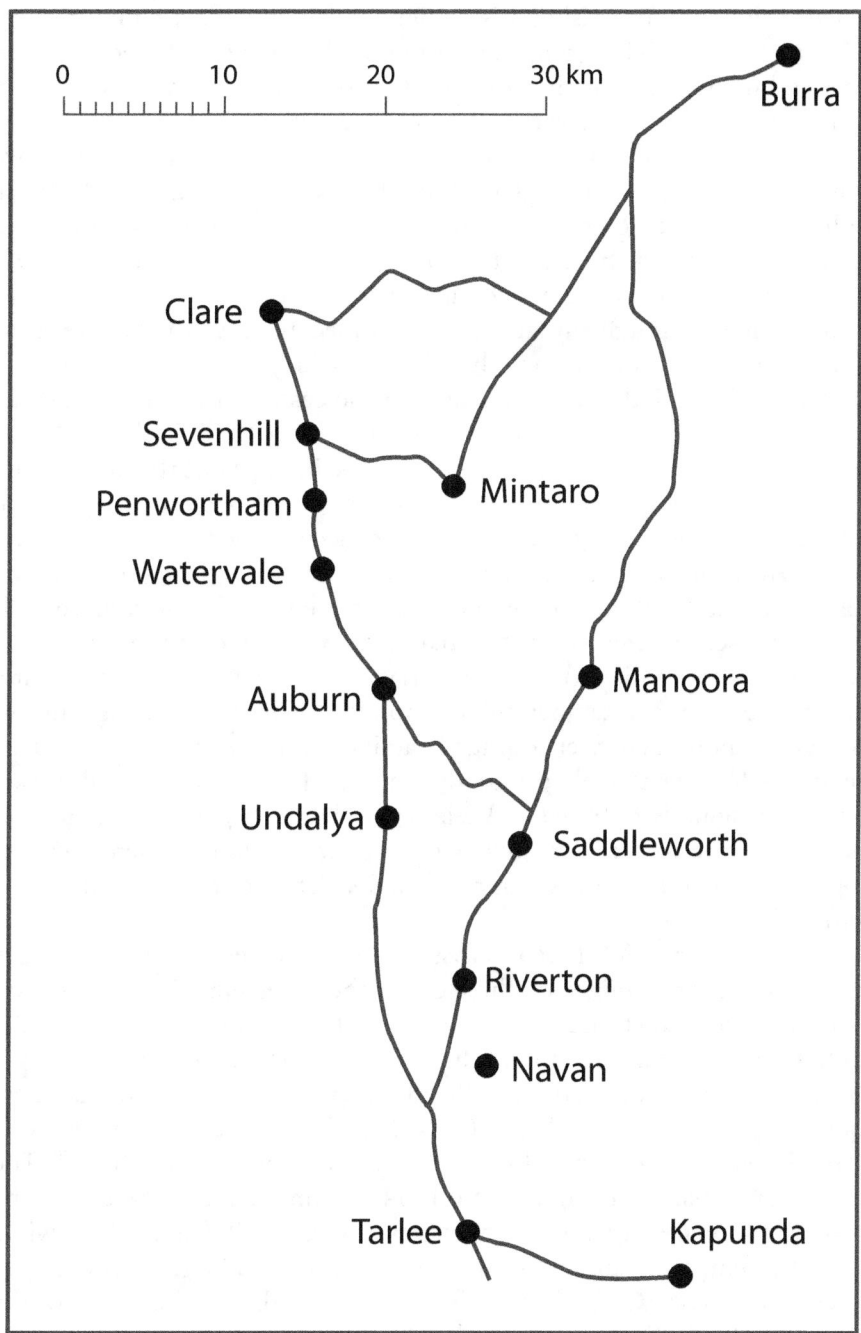

Figure 6.1 Towns of the Clare Valley region of South Australia. (Artwork: J. McEgan)

This notion of minimising Irish migrant numbers was supported by Major Thomas O'Halloran, a Protestant Irishman, who claimed that the early administrators of the colony allowed twenty times more English than Irish settlers to migrate to South Australia.[39]

A severe shortage of workers in the late 1840s, due to the improving economy and increased demand for labourers, caused the near collapse of the colony and resulted in many ex-prisoners and 'poor house' girls being brought to South Australia.[40] About 600 Irish Catholic female orphans arrived in South Australia between 1848 and 1850[41] and, although initially not welcomed because of their religion and their lack of education, the girls were quickly employed until a downturn in available work resulted in the cessation of that particular emigration scheme.[42] The colony's governor from 1855, Richard Graves MacDonnell, planned to spread the Catholic immigrants throughout the countryside to reduce an excess of labourers and overcrowding in the city, as there was insufficient work and accommodation in Adelaide, South Australia's capital. As a result, some of the women shifted to the Clare region, which already had an Irish presence.[43] Further, more Irish girls were sent to that district as part of Caroline Chisholm's scheme[44] to secure work, while arranging marriages for single Irish Catholic girls encouraged a more temperate community.[45] Chisholm, being faithful to her Catholic belief, encouraged families to emigrate together or to reunify when a parent had initially emigrated alone.[46] The St Patrick's Society, originally founded in Adelaide in 1849,[47] began an immigration depot in Clare to care for single women, with a similar scheme operating in Mintaro, both of which employed strict rules to ensure the girls' safety.[48]

Various towns developed across the Mid-North region in response to the influx of immigrants throughout the nineteenth century (Figure 6.1), with six cemeteries in five towns used for this research. Kapunda, initially an agricultural area, advanced with the discovery of copper, while Mintaro developed from Burra's copper industry, being a transport stopover to Port Henry (now Port Wakefield).[49] Mintaro was established in 1849 with Joseph Gilbert subdividing his land.[50] The discovery of slate at Mintaro in 1854 became a major factor in the town's survival after the ore transport bypassed it from 1857, while its development as an agricultural centre further enhanced its continuance.[51] The Irish (Catholics) tended to settle on the northern side of the town, while the English (Methodists) were primarily in the town itself. The Kapunda area saw a large influx of Irish from the 1850s.[52] As in Kapunda, the Irish presence in Mintaro resulted in a strong community, with settlers such as Peter Brady and the Dempsey family, all of County Cavan, becoming leaders in that community, as well as sponsoring many more of their countrymen to settle in the district. This chain migration allowed large kinship groups to develop with support and family nearby while strengthening the bonds among the Irish settlers.

Conversely, Navan was an Irish enclave, named after a town in County Meath, settled in the 1840s by emigrants who fled the Famine.[53] By 1876, Navan was considered more an agricultural district than a township,[54] since the area had reverted mainly to farmland,[55] even though in 1866 it had boasted a population of 300 with a Catholic school and church among its services.[56] The establishment of a segregated Irish community such as Navan was unusual in South Australia. Saddleworth was settled in the 1840s by an English farmer, James Masters, who established a sheep property and named the area after his home town in West Riding, Yorkshire. The town did not appear to have a large Irish population, with only a handful of graves found in the Anglican cemetery, and those all belonging to one extended family. The town developed similarly to Mintaro, being on the transport route from Burra to Adelaide.[57] Riverton, near Navan, was an English community, suggesting that English migrants chose to settle away from the neighbouring Irish. It, too, was established by Masters, in 1856.[58]

Undalya, meanwhile, is on the border of the counties of Stanley and Light, and at the junction of the Wakefield River and Pine Creek.[59] Its two earliest settlers were Englishmen, Captain George Lambert, who is buried in the Undalya Catholic Cemetery, and William Baker, who arrived in the district in 1848, having been a crewman on the *Emerald Isle*, the ship chartered by Gleeson for his migration to South Australia.[60] In what ways, then, did the Irish commemorate their dead in these towns?

PLAIN CROSSES

The use of a cross, other than the Celtic cross, as a headstone form declined among Irish Catholics in South Australia in the 1880s, while its use by Irish Protestants increased slightly. Both groups reversed this trend in the 1890s, suggesting that unique choices by each group may have been occurring. There are two possible explanations: that the use of the plain cross by Catholics and Protestants was a result of adherence to particular religious beliefs or decrees, or that it was an expression of wider political philosophies influencing these two groups.

Elsewhere in the diaspora, Ryan Smith found an avoidance of the cross in Protestant churches in the early-nineteenth-century United States of America,[61] since it was a symbol particularly associated with the Catholic faith. This constraint was generally evident in Protestant graves in this study, except for a minor reversal in the 1880s as previously noted. The acceptance of using a cross in Protestant churches became more accepted in the mid-nineteenth century in the United States,[62] a trend which seemingly filtered to Australia in the following years. But did a developing diasporic nationalist impulse increase the use of crosses among the Irish in South Australia?

In terms of a connection between crosses and political beliefs, Daniel O'Connell's Repeal Association, founded in 1840, with the aim of gaining independence from Britain, firmly associated nationalism with Catholicism to unite the preponderant number of Irish Catholics.[63] Such movements extended across the world, but while some inclination toward such beliefs existed in Australia, Irish migrants seemed more interested with allegiance to family and their county of birth rather than with nationalist connections.[64] This attitude differed from that of Irish-American immigrants who, according to Thomas Brown, were desperate to improve their lives to overcome 'a compulsive sense of inferiority, his sensitiveness to criticism and his yearning for respectability' with the origins of Irish-American nationalism being in the 'loneliness, poverty and prejudice' experienced by the Irish immigrants.[65] Kerby Miller suggests that the Irish considered they were 'in forced exile' from English rule, leading to a steadfast Irish nationalism in America.[66] The involvement of Home Rule campaigners in the murders of English representatives in 1883 in Ireland hindered support for the organisation once news reached the Australian colonies, as did the economic downturn in South Australia in the 1880s.[67] Little archaeological evidence of Irish nationalism has been found in Australia, with the exception of clay pipes sporting Irish slogans and symbols such as shamrocks and the inscription 'Erin Go Bragh' (defined as 'Ireland Forever')[68] found at the excavation of Cadman's Cottage, Sydney in 1988.[69]

Even so, Australia presented abundant opportunities for Irish nationalism to flourish with numerous political prisoners from the 1798 Irish Rebellion transported to the Antipodes and later arrivals following the unsuccessful 1848 revolt.[70] Irish migrants in Australia did have an interest in Irish happenings but were more concerned with supporting those in need rather than political agendas.[71] With the arrival of John Redmond, an Irish National League advocate, to Australia's shores in 1883, support for the nationalist movement met with a mixed reaction. Working-class migrants were more supportive than the eminent members of the Irish Australians. However, as indicated by John Gavan Duffy at the time of Redmond's tour, Irish Australians may have been empathetic but believed 'their first duty [was] to the colony where they lived, together as friends of Englishmen and Scotsmen',[72] a sentiment shared by Patrick O'Farrell arguing that local loyalties and identity, that is to 'family, village and county', held a higher priority than national ties.[73] Malcolm Campbell considers the tyranny of distance in such a large land further weakened the chance of success of Irish nationalism,[74] in contrast with the movement in the United States where the association was more with the working class of the cities. The most critical aspect of Irish nationalism's failure to thrive in Australia, according to Campbell, was the connection with the British Empire. He suggests the Irish Australians were content to accept the governing powers, as to support nationalism would not assist in assimilation into the Australian society, but be 'a potential cause of estrangement'.[75]

While weak nationalist sentiment among the Irish in South Australia helps explain the declining use of crosses, an alternative explanation for the fall in popularity among Catholics in the 1880s may be more prosaic. At this time, South Australia's economy was failing with severe drought decimating the agricultural industry resulting in much financial failure,[76] and this possibly influenced the manner in which the departed were memorialised. Since the Mid-North was an agricultural area, and many of the Irish settlers were farmers, the aftermath of such weather events would have resulted in the loss of, or reduced, cash flow, for the properties. A reduction in the number of cross-form headstones, being that they were among the largest and therefore most costly, could have been due to economics, as could the increasing plainness of headstones from the 1880s, as fewer engraved motifs presumably translated to lower cost. In Victoria, Lindsay Proudfoot and Dianne Hall also found evidence of cost being prohibitive to the headstones erected in Stawell with only 25 per cent of graves featuring a memorial,[77] a situation also encountered in this study with many graves being unmarked. An accurate count of Irish graves cannot, therefore, be determined since burial registers from the time period are incomplete. While O'Farrell stated that Celtic art forms had an increased interest with the Gaelic Revival in Ireland, Celtic crosses increased in popularity on graves in Australian Catholic cemeteries from about the 1880s due to the influence of Irishman Morgan Jaguers, a monumental mason. Such forms, O'Farrell notes, were generally connected with more affluent migrants,[78] though his source of this information is not declared. The lack of examples in this study could be an indication that the financial state of

South Australia, and possibly Victoria, influenced headstone choices. Queensland also presents with Celtic crosses being widespread along with birthplaces.[79]

MOTIFS OF EMOTION

Religious-based motifs symbolising affection and grief demonstrated a distinct difference among South Australian headstones, with Irish Catholic graves exhibiting the bulk of motifs representing affection. Floral motifs were particularly dominant, with roses a symbol of hope, and daisies, representing innocence, being the most often used, especially in the Mintaro and St John's (Kapunda) cemeteries. Wreaths (of both flowers and foliage) and forget-me-nots, each depicting remembrance, also occurred at those cemeteries.[80] In contrast, Irish Protestant headstones were more austere having fewer motifs. Kapunda's Christchurch Anglican Cemetery contained just three emotive symbols, two of which represented grief: a lily with a broken stem (life cut short); and morning glory flowers (mourning).

When considered over time, emotive symbols among Irish Catholics became more popular towards the end of the nineteenth century, ranging from flowers (both affection and grief) to cloth-draped urns (death). There was a steady escalation of such symbols, particularly those of affection, into the 1880s, with a subsequent decline in the 1890s. In contrast, only one or two were found on non-Irish graves in every decade. While a greater numbers of deaths did not occur in the 1880s than other decades, the loss of the early migrants, and thus a direct connection with Ireland, could have accounted for a surge in emotive symbols of affection. This was, however, a choice adopted more by Irish Catholics than by Irish Protestants. The ideology of the different faiths could have been the reasoning behind such a choice rather than the loss of a loved one. In other words, Catholics looked towards healing of the soul with the idea of positive prayer in mourning to allow prompt progress through purgatory[81] while Protestants considered that once life had expired no redemption was possible.

The sentimental association with death was apparent in the language of headstone inscriptions,[82] although this was something that was shared by both Irish Catholics and Protestants. As a whole, however, there was a significant difference in the use of emotive words on Irish Catholic and Protestant graves compared to non-Irish burials in both regions. Figure 6.2 illustrates this difference, showing little use of emotive inscriptions by non-Irish, but a discernible change in the Irish use of inscriptions

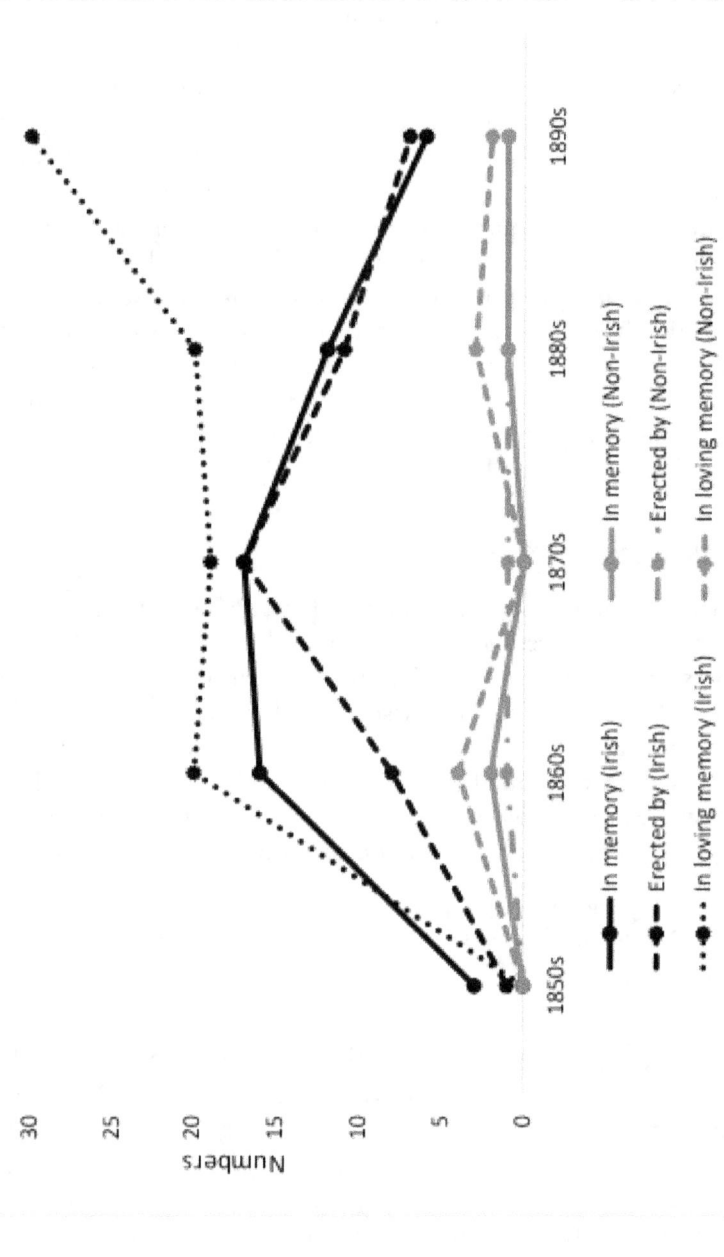

Figure 6.2 Irish vs non-Irish: change over time of introductory phrases in inscriptions. (Data: J. McEgan)

relating to affection over time. So, while the choice of symbolic motifs of affection and grief distinguished Catholics from Protestants, when considered together the use of emotive terms linked the two groups and separated them from the non-Irish around them. In other words, while Irish Catholics tended to use more affectionate terms and Irish Protestants more terms of grief, the Irish as a single group tended to be overtly emotive to a greater extent in comparison to the non-Irish. Nigel Llewellyn's theory of Protestant memorialisation is one explanation for this difference in Irish graves,[83] in that the Protestants used a grave monument as 'a celebration of the social persona of the deceased'[84] and thus grieved the loss of the person. Irish Catholics, however, regard the person's soul as still to be saved and accordingly considered it necessary to treat death as a mere step to resurrection. This variation is comparable to that noted by Sarah Tarlow on Orkney graves in Scotland, where she observed that by the end of the 1880s the use of emotive phrases, such as 'In loving memory' or 'Sacred to the memory', had replaced earlier phrases such as 'In memory'.[85]

RELIGIOUS MOTIFS

When evaluating Irish Catholic and Irish Protestant graves, the presence or absence of religious motifs proved to be statistically significant. Symbols representing Christ (Figure 6.3) and the cross were principally on Catholic graves. In comparison, the few religious motifs found on Protestant graves were analogous to God and the Holy Spirit. Religious motifs used on Catholic headstones peaked in the 1860s, a decade that also saw the greatest use of religious words and quotes in epitaphs, while none were identified on Protestant headstones. For example:

> Immaculate Heart of Mary,
> Your Prayers for them extol;
> Sacred Heart of Jesus.
> Have mercy on their souls!

The inscription of 'IHS'[86] on the cross was encouraged by Jesuit priests,[87] an order well established in South Australia's Mid-North, and so, unsurprisingly, Irish Catholics in the region adopted its use. The maintenance of such strong faith-based imagery in contrast to Protestant belief may have signified more adherences to Catholic orthodoxy.

These results resemble other investigations by Llewellyn and Harold Mytum of Protestant observances of death in the eighteenth and nineteenth centuries, which concentrated on the judgement of a life lived,

Figure 6.3 Engraved stone of the Sacred Heart on Ellen Crowe's grave, 1895, Undalya Catholic Cemetery. (Photo: J. McEgan)

with no prospect of improvement in any afterlife, resulting in few religious symbols being included on headstones.[88]

IRISH SYMBOLS

The use of overtly Irish symbols, such as shamrocks and the Celtic form of the cross, occurred across the timeframe of this study. From the data recorded in the study, the use of such symbols on headstones to demonstrate Irish association was primarily used by first generation immigrants (Figure 6.4), with the lone example of a Celtic cross headstone from the second generation belonging to a nineteen-year-old whose parents erected the death marker. The use of shamrock and Celtic cross motifs proved to be the same, with only one of five graves bearing Irish-type motifs belonging to a second-generation Irishman, whose parents also erected the memorial. In contrast, Irish symbols numbered about 30 per cent of the graves recorded by Proudfoot and Hall in Stawell,[89] with an increase over time. However, similar to the South Australian data, place of birth was the most common inclusion to indicate an Irish connection.[90] Irish Catholic graves in Kilmore, Victoria and the Kiama area of New South Wales do display many Irish markers but few shamrocks or Celtic crosses were found in the areas of high Irish Protestant populations.[91]

Celtic crosses and shamrocks figured prominently as motifs on the cast-iron surrounds of graves with the numbers of shamrocks recorded in South Australia peaking in the 1870s. The shamrocks were most prevalent as fencing motifs rather than on headstones. Again, this could have been due to finances as the shamrock was a less intricate and thus less expensive form to produce than a Celtic cross. The shamrock is a trefoliate leaf,[92] long associated with St Patrick, Ireland's patron saint. The plant's three leaflets are purported to have been used as a metaphor for the Holy Trinity by St Patrick on his quest to convert the Irish to Christianity in the fifth century,[93] with specimens being worn in hats to commemorate St Patrick on his Holy day, as noted by Dr Caleb Threlkeld in 1726.[94] Furthermore, speculation suggests that the ancient Irish Celts revered the plant for its trefoil form, with the numeral 'three' found in many forms in Celtic materials, such as the triskele (Figure 6.5) and the triquetra as well as the shamrock. As noted by Liam Mac Mathúna, Irish folklore had an inherent concept of the cosmos involving a triad of three divisions of the universe being *nem* (sky), *talam* (sea) and *muir* (earth), indicating the importance of the number 'three',[95] a belief also held by the Druids.[96] Christian belief in the Holy Trinity in many ways co-opted such beliefs and entrenched them still further.

Figure 6.4 Michael Dermody's Irish Catholic grave 1861, St John's Cemetery, Kapunda. (Photo: J. McEgan)

The dominance of the shamrock imagery on Irish Catholic graves in the Mid-North region suggests strongly that the connection with religion (and thus St Patrick) was the overriding factor in its use. The Celtic Revival of nineteenth-century Ireland is primarily associated with the Protestant Irish,[97] in which symbols such as the Celtic cross were used 'to establish . . . an Irish national identity'.[98] In contrast, traditional symbols like the shamrock and harp were well represented among the Catholic population during that era.[99] However, the symbols represented different ideas of an Irish heritage. Protestants used such symbols as a means to link to traditional Irish culture in an overall context where they were politically and economically dominant, whereas Catholics associated the images with a chance to reclaim Ireland from the English and restore traditional Irish culture.[100] The results of this study substantiate such observations, as shamrocks were the dominant choice on Irish Catholic graves with the Holy Trinity being a more probable connection than Celtic association. Celtic crosses, however, do have a probable connection with early Christianity. The shape is suggested by Derek Bryce to have evolved from a symbol common in fourth century Christianity – the 'chi-rho' an 'X' (chi) overlaid with a 'P' (rho), being the Greek letters of the first two letters of 'Christ' and used in combination to represent Christ.[101]

SOME UNIQUE GRAVE MARKERS

Spatially, there was little variation in Irish memorialisation of the dead in the Mid-North region. Headstone forms showed little diversity in representation across the six cemeteries in the five Mid-North towns in this study, as with fencing designs and inscription categories over the study area. Motifs had the greatest fluctuation in form. Religious symbols ranged from 40 per cent to 60 per cent in the Catholic cemeteries but were much less frequent on Protestant graves. Motifs of affection had the greatest range in number, from 5 per cent at Undalya to 40 per cent at Saddleworth, while the other cemeteries comprised about 10 per cent. Irish symbols accounted for less than 10 per cent in all cemeteries.

Four early grave markers were unique in style, three of which were Catholic burials at the Navan Cemetery (O'Sullivan, O'Brien and Fahey) and one of which was a non-Irish Catholic burial at the Mintaro Cemetery (an iron cross for Charles Hoffmann, a blacksmith). Two of the Navan headstones, from 1858 (Fahey) (Figure 6.6) and 1863 (O'Sullivan) (Figure 6.7), had the same shape, but were very different to other forms. The O'Brien tablet from the 1860s (Figure 6.8) was the only example

Figure 6.5 Newgrange, Co. Meath, showing triskele designs on entrance stone. (Photo: J. McEgan)

that apparently was hand-carved. The shape of the headstone was not symmetrical, with shapes carved around the edges being irregular. While legible text was neat, it was uneven in size and distribution across the lines, with spelling errors, specifically the words 'REAST' and 'AMN'. The O'Sullivan headstone had distinctive designs not seen on the other three, with two spirals decorating the space above the epitaph (Figure 6.7), which appear to be hand-carved, as they are irregular. The rest of the O'Sullivan headstone had consistently sized text, though some letters had been made smaller to fit on a line, and the additional motifs were regular in form, similar to those on the Fahey stone.

Three forms of foliage decorated the O'Sullivan headstone (Figure 6.7), while the base of the O'Brien headstone (Figure 6.8) included a geometric chevron design between a cross and a chalice. It was the only example in the database to have a painted motif (the heart), and it also bore fern-like engravings similar to those on the O'Sullivan headstone.

There is no indication of the mason for the two similar-shaped headstones but both are assumed to have been made locally, and by the same person since they are the same shape. Both are carved with Botonee crosses inside the rounded finials at the top of the headstone and include a recessed panel in the centre. Each has unique variations, however, indicating that they were not made to precisely the same pattern. The early age of these three headstones, and their uniqueness, is likely to be indicative of a lack of a locally established masonry industry. All three examples display evidence of hand-worked symbols and inscriptions and personal inclusions representative of overt Irish symbolism. The connections made to family, with so much detail of relationships and places of birth, continued the connection with Ireland, while the symbols resembling those of Celtic ancestry, particularly the spirals and geometric designs found on the O'Sullivan and O'Brien graves, highlight the Irish identity of these arrivals in the colony.

CONCLUSION

Recent studies have found that nineteenth-century Irish social identity in the Mid-North was conveyed in different ways, depending on the material remains examined. While Arthure found the Baker's Flat houses to be closely clustered, with indications of a tight-knit, isolated community,[102] the graves in this study suggest that the Irish were interspersed with other ethnicities. Religion was a dominant factor, however, in both studies. This grave study, while not having large numbers of Celtic-related symbols, does show an inclination to overtly Irish images,

Figure 6.6 Fahey headstone, 1858, Navan Catholic Cemetery. (Photo: J. McEgan)

Figure 6.7 Sketch of motifs on the top section of the O'Sullivan headstone, 1863, Navan Catholic Cemetery. Note non-specific motifs and possible Irish spirals. (Artist: J. McEgan)

with religion being an evident factor. Mass-produced items such as headstones reduced the opportunity to express Irishness explicitly in the material form but remained evident through the use of carefully chosen text and motifs.

Further, there is a stereotype that the Irish retain strong ties to their homeland, displayed in overt ways, such as the development of Irish-American nationalism in part because of the immigrant longing for home as indicated by Brown[103] or the maudlin yearning 'for his family and cabin is in the native Irish tradition' through song or verse.[104] This study of Irish graves in the Mid-North region of South Australia does not support such an obvious scenario. In reality, the Irish immigrants studied here used subtle symbolism in motifs and words to invoke

Figure 6.8 Sketch of the O'Brien headstone, 1860s, Navan Catholic Cemetery, showing geometric design at base. (Artist: J. McEgan)

an understanding of their origins. However, their choices do link to wider stereotypes of the Irish being openly emotional and steadfastly Catholic, a characteristic also identified by Brown with Irish immigrants bringing 'intense Catholicism to America'.[105] Furthermore, these Irish migrants demonstrated strong connections with family through their grave markers.

The three headstones at Navan that display personal influences were not mirrored in any later headstones, or at other cemeteries, with the personal symbols and details of lives and origins being particularly poignant. The inclusion of symbols associated with Celtic origins (scrolls on the O'Sullivan headstone and the geometric shape on the O'Brien marker) are indicative of these early Irish migrants maintaining connections with a pre-English past. The detail with which the deceased and their origins were recorded further indicates their need to continue associations with Ireland. Even the Fahey grave, while a simpler memorial, detailed the names, ages and dates of death for each member who had died. These three unique graves expressed family and origins in great detail and align with Miller's argument in which he determines a commonality in Irish Catholic society of the importance of family and tradition.[106] However, these three graves also express distinctiveness in style and motif-use that differs from later memorials in the district.

The individuality of these graves indicates an opportunity for personal memorialisation which diminished in some aspects with the later standardisation of memorials. With mass production, only the choice of wording allowed some individuality, while the physical presentation of monuments became more uniform. This in itself could create a dilemma in determining the individual contribution of the family and the 'Irishness' of material culture. While individuality in graves became less apparent over time, the inclusion of family and relationships in inscriptions does show an adherence to traditions.

The significance of the use of emotion and connection to family, along with adopting Celtic cross and shamrock symbols, shows that the Irish of South Australia's Mid-North emphasised their Irish identity in particular ways, even if not always in an overt manner. Unlike James's study, which stated that a decline in Irish association was apparent after the 1870s,[107] the archaeology indicates stability in the number of symbols and/or words associated with the Irish and a continuance in their use after this time. Emotive text and connection with Ireland or to residence in South Australia changed little. Mentioning relationships with the deceased remained relatively stable although religious style did decrease from the 1870s. Motifs representing emotion and Ireland both increased over time, indicating that representations of Irish culture did not diminish over the duration of the nineteenth century but, as with the text, religious affiliation decreased. This suggests the first-generation migrants and their offspring continued to value their heritage and culture while also maintaining an emotional connection with the early arrivals who had forged a new life in South Australia but were dying out by the end of the nineteenth century.

It was to be expected that there would be variations in the results over the timeframe of this study. Traits may be shared by different groups, which are apparent in the lack of diversity in many aspects of the recorded graves, such as the proximity of family members and the form of the headstones. Differences can occur within a group (in this case, the Irish as a whole) where the type of motifs incorporated on the headstones was a point of religious difference between the two Irish groups. Affectionate symbols were favoured by the Catholics and expressions of grief by the Protestants, while religious motifs were prevalent among the Irish Catholics but not their Protestant countrymen.

As suggested by Stephen Brighton, social identity evolves over time,[108]a concept that is apparent in the Irish communities of the Mid-North. As this research has established, the Irish migrants continued the use of some cultural aspects from their homeland in the burgeoning province of South Australia but also integrated with the diverse population to forge a social identity of an Irish-Australian.

NOTES

1. David Fitzpatrick, *Oceans of Consolation: Personal Accounts of Irish Migration to Australia* (Carlton: Melbourne University Press, 1995), p. 6.
2. Ibid., p. 6.
3. Ibid., p. 10.
4. Malcolm Campbell, 'The other immigrants: Comparing the Irish in Australia and the United States', *Journal of American Ethnic History*, 14:3 (1995), p.7.
5. Fitzpatrick, *Oceans of Consolation*, p. 14.
6. Ibid., p. 6.
7. Eric Richards, 'Irish life and progress in colonial South Australia', *Irish Historical Studies*, 27:107 (1991), p. 216.
8. Richard Reid, *Farewell My Children: Irish Assisted Emigration to Australia 1848–1870* (Spit Junction: Anchor Books Australia, 2011), p. 220.

9. Patrick O'Farrell, *The Irish in Australia* (Kensington, NSW: New South Wales University Press, 1987), p. 16.
10. M. Stephanie James, 'Becoming South Australians? The Impact of the Irish on the County of Stanley, 1841–1871' (MA thesis, Flinders University, 2009); Eric Richards, 'Irish women in colonial South Australia', in Trevor McClaughlin (ed.), *Irish Women in Colonial Australia* (St Leonards: Allen & Unwin, 1998); Richards, 'Irish life,' pp. 216–36; Eric Richards, 'The peopling of South Australia, 1836–1976', in Eric Richards (ed.), *The Flinders History of South Australia: Social History* (Netley: Wakefield Press, 1986); Eric Richards, 'The importance of being Irish in colonial South Australia', in John O'Brien and Pauric Travers (eds), *The Irish Emigrant Experience in Australia* (Dublin: Poolbeg Press, 1991), pp. 62–102.
11. Richards, 'British poverty and Australian immigration', pp. 233–4.
12. James, 'Becoming South Australians?'.
13. Ibid., p. 154.
14. Susan Arthure, 'The Occupation of Baker's Flat: A Study of Irishness and Power in Nineteenth Century South Australia' (MArch thesis, Flinders University, 2014), p. 33.
15. Ibid.
16. Lindsay J. Proudfoot and Dianne P. Hall, *Imperial Spaces: Placing the Irish and Scots in Colonial Australia* (Manchester: Manchester University Press, 2013), p. 226.
17. Richards, 'The peopling of South Australia, 1836–1976', p. 5.
18. Douglas Pike, *Paradise of Dissent* (London: Longmans, Green and Co. Ltd, 1967), p. 52.
19. J. M. Main, 'Social foundations of South Australia: Men of capital', in Eric Richards (ed.), *The Flinders History of South Australia: Social History*, p. 96.
20. Ibid., p. 97.
21. Richards, 'The importance of being Irish in colonial South Australia', in O'Brien and Travers (eds), The *Irish Emigrant Experience in Australia*, pp. 62–3.
22. Eric Richards, 'British poverty and Australian immigration in the nineteenth century', in Eric Richards (ed.), *Poor Australian Immigrants in the Nineteenth Century, Visible Immigrants: Two* (Canberra: Division of Historical Studies and Centre for Immigration and Multicultural Studies, Research School of Social Sciences, Australian National University, 1991), p. 10.
23. Peter Moore, 'Half-burnt turf: Selling immigration from Ireland to South Australia, 1836–1845', in Philip Bull, Chris McConville and Noel McLachlan (eds), *Irish-Australian Studies: Papers Delivered at the Sixth Irish-Australian Conference July 1990* (Bundoora: La Trobe University, 1991), pp. 104–5.

24. Richards, 'The importance of being Irish', p. 67.
25. Moore, 'Half-burnt turf', p. 109.
26. Barry Leadbeater 'South Australian Shipping & Immigration: Passenger Lists', <https://www.familyhistorysa.org/shipping/passengerlists.html> (accessed 24 February 2019).
27. Moore, 'Half-burnt turf', p. 109.
28. Richards, 'Irish life and progress in colonial South Australia', p. 218.
29. Richards, 'The importance of being Irish', p. 84.
30. Ibid., p. 69.
31. Spencer Thomas, 'Colonel George Wyndham, 1st Lord Leconfield, and his agency in the fledgling colony of South Australia, 1838–1860', *South Australian Geographical Journal*, 97 (1998), p. 3.
32. Richards, 'The importance of being Irish', p. 84.
33. Moore, 'Half-burnt turf', pp. 111–12.
34. Eric Richards, 'The peopling of South Australia, 1836–1976' p. 123.
35. Moore, 'Half-burnt turf', p. 112.
36. M. Niesingh and A. Shackley, 'Revegetation Action Plan, Clonlea Park' (Report for Town of Gawler Council and the Adelaide and Mount Lofty Ranges Natural Resources Management Board, 2009), pp. 4–5.
37. Moore, 'Half-burnt turf', p. 110.
38. Richards, 'Irish life and progress in colonial South Australia', p. 216.
39. Major O'Halloran, et al., 'St Patrick's Society of South Australia', supplement to *Adelaide Observer* (14 July 1849), <http://trove.nla.gov.au/ndp/del/page/18836007> (accessed 24 February 2015).
40. Richards, 'The peopling of South Australia, 1836–1976', p. 126.
41. O'Farrell, *The Irish in Australia*, p. 74.
42. Richards, 'Irish women in colonial South Australia', pp. 83–5.
43. Ibid., pp. 91–2.
44. Jean V. Moyle, *The Wakefield, its Waters and its Wealth: The Story of a Winding River* (Riverton: Moyle, 1982), pp. 16–17.
45. Pat Gallasch, 'Damned whores & God's people', *Off Our Backs*, 13:3 (1983), p. 4.
46. Anonymous, 'Nation building and immigration', *Journal of the Australian Population Association*, 5:1 (1988), p. 54.
47. O'Farrell, *The Irish in Australia*, p. 143.
48. Gerald Lally, *'A Landmark of Faith': Church of the Immaculate Conception, Mintaro – its parishioners, 1856–2006* (Clare: Lally, 2006), pp. 5–6.
49. Robert James Noye, *Clare: A District History* (Coromandel Valley: Lynton, 1975), p. 20.
50. State Heritage Branch, Department of Environment and Natural Resources *Mintaro: State Heritage Area*, 1990, <www.environment.sa.gov.au> (accessed 14 April 2014).

51. Noye, *Clare: A District History*, p. 125.
52. Rob Charlton, *The History of Kapunda* (Melbourne: The Hawthorn Press, 1971), pp. 42–3.
53. Mary Burrows, *Riverton – Heart of the Gilbert Valley* (Riverton: District Council, 1965), p. 29.
54. Frank S. Carroll (compiler), *The District Atlas of South Australia and Northern Territory, 1876* (Adelaide: E. S. Wigg & Son, 1876), p. 4.
55. Burrows, *Riverton – Heart of the Gilbert Valley*, pp. 29–30.
56. Robert P. Whitworth (compiler), *Bailliere's South Australian Gazetteer and Road Guide* (Adelaide: Bailliere, 1866), p. 157.
57. History Trust of South Australia, <http://explorehistory.com.au/organisation/saddleworth-district-historical-society-museum> (accessed 16 April 2020).
58. Burrows, *Riverton – Heart of the Gilbert Valley*, p. 1.
59. Whitworth, *Bailliere's South Australian Gazetteer*, p. 256.
60. Moyle, *The Wakefield, its Waters and its Wealth*, p. 98.
61. Ryan K. Smith, 'The cross: Church symbol and contest in nineteenth-century America', *Church History*, 70:4, 2001, p. 706.
62. Ibid., pp. 720–1.
63. Jeanne Sheehy and George Mott, *The Rediscovery of Ireland's Past: The Celtic Revival, 1830–1930* (London: Thames and Hudson, 1980), p. 29.
64. O'Farrell, 'The Irish in Australia', p. 30, cited in Campbell, 'Irish nationalism', p. 33.
65. Thomas N. Brown, 'The origins and character of Irish-American nationalism', *The Review of Politics*, 18:3 (1956), p. 333.
66. Kerby A. Miller, 'Emigrants and exiles: Irish cultures and Irish emigration to North America, 1790–1922', *Irish Historical Studies*, 22:86 (1980), p. 104.
67. Fidelma E. M. Breen, '"Yet we are told that Australians do not sympathise with Ireland": A study of South Australian support for Irish Home Rule 1883–1912' (MPhil thesis, University of Adelaide, 2013); Malcolm Campbell 'John Redmond and the Irish National League in Australia and New Zealand, 1883', *History*, 86:283 (2001), p. 356.
68. Encarta World English Dictionary 2009, <https://www.webcitation.org/5kwbrFM3c?url=http://encarta.msn.com/dictionary_18616898 51/Erin_go_bragh.html> (accessed 6 April 2018)
69. Denis Gojak and Iain Stuart, 'The potential for the archaeological study of clay tobacco pipes from Australian sites', *Australasian Historical Archaeology*, 17 (1999), p. 45.
70. Campbell, 'Irish nationalism and immigrant assimilation', pp. 29–30.
71. Ibid., p. 32.
72. Campbell, 'John Redmond and the Irish National League in Australia and New Zealand, 1883' p. 355.

73. Campbell, 'Irish nationalism and immigrant assimilation', p. 33.
74. Ibid., p. 34.
75. Ibid., p. 36.
76. M. Stephanie James, 'Mobility patterns of Irish immigrants in the Clare Valley', in Margaret A. Kleinig and Eric Richards (eds), *On the Wing: Mobility Before and After Emigration to Australia. Visible Immigrants:7* (Spit Junction, NSW: Anchor Books Australia, 2012), p. 110.
77. Proudfoot and Hall, 'Sites of faith and memory', p. 227.
78. O'Farrell, *The Irish in Australia*, p. 173.
79. D. A. Larkin, *Memorials to the Irish in Queensland* (Brisbane: Genealogical Society of Queensland Irish Group and the Queensland Irish Association, 1988)
80. Amanda Norman and Mark Kneale, 'Headstone symbols and meanings', 2017 <https://headstonesymbols.co.uk>; Lorine M. Schulze, 'Graven images: Gravestone motifs and their meanings', 2014, <http://www.olive treegenealogy.com/misc/grave.shtml> (accessed 14 September 2014).
81. Phillippe Ariès, *The Hour of Our Death*, trans. H. Weaver (New York: Knopf, 1981), p. 463.
82. Edwin S. Dethlefsen, 'The cemetery and culture change: Archaeological focus and ethnographic perspective', in Richard A. Gould and Michael B. Schiffer (eds), *Modern Material Culture: The Archaeology of Us* (New York: Academic Press, 1981), p. 140.
83. Nigel Llewellyn, *Funeral Monuments in Post-Reformation England* (Cambridge: Cambridge University Press, 2000).
84. Ibid.
85. Tarlow, *Bereavement and Commemoration*, p. 66.
86. One explanation of this abbreviation is *Iesus Hominum Salvator* – 'Jesus Saviour of Mankind', Colm J. Donnelly, 'The I.H.S. monogram as a symbol of Catholic resistance in seventeenth-century Ireland', *International Journal of Historical Archaeology* 9:1 (2005) p. 39.
87. Harold Mytum, 'Faith in action: Theology and practice in commemorative traditions', in James Symonds, Anna Badcock and Jeff Oliver (eds), *Historical Archaeologies of Cognition: Explorations into Faith, Hope and Charity* (Sheffield: Equinox Publishing, 2013), p. 167.
88. Mytum, 'Faith in action', p. 162; Llewellyn, *Funeral Monuments in Post-Reformation England*; H. Mytum, 'Popular attitudes to memory, the body, and social identity', *Post-Medieval Archaeology*, 40:1 (2006).
89. Proudfoot and Hall, *Imperial Spaces*, p. 227.
90. Ibid., p. 227.
91. Ibid., p. 229.
92. Lizzie Deas, *Flower Favourites: Their Legends, Symbolism and Significance* (London: Jarrold and Sons, 1898), p. 104.
93. Thomas H. Porter, 'The shamrock', *Ulster Journal of Archaeology*, 5 (1857), p. 12.

94. W. Frazer, 'The shamrock: Its history', *The Journal of the Royal Society of Antiquaries of Ireland*, 4:2 (1894), p. 133.
95. Liam Mac Mathúna, 'Irish perceptions of the cosmos', *Celtica*, 23 (1999), pp. 174, 177.
96. Deas, *Flower Favourites*, p. 105.
97. John Hutchinson, 'Archaeology and the Irish rediscovery of the Celtic past', *Nations and Nationalism*, 7:4 (2001), p. 505.
98. Ibid., p. 510.
99. Ibid., p. 510.
100. Ibid., pp. 513–4.
101. Derek Bryce, *Symbolism of the Celtic Cross* (Felinfach: Llanerch Enterprises, 1989), chapter 5.
102. Arthure, 'The occupation of Baker's Flat', p. 112.
103. Brown, 'The origins and character of Irish-American nationalism', p. 331.
104. Mary Helen Thuente, 'Development of the exile motif in songs of emigration and nationalism', *The Canadian Journal of Irish Studies*, 26:1 (2000), p. 19.
105. Thomas Brown, *Irish-American Nationalism, 1870–1890* (Philadelphia: Lippincott, 1966), p. 16.
106. Miller, 'Emigrants and exiles', pp. 122–5.
107. James, 'Becoming South Australian', pp. 198–9.
108. Stephen Brighton, 'Symbols, myth-making, and identity: The Red Hand of Ulster in late-nineteenth-century Paterson, New Jersey', *International Journal of Historical Archaeology*, 8:2 (2004), p. 157.

7

Memorialising the Diasporic Cornish

Philip Payton

And Shall These Mute Stones Speak? asked Professor Charles Thomas in his seminal book of the same name, arguing that in the early medieval period, with its paucity of documentary records (the so-called 'Dark Ages'), the inscribed standing stones of Cornwall were the best surviving evidence for the existence of named early Cornish people.[1] In comparing this period, with its scant documentary evidence, with the modern era and its almost embarrassment of riches drawn from a multiplicity of data and sources, the inference was that it was hardly necessary to resort to such devices to seek information about the lives (and deaths) of individuals and communities in recent centuries. Given the vastness of modern archives and repositories, one need not search for silent, fragmentary remains cast in stone to illuminate life stories.

However, alongside the myriad newspaper reports, census returns, marriage registers, shipping lists, posters, leaflets, emigrants' letters, diaries and other material, there is in fact an array of similarly 'mute stones' in cemeteries large and small across the world which, as any genealogist will explain, can reveal a surprising amount of information to complement more conventional sources. Indeed, in New World settler societies, especially (but not exclusively) in the Anglosphere, such cemeteries have been elevated to almost totemic status, meccas for genealogists and others today piecing together the pioneer lives of early migrants, and monuments themselves to the arrival, establishment and survival of Europeans in distant lands. The latter role was not lost on the early migrants themselves, who saw cemeteries as markers of territorial possession and individual graves as memorials to their own pioneering efforts. At one level, as Robert Nicol put it in his pathfinding *At the End of the Road*, a history of interment in Adelaide and South Australia, the study of any individual settler cemetery served to illuminate 'the story of how one relatively new and isolated European society has coped with the complex problem of disposing of human remains'.[2] But alongside the practical and prosaic, there was also deep cultural meaning. As Janine McEgan outlines in her contribution within this volume, cemeteries in the Irish communities of South Australia's rural Mid-North reveal widespread use of Irish, Celtic and Catholic symbolism on individual gravestones – shamrocks, Celtic crosses and knotwork, even a Sacred Heart – designed to imbue these sites with an enduring Irishness.[3]

More generally, for Anglophone settler societies, such memorialisation – and the attendant commemoration and remembrance – became a major preoccupation as those societies became more permanent, marking (even celebrating) the territorial dispersal of the British and Irish diasporas across the globe, from North America to the Antipodes. Early graves were revered as the final resting places of 'pioneer families', acquiring shrine-like status, and becoming sites of intrinsic historical importance. Cemeteries, as they emerged on the outskirts of new settlements, especially in rural and remote areas, achieved a particular civic significance, evidence of the successful establishment of townships and communities on the frontier, proclaiming their amenity value, stability, continuity and presumed permanence. Later, war gave a new imperative to the desire to memorialise, again especially in settler societies geographically far removed from the battlefield. Although in the Great War of 1914–18 soldiers who had lost their lives were almost always buried where they fell, usually in Europe or the Middle East, each of the belligerent nations sought to commemorate their dead, not least in the Antipodes – half a world away – where war memorials sprang up in even the tiniest or most far-flung localities.[4]

This desire to memorialise and commemorate through cemeteries and individual graves was, not surprisingly, one aspect of the complex Cornish transnational identity that had emerged during the nineteenth and early twentieth centuries. Like the Irish, the Cornish overseas sought to differentiate themselves in death as in life, presenting themselves as a distinct ethno-occupational and ethno-religious group – many of them were hard-rock miners and most were Methodists – and asserting their identity through the 'myths' of Cousin Jack and Cousin Jenny. Put simply, a Cousin Jack was a male Cornish migrant, and his myth insisted that the Cornish were innately imbued as superior hard-rock miners, especially when compared to competing nationalities. Likewise, the myth of Cousin Jenny claimed that emigrant Cornish women were especially suited to the rigours of the international mining frontier, bringing order and domesticity, and succeeding where lesser women might fail. In death, the clannishness of Cousin Jack and Cousin Jenny often extended to the manner in which they were memorialised.[5]

In this way, the physical evidence of the nineteenth- and early-twentieth-century Cornish diaspora – the gravestones of Cornish emigrants in Cornish cemeteries as disparate as Real del Monte in Mexico and Moonta in South Australia – have proved to be vivid insights into the Cornish diasporic experience, and are tangible reminders in the landscape of Cornwall's emigration story in the nineteenth and early twentieth centuries. Their location in often remote areas is testament to the extent of Cornish diasporic dispersal, while the inscriptions on individual gravestones are often themselves important sources of social and cultural history. Moreover, these cemeteries and gravestones have served, collectively and individually, as specific memorials to the diasporic Cornish, often organised into distinctive 'Cornish' sections in graveyards. Today, as we shall see, they are explicit sites of remembrance – as in the 'Dressing the Graves' ceremony performed at Moonta, Wallaroo and Kadina during the biennial 'Kernewek Lowender' Cornish festival on South Australia's northern Yorke Peninsula. Yet, as we shall also see, Cornish gravestones were often plain and simple, as Cornish religious nonconformity dictated, with little in the way of symbolism (with the interesting exception of Masonic insignia), although often with an appropriate biblical text.

Among the distant destinations of early Cornish emigration was Mexico where, in the 1820s, skilled Cornish miners had been brought in to develop the country's silver mines.[6] Although many had envisaged a temporary sojourn, with the expectation of returning to Cornwall on the expiry of their contracts, there were, inevitably, those who succumbed to disease or accident, finding an early grave at Pachuca or Real del Monte, while others decided to stay on, making Mexico their home for life. Alongside (chili-flavoured) pasties and telltale Cornish mine engine-houses, among the enduring signifiers of Cornish influence, was (and is) the so-called 'English cemetery' at Real del Monte, where most of those interred were actually Cornish rather than strictly English. Although most nineteenth-century Cornish adhered to the view that they hailed from 'Cornwall, near England',[7] like most Britons at the time they were also content to equate 'England' with England-and-Wales, Great Britain, the United Kingdom or even the Empire, while 'England's flag' was the Union Jack rather than the cross of St George.[8] Sometimes this hazy hybridity was reflected on gravestones, with references to 'Cornwall, England' but more often 'Native of Cornwall' was sufficient, as in the case of the gravestone of Edward Bowden at Real del Monte, dating from the mid nineteenth century.

Many of the gravestone inscriptions bear witness to the hard and sometimes tragic lives of the Cornish emigrants, with their telltale Cornish surnames more than a clue to their Cornish origins.[9] There is Edward Richards, from Breage, who was killed in the Santa Gertrudis mine in 1896, aged only twenty-six years. There is Isaac Prout, who was assassinated on the road from Real del Monte to Pachuca on 31 July 1864, aged thirty-one years. His gravestone recalls the words of Psalm 102:25: 'They weakened my strength in the way / They have shortened my days'. Sometimes whole families were afflicted by such shortened days, as the Pengilly grave testifies:

Sacred to the memory of
THOMAS PENGILLY
Beloved husband of
ELIZABETH PENGILLY
who died at Pachuca
November 22 1893
Aged 48 years
and also of:
Their dearly beloved son
THOMAS ALVINO
WHO DIED AT PACHUCA
March 12th 1888
aged 4 years 3 months[10]

Even more desolate in its brevity is the headstone of 'John the son of MARY RULE / January 2nd 1871 aged 1 year and 6 months'.[11] Perhaps Mary was a widow; probably she was a single mother.

When historian A. C. Todd visited Real del Monte and Pachuca in 1968, researching material for his book *The Search for Silver: Cornish Miners in Mexico 1824–1947*, he visited the cemetery and was greatly moved by what he found. 'Many of the Cornish never returned to the land of their fathers', he wrote, 'but finished out their time on the top of a hill that is known today as "the English cemetery", carried there by Cornish bearers and accompanied by friends who sang Cornish hymns'.[12] According to legend, the graveyard had originally been known as 'Jew's Hill', reflecting the unwillingness of the predominantly Catholic population to allow those of other faiths to be buried in their cemetery, and when the Cornish arrived in the locality it was thought appropriate for their dead to share the hill with their Jewish neighbours. For Todd, 'this is "some corner of a foreign field that is forever Cornwall"', where 'one meditates upon its Cornish character and the sense of a final withdrawal from a Mexico within Mexico. If any place demonstrates the continuity of the Cornish ability to adapt themselves to a new country, so very different from their own, then this is it.'[13] The date on the corner-stone of the arch over the cemetery entrance gates was 1851, Todd noted, although the gates themselves were erected in 1869 and carried a religious text picked out in iron letters: 'Blessed are the Dead who died in the Lord'.[14]

Ironically, a few weeks later 'the Cornish lady, who had brought us [Todd and his wife] to Pachuca from the City of Mexico, was herself buried here. She originally came from Twelveheads [in Cornwall] and will now be remembered, like the others, in the art of the Mexican stonemason who has carved his angels and incised their names, though more in the English and Cornish style of lettering than the Spanish and Mexican'.[15] As A. C. Todd concluded, writing forty years ago at Real del Monte, the 'Cornish dead lie in their abundance, proclaiming their Celtic ancestry and their Mexican affinities: Carlos Richards, Nazario Skewes, Senor Alberto Del Rosa, Frederico Hosking and Roberto Noble from St Hilary near Penzance'.[16] Todd was not Cornish but he felt an acute connection and sympathy, partly from his Scottish (that is pan-Celtic) roots and partly because of his role over many years as a university extra-mural tutor in Cornwall. Following his visit to the cemetery, he wrote to his friend and mentor, the Cornish historian A. L. Rowse, describing what had been an intensely poignant occasion:

> I understand what you mean when you say you are writing about your own people. On Christmas Day we visited the Cornish cemetery at Real del Monte, 10,000 feet up in the mountains and ringed by pines. An old Mexican woman tends the grass. She took us into a clean but inadequate cottage – no light, no water. On the walls were photographs of her ancestors and, in striking contrast, propped up in the corner the iron cross of a Cornish miner that she had brought out of the cemetery – why? I don't know, but I felt that there was some connection between RABLING [a well-known Cornish family] and this dear old lady who had no meat to put in her tacos.[17]

Many of the Cornish gravestones at Real del Monte sported Masonic inscriptions, reflecting the attraction that Freemasonry, along with the Oddfellows and other friendly and temperance societies, had had for the emigrant Cornish, vehicles for the myth of Cousin Jack and mechanisms to stick together and promote their interests in the new lands. The same was true north of the Rio Grande, where the Cornish had arrived in large numbers since the 1830s, playing a major role in the expansion of the American mining frontier. As Sharron Schwartz has observed, Masonic lodges were a prominent feature of life in nineteenth-century Cornwall, and the 'continuance of the Masonic tradition abroad, particularly in the USA, must have served the Cousin Jacks well with its expressed aims of social philanthropy and welfare, which would also have strengthened the kin network and provided a degree of security'.[18] Indeed, a great number of Cornish burials in public cemeteries in the United States were in sections reserved for Freemasons and Oddfellows. Schwartz notes an exemplar: 'Carn Marth miner Joseph Kemp, buried at the Glenwood Cemetery in Park City, Utah, has Masonic insignia on his headstone'.[19]

The rapid expansion of the North American mining frontier drew the Cornish to a multiplicity of mining destinations from the 1830s – to California, Wisconsin, Michigan, Nevada and a host of other areas as they toiled for gold, silver, copper and other metals. Sometimes their influence was permanent, at others fleeting, as the relative fortunes of the mines and mining districts rose and fell. The Comstock silver-lead mining district of Nevada, with Virginia City as its focus, was a magnet for the Cornish in the second half of the nineteenth-century yet by the time A. C. Todd visited in the 1960s, they appeared to be all but forgotten, many having moved on decades before. 'Today the Cousin Jacks of the Comstock', he opined, 'will only be remembered perhaps in their eleven cemeteries on Decoration Day'.[20] Nowadays the latter is often conflated with Memorial Day, when the graves of those who have fallen in military service are decorated with flowers and American flags. Decoration Day predated the American Civil War, and remains in some areas an opportunity to tidy up cemeteries and tend individual graves, dressing them with floral tributes and honouring family ancestors, irrespective of their military service. On such occasions, Todd averred, the Cornish might at last be remembered in their erstwhile Nevada homes. Indeed, by the early twenty-first century, Cornish enthusiasts were now making their way routinely to the remote cemeteries of Nevada, searching for evidence of their forebears. Among their number was Heather Pearce, who combed the Oddfellows' section of the cemetery at Virginia City, and to her delight found 'a marble headstone in very good condition' on the grave of Henry K. Rowe (who had died in 1885), with the legend 'Erected by his brother Thomas'.[21]

As historian John Rowe observed, the Cornish, perhaps, had been better remembered by observers in the United States for their distinctive funeral practices, certainly in the copper-mining region of Upper Michigan where 'coffins were borne from church to graveside by pallbearers', just as in Cornwall, and 'the sombre hymn *Nearer My God to Thee* was sung'. From Cornwall, too, added Rowe, 'came the customs of long funeral cortèges and crowded attendances at funerals besides the wearing of deep mourning as token of respect for the deceased'.[22]

And, unlike the Comstock, the memory of the Cornish burned bright in Upper Peninsula of Michigan for years to come. When A. L. Rowse toured the district in the 1960s, collecting material for his *The Cornish in America*,[23] he visited the Pine Grove Cemetery at Eagle Harbour, noting details in his diary. He pondered the tragedy of many Cornish lives blighted and cut short. There was the grave of 'Thomas R. Job, 1870, aged 24, wife 22: "Weep not for me my wife so dear"', the inscription read. Then there was 'Peter Opie, son of James Opie and Jane Roberts, 1869–85, aged 16. Bessie, their daughter, aged 3'. As in Cornwall, headstones often gave a wife's maiden name. As he wandered among these tombstones, Rowse encountered the graves of 'Any number of small children at two and three, and young people in their twenties – those ferocious winters and insanitary conditions, poor folk with their hard-bitten lives'. He recognised the telltale Cornish surnames on the headstones – Rosewarne, Martin, Cocking, Rule, Paull, Sampson, Nicholls, Williams, Barrett, Kellow, Bawden, Richards, Angove, Saunders, Collins, Uren – 'And then there was a tough old girl who lived through the whole period, from beginning to its end, dying at a hundred when I was a growing boy: Harriet Uren, 1808–1909'. Also, as Rowse observed, there were the inevitable mining accidents. 'Sacred to the memory of William Roberts who came to his death while performing his daily labor in the Amalgamated Mine, May 18, 1869, aged 28 years', recorded one memorial stone. Another was to Thomas and John Berryman, both killed in the Central Mine on 29 April 1872. Rowse read the inscription, noting it in his diary: 'They fought the fight'.[24]

A decade later, the Cornish poet and novelist D. M. Thomas followed in Rowse's footsteps, visiting the same cemetery, an experience which led to the composition and subsequent publication, in the *Cornish Review* in 1973, of his poem 'A Cornish Graveyard at Keweenaw'. Like Rowse, Thomas was struck by the familiarity of Cornish surnames in this unfamiliar place, a strange and distant shore but where the Cornish (a Celtic people, as he noted) were now rooted for all time, the graveyard – and death itself – hardly able to suppress their defining characteristics:

>   Rosewarne
> Opie, Paull, Rule.
>   Trethewey.
>   Berryman.
>   Curnow.
> Mineral is their true root, and now their night.
> Rickard is turned to rickardite, to a tellurite.

> Of copper immortalised, Pearce to pearcite.
>   This graveyard
>   at Eagle harbour
>   by Superior's groundroar
> Makes heavy weather quelling the continuous drama
> Of Celtic hands and features, dry humour,
> Cough and gob of spit, a quiet snicker,
>   and cannot quell
> their deep and daring harmony.[25]

Like A. C. Todd and D. M. Thomas, A. L. Rowse was sensitive to the deep pathos of the Cornish emigrant graveyards, with their half-articulated stories of tough and sometimes lonely lives acted out far from home. Although Rowse had never visited South Africa, he knew that it was the final resting place of many Cornish miners and their families – Graham Dickason found identifiably Cornish headstones (based on place of birth and Cornish surnames) in more than forty cemeteries from Cape Town to Johannesburg[26] – and remembered as a boy in Cornwall before the First World War the miners returned from the Rand with quartz dust in their lungs, men old before their time but condemned to a lingering, rasping death. His own father had been in Johannesburg for a while, and his Uncle Tom had died out there – from 'phthisis and drink'.[27] Rowse's youngest uncle, 'Cheelie' (the 'cheeld' of the family, in Cornish dialect), also emigrated to South Africa and, according to Rowse, had stayed with his parents – Richard and Annie Rowse – before leaving Cornwall. During those few weeks, Cheelie tinkered incessantly with an old clock that no longer worked. Rowse takes up the story:

> One morning about eight o'clock, some months after he had gone away, while my mother and father were sitting at breakfast, the clock suddenly struck 'one' out loud. 'That's funny', said my father, 'there must be a mouse in 'n' [in it]. He got up and looked; there was no mouse there. Three weeks later they got the news that Cheelie had been killed on that day, at about that time. They ever after took it as a 'token', a signal of his death: there are many such stories in Cornish families. When the poor boy was brought up to surface dying – he was almost cut in two by the crashed skip – he said these last words: 'I've no father nor mother to grieve for me, so it's all right.'[28]

The 'token' of violent death and the courageous stoicism of the lonely emigrant miner expiring in a foreign land, were, as Rowse noted, integral to the lore of 'diasporic death' in many Cornish families. And if distant graveyards could not be visited, they could at least be imagined. As Rowse put it: 'He was a brave spirit, Cheelie, and has left a fragrant and beautiful memory in my family and among all who knew him.'[29]

Individual memory, then, could be a precious part of memorialisation, intangible and intensely personal but vibrant and meaningful nonetheless.

As John Rowe had intimated, funerals and burial services were also essential components of the memorialisation process overseas, in some respects more important even than the subsequent erection of inscribed headstones. Moonta, in the copper-mining district of northern Yorke Peninsula in South Australia, an area known as 'Australia's Little Cornwall', was renowned for such events. In 1902, the Revd W. F. James, a Bible Christian minister, born in Cornwall in 1846 and for many years active on Yorke Peninsula, recalled the spectacle of the old-time Cornish burial service. At Chacewater, in the heart of Cornwall's Gwennap mining district, funerals were, he recalled, 'largely attended and the singing was memorable. Never shall I forget', he added, 'the sight of a funeral procession turning the corner of the street leading to the churchyard. The corpse was preceded by some twenty or thirty men, having good voices, with measured step and slow'. They were, James said, 'singing a solemn hymn to an appropriate tune. I have never heard anything like it, save at Moonta.'[30]

A favourite at Moonta funerals was Isaac Watts' hymn 'Thee We Adore', set to the tune 'Rapture', a piece by 'Fiddler Jim' Richards, a local composer of Cornish carols and sacred music, who was born at Perranporth in Cornwall in 1828 and emigrated to South Australia around 1857. A ritual developed at Moonta whereby the coffin was picked up by the bearers during two lines from the third stanza of the hymn – 'What e're we do, where'er we be, / We are travelling to the grave' – always a moment of high religious drama and intense emotion.[31] Geoffrey Blainey, writing in 1963 in his *The Rush That Never Ended: A History of Australian Mining*, explained that at Moonta the funeral processions also invariably sang 'the slow burial tune that had been sung at miners' burials in Cornwall for unmeasured years':

> Sing from the chamber to the grave,
> I hear the dying miner say;
> A sound of melody I crave
> Upon my burial day
>
> Sing sweetly while you travel on,
> And keep the funeral slow;
> The angels sing where I am gone
> And you should sing below.[32]

The miners' 'burying tune' was often sung for those killed in the mines. The mourners, suddenly and tragically bereft, were urged to exult in the passage of their loved ones to heaven. Of course, the ever-present prospect of death cast a perpetual shadow over the mining communities. Periodic epidemics of 'colonial measles', typhoid, diphtheria, and other diseases decimated the infant population, leading to great Methodist revivals, such as those of 1874–5, as the community rallied to confirm and proclaim its religious faith.[33] At Moonta Mines, situated east of Moonta township, the revival in April 1875 was precipitated by the untimely death of Kate Morcombe, a young Bible Christian Sunday-school teacher whose sudden loss was felt keenly by the community at large. Similarly, at the nearby Wesleyan chapel an intense religious revival was triggered by the tragic death of Captain Hugh Datson, a mine manager, in a rockfall underground in March 1875. Curiously, only a few days before the accident Datson had felt compelled to confess his Christian faith anew, after which, it was said, a 'strange awe filled every church in Moonta', the people 'instinctively called to prayer'.[34]

Here was 'triumphant death', something to be treasured, Methodists insisted, where the dying person remained, even in his or her last moments, and despite all pain, serenely confident in the salvation of life everlasting. At the chapels they sang Charles Wesley's words – 'Rejoice for a brother deceased / Our loss is his infinite gain' – and the manner in which a person had died was a source of endless fascination. It was important that Methodists should 'die well', as John Wesley had put it, and on the bleak frontier of northern Yorke Peninsula his stricture had especial weight. It helped people, those dying and those loved ones left behind, to bear their predicament.

Disease, of course, was no respecter of rank or station, and among those to succumb to typhoid in June 1870 was Sarah Hancock, wife of Captain Henry Richard Hancock, the far-famed chief captain of the Moonta mine. Following her funeral and interment, her grieving husband arranged for the headstone to be placed on her grave at Moonta Cemetery. 'Shortly before the hour of dissolution', said the inscription composed by Captain Hancock himself, 'she calmly and distinctly expressed her humble trust in the Saviour in the following words: "Christ our wisdom, righteousness, sanctification and redemption"'. Aged only thirty-two, Sarah had 'died well': at four o'clock in the morning, as she had begun to fade, she had been 'filled with heavenly consolation', it was reported, and she joined with her husband Henry in whispering the words of the hymn 'Jesu, lover of my soul'. Shortly after seven o'clock, as the morning light dawned, she departed this world.[35]

Sarah's death was a gratifying example of 'the fullness and sweetness of Christian triumph', as the Revd Charles Tresise described it in 1885, when commenting on the similar passing of Eliza Thomas, aged only twenty, at nearby Wallaroo. 'In her case,' said Tresise, 'the Jordan valley rang with songs of faith and joy ... There was no cessation for the whole 36 hours of this spiritual animation, except when she laid her head on her mother's lap and sank to sleep, saying "I'm so tired".' Then, rallying from her slumber, she announced that she wished to 'sing all the way to heaven'. Turning to her sister, Eliza asked: 'Annie, don't the angels sing when they see another coming?' Annie replied that it was so, and Eliza answered, 'I can hear them singing beautifully now. I shall soon be through the pearly gates.'[36] It was another good death.

There were cemeteries at both Wallaroo and Kadina but it was Moonta that created its early and enduring mystique, which Geoffrey Blainey felt keenly in the 1960s when he visited 'that stone-walled graveyard where Methuselah Tregonning and Ephraim Major lay with a thousand Cornish dead'.[37] As Oswald Pryor recalled, such was the exalted place of Moonta Cemetery in local lore, that a 'surprising number of former residents of the district left instructions that their remains were to be taken back to Moonta for burial there'.[38] The most famous, perhaps, was John Verran, born in Gwennap, erstwhile leader of South Australia's (and the world's) very first Labor government, who had retired to the Adelaide suburb of Unley but who in death (he passed away in 1932) returned to Moonta for his state funeral.[39] An earlier exemplar was in the poignant account, published in the Moonta *People's Weekly* newspaper in 1893, of the ill-fated romance between a Moonta girl at Broken Hill (across the New South Wales border) and her lover, a miner in the local Block 11 mine:

> And when I'm dead and gone, this one request I crave,
> You'll take my bones to Moonta and lay them in the grave,
> Some words write on my tombstone to tell the passer-by,
> I died all broken-hearted through that 11 Block miner boy.[40]

In the earliest days, Moonta Cemetery was a chaotic affair, with relatives of the deceased 'simply choosing any spot they wished, without any thought for order in the arrangement or position of the graves'.[41] This was a practice that mirrored the ad hoc erection of miners' cottages on the adjoining mineral leases at Moonta Mines, where miners and their families chose plots randomly and at will on which to build their impromptu homes. Yet order was soon imposed on this rapidly expanding cemetery, as the *Wallaroo Times* observed in August 1865 when commenting on the 'very large number of friends and others [who] visited the cemetery at Moonta on Sunday last, on the occasion of the funeral of Mrs Roach; it was estimated that there were one thousand five hundred persons present'.[42] As the newspaper added:

> This cemetery is becoming the chosen place of resort by the inhabitants of the town for spending the quiet hours of Sunday afternoon. It was computed that throughout the whole of last summer, the average number of visitors on each Sunday was not less than two hundred, irrespective of those who were to follow friends to their last resting place. The curator has had it carefully cleared and grass cut, besides placing seats at every short distance for the accommodation of those who chose 'to rest and be thankful'. Several choice plants and shrubs have been planted, amongst which may be noticed the Moreton Bay (Queensland) fig.[43]

As Oswald Pryor noted, many of the early gravestones at Moonta were careful to 'bear witness to the birthplace of most of those buried there', a practice that gradually declined over time. There was, for example, Richard Eddy from Porthleven, together with William Arundel Paynter from Gwennap, Elizabeth Beaglehole from Helston, Stephen Brown from Redruth, Edward Glasson from St Just, and James Jeffery, 'born at Illogan, and forty years a local preacher' according to his epitaph.[44] By 1867 the twenty-eight bodies that had been buried outside the boundary of the cemetery in the early days were exhumed and reinterred within the cemetery proper. Two years later James Lander (a Cornish surname) was appointed the new curator, and he successfully negotiated a grant of an additional ten acres for the cemetery. The front wall of the cemetery was constructed in 1871, with large iron gates erected. Cemetery records for 1873 showed 327 burials at Moonta, mostly typhoid victims, while between 1 and 20 December 1874 alone, during the 'colonial measles' outbreak, there were seventy-four interments, mainly of children.[45] Overall, during 1873 and 1874, there were 435 deaths of children under ten years old at Moonta, the result of typhoid and measles epidemics.[46]

Liz Coole and colleagues have investigated the lives of many of the early 'Pioneers from "Australia's Little Cornwall"', as they term them, marshalling biographical details from newspaper obituaries and noting precisely their burial plots in Moonta Cemetery. A wooden headboard, said to be the oldest grave marker in the cemetery, is that to Samuel Jones (died 1865, aged fifty years) and his wife Eliza Williams (died 1874, aged sixty-four years). 'Christ is All and All', proclaims the headboard: 'Farewell dear children and friends Farewell for we shall meet no more till we are raised [?] with Christ to dwell on Zions peaceful shore'.[47]

Detailed research by Coole and her team has allowed the accumulation of other forensically acquired data. Thomas Yelland, for example,

Figure 7.1 The lonely grave of Annie Trevithic[k], from Lelant in Cornwall, near the entrance to the Blinman copper mine in the northern Flinders Ranges in outback South Australia. Annie died in childbirth aged twenty-four on 14 March 1866, and she shares her grave with her two sons, one who predeceased her in 1865 aged six months, the other in May 1866 just eight weeks after her own death. See Nic Klaassen, *The Northern Flinders Ranges: Mountains, Minerals and Mines 1850–1920* (Adelaide: Nic Klaassen, 1991), p. 130, and Liz Coole and J. R. Harbison, *Mine Captains of the Copper Triangle, Yorke Peninsula, South Australia* (Moonta: National Trust of South Australia, Moonta Branch, 2006), p. 4. (Photo courtesy of Dee Cleary)

was killed in an underground accident in the Moonta mine in 1889 when only twenty-six years of age. It was reported that his funeral was one of the largest seen at Moonta, some 500 men from the Amalgamated Miners' Association, the Rechabites and the Young Turks Football Club preceding the coffin to its grave.[48] The mix of attendees was an intriguing insight into Yelland's cultural affiliations, and that of the wider community. The Amalgamated Miners' Association, an Australia-wide trade union, had several branches in the locality, and had subsumed the Moonta Miners' and Mechanics' Association formed in the early 1870s becoming now a powerful institutional presence on northern Yorke Peninsula.[49] It developed close links with the local Methodist chapels and with the various friendly and temperance societies, notably the Rechabites of which Thomas Yelland was evidently a member. If this sounds very Cornish, then the Young Turks reference is testament to the increasing popularity on the Peninsula of Australian Rules football and, perhaps, to an emergent cultural hybridity.

Fortunes of a very different sort are evident in West Side Row 4 – Grave Block 210 at Moonta Cemetery, where Thomas Woolcock is interred. He died in 1873, aged thirty-four years, having been slowly poisoned with mercury by his wife Elizabeth, whom he had treated abominably in life. She was found guilty of Thomas's murder and, despite a wave of public sympathy for her predicament, was hanged in Adelaide Gaol, the only woman to be executed in South Australia. Thomas Woolcock's headstone epitaph is enigmatic, to say the least: 'Dangers stand thick through all the ground to push us to the tomb and fierce diseases wait around to hurry mortals home'.[50] Incremental poisoning by tiny mercury doses might just be considered 'fierce diseases' but the coy inscription (lifted from a Methodist hymn) disingenuously suggests natural causes rather than murder, protecting both victim and perpetrator. For all the tragedy so evident in cemeteries, a certain decorum needed to be maintained, especially if they were to fulfil their roles as places of quiet reflection and retreat. Yet epitaphs were not above making moral points, as on the gravestone of William Jenkins, from Gwennap, who was killed in the Karkarilla mine, near Moonta, when caught in a rockfall underground in February 1867. He was only aged twenty-eight, in the prime of life. But as his headstone warned: 'Boast not young man of health or might / Well in the morn but dead at night'.[51]

Other gravestones at Moonta bore biblical inscriptions or lines from favourite hymns, with frequent references to crossing the Jordan and angels singing their welcomes:

We've crossed the River Jordan,
Hallelujah, Hallelujah,
We're over the River Jordan, Happy in the Lord.

Likewise:

Home at last, my labour done,
Safe and Blest, the victory won,
Jordan passed, from pain set free,
Angels now have welcomed me.[52]

Christian faith was often proclaimed – 'I now enjoy what I lived for' – with reward for good works on Earth a favourite theme: 'She rests from her labours / And her works do follow her'. Sometimes there were references to slow agonising deaths, often experienced by miners suffering from pulmonary diseases:

He faded like a flower that wasted by slow decay,
Not snatched in an untimely hour but withered day by day,
With tearful eyes we watched him and saw him pass away,
And though we dearly loved him we could not make him stay.[53]

Glimpses of the mobility of mining families, and of the complexities of the Cornish transnational identity, were evident on some gravestones and in the stories that lay behind them. On some gravestones there were allusions to places of former residence in Victoria and New Zealand, as well as Cornwall itself, and hints of global careers. James Michael Whitburn, for example, was born in Camborne and arrived in Australia after a brief sojourn in Chile. He toiled in the Old Geraldine copper mine, near Geraldton in Western Australia, and from there crossed the continent to the Great Cobar mine in New South Wales, before moving on to Broken Hill and later to the Western Australian goldfields, eventually settling at Moonta. He died in September 1912, and was buried in Moonta Cemetery with his wife Jane. Tellingly, adjacent memorials were to their two sons, John and Charles Whitburn, who both died in South Africa and were buried out there.[54]

Although the copper mines of northern Yorke Peninsula closed in 1923, the communities of Moonta, Wallaroo and Kadina remained intensely conscious of their Cornish identities, epitomised in the publication in 1962 of Oswald Pryor's delightful local history *Australia's Little Cornwall* and institutionalised in the Kernewek Lowender Cornish festival, held biennially since 1973.[55] A popular addition to the repertoire of festival activities, first introduced during the 2001 Kernewek Lowender, was the ceremony of 'Dressing the Graves' (or 'Dressing of the Graves',

Figure 7.2 The gravestone of William Tremaine in the cemetery at Silverton, a small mining town near Broken Hill in outback New South Wales. Although the gravestone does not tell us, William Tremaine was born in Cornwall in about 1820. His epitaph includes a religious text, typical of Cornish Methodist gravestones. See G. J. Drew, *Captain Bagot's Mine: Kapunda Mine 1844–1916* (Kapunda: Light Regional Council, 2017), p. 162. (Photo courtesy of Dee Cleary)

as it was sometimes more clumsily rendered). As the booklet published in 2007 to review their progress explained, separate ceremonies were performed in the cemeteries at Moonta, Wallaroo and Kadina, and were held to:

> draw attention to the pioneers and the esteem in which each was held. The ceremony at each cemetery takes just over an hour. At each grave a floral tribute is laid on the grave and the citation is read and then placed on the grave for the duration of the [Kernewek] Lowender. The whole event takes five and a half hours, including time for lunch and travelling between cemeteries. During each festival ten people buried in each of the three cemeteries are honoured [having been nominated by descendants or other interested persons] ... at Moonta ... the babies and young children who died in the diphtheria and typhoid plagues of the 1870s and 1880s are also remembered.[56]

Here the role of 'pioneers' in establishing the settlements was saluted, the physical act of traversing the cemeteries and laying tributes an affirmation of territorial possession by a settler society. But while 'Dressing the Graves' might echo the rituals of other settler societies (such as Decoration Day in the United States), it was explained emphatically that the 'ceremony is not a traditionally Cornish event as many would assume'.[57] And yet, sponsored by the Cornish Association of South Australia and soon enjoying a prominent role in the festival, 'Dressing the Graves' swiftly acquired a Cornish patina, at least in this South Australian context. In the same way, it was noted that 'a large number of the graves recognised in this event are not Cornish. It is believed that the festival exists for all people of various ethnic backgrounds. Cornishness is not a pre-requisite for inclusion.'[58] While many of those honoured were indeed Cornish or of Cornish descent – John Davey Beare from Egloshayle, Richard Borlace from St Austell, Paul Roach from Ludgvan, Thomas Trevan from Illogan, Samuel Phillips from St Agnes, and so on – there were numerous others from England, Ireland, Scotland and Wales, as well as from Germany, together with the Australian-born. Included in the latter was 'King Tommy', an Aborigine buried in Kadina Cemetery. Moreover, in the cemetery at the more cosmopolitan port of Wallaroo, there 'are Chinese and Japanese memorials to dead seamen. As well, Swedish and Finnish sailors ... are also to be found there.'[59] Yet, notwithstanding the disclaimers, all these diverse individuals had been co-opted within the Cornish narrative of the Kernewek Lowender festival and, like the 'Dressing the Graves' ceremony itself, had been accommodated within the widening story of the diasporic Cornish.

Authentically 'Cornish' or not, 'Dressing the Graves' was a major element of the 2019 Kernewek Lowender. At Wallaroo Cemetery, the festival's 'official program' announced, this 'year will have a World War I Theme. Local school choirs sing and place flowers and the KWM [Kadina–Wallaroo–Moonta] Band plays in support.' At Kadina, this 'year will have a Pioneer Children Theme – honouring the many children interred in common graves'. Meanwhile, 'Moonta's ceremony begins with a re-enactment of a funeral procession of the era'. Additionally, at nearby Greens Plains, where many miners-turned-farmers and their families had settled in the later nineteenth century, 'this year's ceremony will have a farming theme', an initiative to expand the 'Dressing the Graves' formula to other cemeteries and communities in the locality.[60]

Brass bands, children's choirs and themed events had by the end of the second decade of the twenty-first century introduced new dimensions to the commemoration of northern Yorke Peninsula's diasporic graves, mediating and enriching the complexity of the symbiotic relationship between the headstone inscriptions and the real lives they represented. Nearly eighty years before, in 1942, Phyllis Somerville, born at Kadina with three Cornish grandparents, had published her minor classic, the novel *Not Only in Stone*. The heroine is the fictional Mary Elizabeth 'Polly' Thomas, a literary amalgam of the many independent-minded Cornish women Phyllis Somerville had known as a child, and her story is that of a 'simple but stout-hearted woman' who 'stands fast in the face of many tragic set-backs'.[61] The book's title reflects Somerville's main point, that Polly's supposed headstone acts as a window to her former life beyond the grave: 'The story of Polly Thomas is not graven only in the stone over her clay, but abides with visible symbol, woven into the stuff of other lives. And this is her story.'[62] Somerville imagines Polly's headstone:

> MARY ELIZABETH THOMAS
> Born St Ives, Cornwall 1838
> Died Adelaide 1927
> Arrived in Australia by ship
>   *Lady Milton* 1865
> ''Tis not the whole of life to live,
> Nor all of death to die'.
> This memorial erected by her sons[63]

But Phyllis Somerville is also careful to include the telling quotation from Thucydides, the fifth-century BC Athenian historian, which had first inspired her work and, which one might argue, stands as a permanent insight into the nature and purpose of diasporic memorialisation,

Cornish and otherwise: 'The whole earth is the tomb of heroes. Their story is not graven in the stone over their clay, but abides everywhere with visible symbol, woven into the stuff of other men's lives.'[64] Like other emigrant peoples, the Cornish had used individual gravestones and sometimes (as at Real del Monte and Moonta) whole cemeteries to mark their progress and assert their identity in far-off lands, determined that they should not be forgotten.

NOTES

1. Charles Thomas, *And Shall These Mute Stones Speak? Post-Roman Inscriptions in Western Britain* (Cardiff: University of Wales Press, 1994).
2. Robert Nicol, *At the End of the Road* (St Leonards, NSW: Allen & Unwin, 1994), p. xi.
3. See also Janine McEgan, 'Irish graves in mid North South Australia, 1850–1899', in Susan Arthure, Fidelma Breen, Stephanie James, and Dymphna Lonergan (eds), *Irish South Australia: New Histories and Insights* (Adelaide: Wakefield Press, 2019), pp. 74–89.
4. Philip Payton, *Regional Australia and the Great War: 'The Boys from Old Kio'* (Exeter: University of Exeter Press, 2012), pp. 1–2 and pp. 207–9.
5. For a discussion of the myth of Cousin Jack, see Philip Payton, *The Cornish Overseas: A History of Cornwall's Great Emigration* (Exeter: University of Exeter Press, 2020), p. 13.
6. A. C. Todd, *The Search for Silver: Cornish Miners in Mexico 1824–1947* (Padstow: Lodenek Press, 1977).
7. *Yorke's Peninsula Advertiser*, 25 February 1876.
8. Philip Payton, *Making Moonta: The Invention of Australia's Little Cornwall* (Exeter: University of Exeter Press, 2007), p. 59.
9. For a comprehensive discussion of Cornish surnames see Bernard Deacon, *The Surnames of Cornwall* (Redruth: Cornish Social & Economic Research Group, 2019).
10. Payton, *The Cornish Overseas*, p. 108.
11. Ibid.
12. Todd, *Search for Silver*, p. 14.
13. Ibid.
14. Ibid.
15. Ibid., pp. 14–15
16. Ibid., pp. 14–15.
17. Exeter University Library (EUL), Rowse Collection, MS113/3, Correspondence/1/Todd to Rowse, 16 March 1969. See also Philip Payton, *A. L. Rowse and Cornwall: A Paradoxical Patriot* (Exeter: University of Exeter Press, 2005), p. 196.

18. Sharron Schwartz and Roger H. Parker, *Lanner: A Cornish Mining Parish* (Tiverton: Halsgrove, 1998), p. 152.
19. Ibid.
20. A. C. Todd, *The Cornish Miner in America* (Truro: D. Bradford Barton, 1967), p. 204.
21. Heather Pearce, 'ROWE Virginia City NV and Grass Valley CA', *Journal of the Pacific Northwest Cornish Society*, 11:3 (2009), p. 4.
22. John Rowe, *The Hard-Rock Men: Cornish Immigrants and the North American Mining Frontier* (Liverpool: Liverpool University Press, 1974), p. 279.
23. A. L. Rowse, *The Cornish in America* (London: Macmillan, 1969).
24. EUL, MS113/2, Journals and notebooks 5/2, September 1966; Payton, *A. L. Rowse and Cornwall*, pp. 183–4.
25. D. M. Thomas, 'A Cornish graveyard at Keweenaw', *Cornish Review*, 24 (1973), pp. 65–6. See also Payton, *The Cornish Overseas*, pp. 412–13.
26. Graham B. Dickason, *Cornish Immigrants to South Africa: The Cousin Jacks' Contribution to the Development of Mining and Commerce, 1820–1920* (Cape Town: Balkema, 1978), p. 115.
27. A. L. Rowse, *A Cornish Childhood: Autobiography of a Cornishman* (London: Jonathan Cape, 1942), p. 34.
28. Ibid., pp. 38–9.
29. Ibid.
30. *Burra Record*, 13 August 1902; Payton, *Making Moonta*, pp. 162–3.
31. Philip Payton, *Cornish Carols from Australia* (Redruth: Dyllansow Truran, 1984), pp. vi–x.
32. Geoffrey Blainey, *The Rush That Never Ended: A History of Australian Mining* (Melbourne: Melbourne University Press, 1963, revised edn 1964), p. 120.
33. See Payton, *Making Moonta*, especially chapter 5.
34. *South Australian Bible Christian Magazine*, August 1975; Payton, *Making Moonta*, pp. 159–60.
35. Mandie Robinson, *Cap'n 'Ancock: Ruler of Australia's Little Cornwall* (Adelaide: Rigby, 1978), pp. 85–6.
36. *South Australian Bible Christian Magazine*, November 1885; Payton, *Making Moonta*, p. 162.
37. Blainey, *The Rush That Never Ended*, p. 120.
38. Oswald Pryor, *Australia's Little Cornwall*, (Adelaide: Rigby, 1962), p. 170.
39. For an account of John Verran's career, see Philip Payton, *One and All: Labor and the Radical Tradition in South Australia* (Adelaide: Wakefield Press, 2016).
40. *People's Weekly*, 17 June 1893; see also Payton, *The Cornish Overseas*, p. 314.
41. Nicol, *At The End of the Road*, p. 122.

42. *Wallaroo Times*, 15 August 1865.
43. Ibid.
44. Pryor, *Australia's Little Cornwall*, p. 169.
45. Liz Coole, Jim Harbison, Judith Hayde, and Rosemary Gray, *Moonta Cemetery: A Walk through the Lives of the Pioneers from 'Australia's Little Cornwall'* (Moonta: National Trust of South Australia, Moonta Branch, Moonta, 2009), pp. 5–6.
46. Ibid.
47. Ibid., p. 80
48. Ibid., p. 15.
49. Payton, *Making Moonta*, chapter 4; Philip Payton, *One and All*, chapter 4.
50. Ibid., p. 18.
51. Ibid., p. 22.
52. Roslyn M. Paterson (ed.), *Dressing of The Graves: A Collection of Citations from 2001–2007 of the district's pioneers buried in the Kadina, Moonta and Wallaroo Cemeteries* (Adelaide and Kadina: Cornish Association of South Australia and Kernewek Lowender Inc., 2007), pp. 99–100.
53. Ibid., p. 100
54. Ibid., p. 140.
55. Payton, *Making Moonta*, pp. 215–19.
56. Paterson, *Dressing of the Graves*, p. 5.
57. Ibid.
58. Ibid.
59. Ibid., p. 10.
60. *Kernewek Lowender Copper Coast Cornish Festival, May 13–19 2019, Official Program*, pp. 6–8.
61. Phyllis Somerville, *Not Only in Stone* (Sydney: Angus & Robertson, 1942; repub. Adelaide: Seal Books, 1973), backcover notes; see also Charlotte White, 'Cousins Jack and Jenny in Phyllis Somerville's *Not Only in Stone*', in Philip Payton (ed.), *Cornish Studies: Nineteen* (Exeter: University of Exeter Press, 2011), pp. 225–34.
62. Somerville, *Not Only in Stone*, p. viii.
63. Ibid.
64. Ibid., p. i.

8

Documents in Stone: Records of Lives and Deaths of Scots Abroad and in Scotland

John M. MacKenzie

If tombs and gravestones are anything to go by, it would seem that the deaths of Scots abroad (and especially in the British Empire) had a striking resonance. An imperial death seems to have been particularly poignant for a variety of reasons. It was a death that was far from home. It was a death that was viewed almost as a martyrdom in the cause of what was then seen as the noble and even elevating cause of imperialism and this was true of both military and civilian deaths. Above all, it was generally a death that was premature, either because of violence in colonial warfare and revolt or because of the supposedly dangerous exotic environments which resulted in potentially fatal diseases. It might also be, tragically, a death in childbirth or in infancy. Any modern traveller, particularly in India and elsewhere in Asia, cannot fail to notice the attention given to memorialise the deaths of some Scots invariably but not exclusively from the elite. Meanwhile, in Scotland deaths overseas were sometimes commemorated on family gravestones, as though there was an imperative to bring family members together in carved memorialisation in their place of origin or of their upbringing. Where death had occurred after imperial service and a return to the homeland, stones often included elaborate inscriptions detailing an overseas career, often as though such a trajectory seemed a great deal more worthy than one spent more conventionally at home. In some cases, there were special memorials, both in imperial and in Scottish settings, to record elite imperial lives.

This chapter analyses the varied forms of inscription, mainly from the nineteenth and early twentieth centuries, reflecting the manner in which an imperial Scottish death could provoke an interaction between the exotic locale in which the life had been led and the familiar home from which it had sprung. It will also reveal the longer timescale of these phenomena, going back at least to the eighteenth century. Given the geographical range of such graveyards, it will be necessary to concentrate on some locations, particularly those in India and, specifically, in Penang. As will be demonstrated below, some scholarly (as well as genealogical) attention has already been given to Indian cemeteries, but here the focus will be on the Scots as a specific ethnic (and Protestant) group. Since we need a domestic as well as an imperial perspective, some notice will be taken of intriguing graves within Scotland.

If we deconstruct these various elements of imperial diasporic deaths further, there is little doubt that exoticism was particularly potent in representing distance from Scotland and hence a translation from the domestic familiarity of origins to the unfamiliar contexts of a different continent. This was mainly true of sojourners (intended temporary residents) in the dependent empire, and less true of settlers or permanent migrants whose intention was to create a new domesticity, a fresh and hopefully safe home. While there were some settlers (mainly on plantations) in Asia, most had the intention to return. Settlement was generally precluded by the dense indigenous demographics of Asia, as well as by a whole range of environmental, political and cultural reasons. In both cases, deaths were all the more touching when opportunities for return journeys were less common and convenient. To some extent, this remained true until the late nineteenth and early twentieth centuries, when transport became safer, faster and more regular. Until then, movement to imperial territories was often irreversible, except in a few unusual cases.[1] Moreover, in Victorian times particularly, exotic locales formed an important backdrop for adventure stories, for publications about Christian evangelisation, for theatrical productions and panoramas, and for accounts of events in newspapers and the illustrated journals.[2]

The brevity of lives in imperial contexts was an affecting phenomenon that was to continue into the twentieth century. Violence remained a central characteristic of empire throughout its history, while tropical diseases only became more clearly understood from the last decade of the nineteenth and early years of the twentieth centuries with the advances in microbiology and the foundation of schools of tropical medicine in Liverpool (1898) and London (1899).[3] Hence, lives were rendered all the more heroic because so short and therefore worthy of greater memorialisation. For contemporaries thrilled by the imperial advance, it took courage as well as cupidity, duty or religious zeal to go East, later to Africa or even to the territories of settlement. Graveyards and memorials became the object of visits but not for the bereaved. Instead, they drew the interest of imperial travellers, particularly if associated with specific events such as the Indian Uprising or 'Mutiny' of 1857 or warfare such as the Zulu and Anglo-Boer wars in South Africa. By the late nineteenth century, such visits come to be featured in guidebooks.[4]

As well as the evidence of the memorials themselves, the 'documents in stone', it is clear that interest in the commemoration of imperial deaths started at an early date. Significant sources therefore include the extraordinary publications produced in Calcutta (Kolkata) during the nineteenth century, *Asiaticus* (1803) and *The Bengal Obituary* (1851), both of which are available online. Various organisations have also been active in recording inscriptions and in attempting to protect graveyards, including the British Association for Cemeteries in South Asia (BACSA) and the Kabristan Archives; the work of both is examined in this chapter. They have produced extensive materials for the aid of genealogists, but it is apparent that their objectives have some ideological content too. In preserving and celebrating lives, there is an element of celebrating the imperial service of those lives. The existence of these various sources and organisations has helped to produce scholarly articles by Robert Travers and Elizabeth Buettner, though the Kabristan Archives have been little noticed. In addition, a number of websites have recorded surviving inscriptions and offer archaeological surveys such as the Scots graveyard in Kolkata. The use of graveyards and cemeteries as significant sources for the lives and deaths of Scots (and other Britons) in the East is, therefore, now well developed. This is less true of graveyards in Scotland, where the material used below has been taken from a personal database. The recording of imperial careers on gravestones in Scottish domestic contexts provides a significant balancing source to those identified overseas.

My own conversion to the importance of graveyards as a historical source came in a particularly exotic context. On a visit to the (still) Portuguese territory of Macao (now Macau) in 1980, I visited the 'Protestant Graveyard' where the memorials recorded deaths that had occurred far from Europe.[5] One notable individual buried there is the missionary and sinologist Robert Morrison (1782–1834). His birth in Northumberland and his career are recorded on the gravestone, but not the fact that he was of Scots parentage and was ordained in the Scotch Church in London, after which he became a noted sinologist.[6]

Since then, the search for and recording of grave inscriptions in South Asia, South-East Asia and the Far East, together with Africa and in Scotland itself, has become a major research interest. The significance of these commemorative inscriptions is that they operate at a number of key social and ideological levels. On the one hand, they represent family life, affection, love, pride and loss, but on the other they also project the ideology of the age, the sense of the rightness of the enterprise in which the deceased person had been involved. At yet another level, they can constitute major exercises in propaganda. This is particularly true of the grander public monuments that highlight the lives of significant figures, some of whom became famous in their own day, but are now scarcely remembered. In the Christian context of cathedrals and churches, this mix of emotions, of tragedy, loss, admiration of family, friends and colleagues, and the powerful justification of a propagandist ideology central to the age is particularly apparent. It is also in the interior space of such ecclesiastical buildings that such monuments are more likely to survive, free of the many dangers to be found outside, both of deterioration from environmental causes or from human action. Such is the case both in Scotland itself and in the wider world of the former and now rejected empire. It is certainly the case that the ideological dimensions so consonant with the era in which they were prepared, carved and erected are now seen as representing outmoded and unacceptable ideas of the past, even at a distance of not much more than a century.

In former colonial territories, such ideas can appear to be part of what we may consider to be 'dissonant heritage', that is, a surviving material presence which reflects aspects of an inescapable historical period, but displays the rebarbative (to some at least) notions of another time no longer chiming with current generations and modern nationalisms. Such reactions may be less powerful in Scotland itself, where the ideology may often seem like little more than quaint survivals, even ideas that some continue to accept in an atavistic way. At any rate, it is the expression of so many emotions and values on gravestones and monuments which ensure that they constitute 'documents in stone', important records which have added value to the facts of the life lived and certainly to the bare burial records that constitute (where surviving) the prime written source for the respective graveyard. In addition, it is also the case that the encounter with the monument to the death of an individual may be seen to provide an emotional connection with the person commemorated in a manner far more powerful than a simple text. In surveying and analysing a few examples that follow it is essential to remember two things: first, that the Scots were of course in a minority everywhere except in a specifically Scots cemetery, and, second, that the examples here represent a tiny proportion of the vast numbers existing throughout the former imperial territories and at home.[7] These examples are conditioned by the survival of gravestones, by the striking nature of the commemoration, and by the significance of the life of the individual commemorated.

MONUMENTS AND INSCRIPTIONS OVERSEAS

The particular resonance of imperial burials seems to have resulted in the grandeur of many funerary monuments in the British Empire, particularly in India and in some other parts of Asia. The striking structural character of such tombs seems to reflect a desperate search for immortality, the often vain hope that the monumentality of the entombment or the memorial will preserve the record of the life for many years. Almost a means of extending that life, it emphasises the self-regarding sense of being involved in extraordinary events and striking contexts: geographical, military, religious, social and political. But there is also a racially distancing effect, marking out the deceased individual as someone of a different religion, a contrasting and, for them, superior race, a member of the ruling group. Many such graves supposedly marking racial distance are also symbolic of upward social mobility at a distant periphery, the life of an individual who was a Christian in non-Christian surroundings, and who deserved the preservation of their supposedly superior racial and social status in death. In India, Europeans may also have been striving to emulate the great mausoleums of Indian rulers like the Mughals, an attempt at a form of aristocratic emulation. This becomes particularly apparent given the contrast between Hindu and Muslim funerary practices, between cremation and burial. To these apparently high-flown ideological reasons, we can add practical ones, such as the comparative cheapness of materials and labour, combined with the fact of the superior financial status of the white people so commemorated. On the other hand, it must be noted that some of the magnificent memorials in cathedrals in India are by Flaxman, Bacon and other leading London sculptors and the commissioning and transport to Asia must have been costly.[8]

That India had a very special resonance in the commemoration of death is readily apparent from the fact that there is nothing new about collecting and recording the inscriptions on gravestones in the subcontinent. It may well be that this had its origins in India in the early nineteenth century and the practice has been given a name, 'Epitaphy'.[9] The remarkable *Asiaticus* by John Hawkesworth (1803) revealed the objectives of such a compilation. It was divided into two parts, the first offering 'Ecclesiastical, Chronological and Historical Sketches respecting Bengal', and the second containing the epitaphs of the different burial grounds 'in and about Calcutta'. The first part offered, among other material, anecdotes of the founder, the history of the church of St John, the Protestant Mission, a list of chaplains, the military orphanage, as well as an intriguing survey of the (European) cosmopolitanism of this key East India Company (EIC) settlement, with notes on the Portuguese, Armenian and Greek communities. Significantly, there was a chapter on the yearly mortality in Calcutta. The second part contained the grave epitaphs of some seventeen burial grounds, several of them associated with Roman Catholic institutions. The most important British Protestant ones included that of the Anglican St John's Church and the original Chowringhee burial ground. It is an extraordinarily valuable record since many of these were swept away either during the continuing building of the city in subsequent decades or for medical reasons since it was thought that burial grounds associated with residential buildings could pose a risk to health. The extraordinary number of inscriptions in this publication therefore constitutes a strikingly valuable historical document. But its significance also lies in the fact that Hawkesworth clearly sought to demonstrate the manner in which EIC activities in Calcutta were pursued against a background of a hostile environment (as well as resisting indigenous rulers) and a record of high mortality. As such, the recording of deaths was laid out as part of an imperial martyrology, a record of 'heroism' in the creation of the British Empire.

Among the many Scots commemorated in the pages of *Asiaticus* is George Bogle (1746–81), the son of a wealthy Glasgow tobacco merchant, who was educated at Edinburgh University and in London. Bogle became a writer in the EIC in 1770 and was celebrated as a lively social adornment to Calcutta society. He became private secretary to Warren Hastings, who decided to send him on a mission to Tibet to attempt to open up trade with China.[10] Bogle's diplomatic mission constituted one of the first encounters with Tibet. He died in Calcutta in 1781 and his epitaph is recorded in *Asiaticus:*

> In sincere attachment to the memory of Mr. George Bogle, late Ambassador to Tibet, who died the 3rd April, 1781, this monument is erected by his most affectionate friends, David Anderson and Claud Alexander.[11]

Both Anderson and Alexander were fellow Scots which reveals the manner in which Scots overseas tended to hang together. They were the executors of Bogle's will and also made arrangements for Bogle's children to be looked after, possibly by a Tibetan woman.[12] The epitaph also gives some of the flavour of the sociability of this typical EIC group of Scots. Bogle's tomb, with this touching inscription, can still be seen in South Park Street Cemetery. *Asiaticus* contains the epitaphs of many other Scots in Calcutta, particularly the many Wedderburns who were merchants there at that time. Not all are identified as Scots, but names that can be verified as Scottish-born and information from other sources betray their Scottish origins.

Half a century after the publication of the extraordinary *Asiaticus*, the Calcutta undertaker Holmes and Company compiled a large compendium of epitaphs with the title *Bengal Obituary* (1851), which was presumably intended as a sort of advertisement for their trade but which they justified rather differently. They intended to memorialise the dead as a 'spur to emulate patriotic endeavours'. The elaborate title, redolent of the age, reads:

> A Record to perpetuate the Memory of Departed Worth being a compilation of tablets and monumental inscriptions from various parts of the Bengal and Agra Presidencies to which is added Biographical Sketches and Memoirs of such as had pre-eminently distinguished themselves in the history of British India being the formation of the European settlement to the present time.[13]

They brought together tomb inscriptions from different European settlement and burial grounds, over a considerable area of northern India, collating and disseminating them for the benefit of British readers when visiting the Empire. The whole compendium runs to no fewer than 426 pages and inevitably contains the records of many Scots active in the era of the EIC.[14]

This urge to collect, record and preserve such material very much continues into the modern era. BACSA was founded in 1976 with a mission to preserve and record the graveyards of the British in India. One of its founders, Theon Wilkinson, immediately published a work with the title *Two Monsoons*, the phrase long intended to convey the lifespan of many sojourners in India. Among the Scots that Wilkinson identified in the cemeteries surveyed were James Anderson, Mungo Park (son of the famous African explorer) and Jonathan Duncan (see below). Anderson, like so many Scots in India, was a doctor whose epitaph on his grave in Madras (he died in 1809) was in Latin, starting *Jacobus Anderson, Scoto-Britannicus, MD*. His name was also recorded in three Indian languages – Tamil, Telugu and Hindustani (as well as in Latin and English) – and it is recorded that he introduced a number of botanical economic products to India.[15] The inscription alludes to the eighteenth-century skill with language that was one of Anderson's accomplishments (shared by many other Scots) together with the fact that medical training in the period stimulated interests in botany that could have significant economic benefits. Park, on the other hand, was commissioned in the Madras Medical Service in 1822 and died of cholera in 1823, a perfect example of 'two monsoons' syndrome. Wilkinson records the graves of many other Scots, including for example the Revd James Gray, who had been a schoolmaster in Dumfries when Robert Burns had been at school and whose life ended when he was tutor to the Rao of Cutch.[16] Presumably, he moved to India not only to educate (as he would have seen it) an Indian ruler, but also to seek the expansion of Christianity. Many Scots were planters and their deaths are duly recorded by Wilkinson, as well as those commemorated in the Scottish and Dissenters' Cemetery in Calcutta, the importance of which will be highlighted below.

The objectives of BACSA were many and varied.[17] Apart from the principal desire to preserve and archive cemeteries perceived to be fast disappearing, there were other significant elements. Their activities, which included meetings, lectures and various publications including a newsletter called *Chowkidar* ('Watchman'), coincided with a new wave of Raj nostalgia, reflected in publications of personal histories, novels and the making of television programmes and films.[18] There was certainly a celebratory element to all of this, a desire to unveil the sacrifices endured by the British in India and elsewhere. These were objectives which ran directly counter to the developing post-colonial school of history in the period. All of this also accompanied the significant rise of the fascination with family history and genealogy, while BACSA was one of several Indian conservation bodies that appeared around the same time. For instance, the Society for the Preservation of Archival Materials and Monuments of Calcutta was founded in 1981, with the nationally important non-profit charity, the Indian National Trust for Art and Cultural Heritage following in 1984. The Delhi Conservation Society together with, in South-East Asia, the Penang Heritage Trust, significantly, was founded in 1986 on the two-hundredth anniversary of the island's annexation by Britain. Obviously, the South Asian bodies were principally concerned with the preservation of Indian buildings and other aspects of material culture, but they also became interested in the inheritance from the British period (ranging from the mid-eighteenth to mid-twentieth century). The latter was more prominent in Penang, where pre-colonial structures were less prominent.

However, a focus on BACSA should not obscure the fact that there are other players in this field of collecting burial commemorative and other records. The Kabristan Archives (*kabristan* is the Turkish word for cemetery) was also founded in the 1980s (and has certainly been

Figures 8.1a and **b** The monument to Jonathan Duncan (1756–1811), Governor of Bombay, 1795–1811, St Thomas's Cathedral, Bombay. (Photo: John MacKenzie)

b

selling books since 1987). It declares itself to be 'dedicated to the preservation of memorial inscriptions from graveyards in Ireland, the Indian sub-continent, Sri Lanka, and Jamaica' (and has also shown interest in the Himalayan regions).[19] It claims that as of May 2019 it has logged 84,428 burial records, as well as marriage, birth and baptism records. In its lists of publications, it includes no fewer than fifty titles relating to Sri Lanka alone. More overtly concerned with family history and genealogy, many of the issues that concern BACSA are included in the Kabristan Archives' remit, if less prominently.

The deterioration and disappearance of cemeteries and graves throughout India is a phenomenon matched elsewhere in Asia and also in Africa. There are many reasons for such problems. The most important is the hunger for urban growth which often leads to the building over of valuable land taken up by seemingly irrelevant graveyards, perhaps particularly significant in Hindu areas of India where cremation has always been the norm. There are also issues of health and social deprivation. It is well known that open land such as graveyards had become locations for the homeless to congregate, perhaps even seeking shelter in tombs, but also where drinking, drug-taking and other activities regarded as anti-social might occur. Gravestones, some of them valuable marble, were also removed to constitute building materials elsewhere, or as saleable items. Some graveyards became infested with animals, while others were even being used for laundry activities since stones, as in rivers, offer useful surfaces for the traditional pounding and rubbing, to the obvious detriment of the survival of inscriptions.[20] In personal travels, I was advised not to visit a graveyard in Delhi because it had no watchman and was used for drug-taking (I found it to be locked in any case, though as I peered through the gate an individual came along and crawled through the gap at the bottom). A desire to visit the large Happy Valley graveyard in Hong Kong was also frustrated by gates and padlocks. In the Burma hill stations of Maymyo and Kalaw, the evocative British cemeteries were much overgrown and tended to be repositories of rubbish. In South Africa, Anglo-Boer war cemeteries often contained iron crosses over the graves of British troops (the Commonwealth War Graves Commission only protects military cemeteries from the First World War onwards). These had naturally become in effect a quarry for iron for African use or sale, as in the small cemetery in Wynberg in the (formerly Orange) Free State.

Such problems of survival are less apparent inside Christian churches. Some of the most impressive memorials in India are to be found in St Thomas's Cathedral, Bombay (Mumbai), where there are some magnificently extravagant memorials.[21] The monuments there seem to reflect the notion that everything in the East has to be done on a noble scale. One commemorates Jonathan Duncan (1756–1811), a linguist proficient in Persian and Hindi, who was baptised in Lethnott (now in the County of Angus) and joined the EIC at the age of fifteen.[22] He later became the Resident at Benares (Varanasi), where he founded the Sanskrit College in 1791 and served as governor of Bombay from 1795 to his death (it is thought that he never returned to Scotland at any time during this thirty-nine-year career). His immensely impressive monument records his efforts to eliminate infanticide in 'Benares and Varanasi' and offers an encomium upon his service.

The ideology of imperialism is made even more explicit in the memorial to Lt Col. John Campbell, born in Edinburgh in 1750, the son of the Scottish judge Lord Stonefield. This seems to have been erected by the East India Company and declares that it 'dedicates this memorial to British Justice to the Merits and Services' of Campbell,

> Who in the Crisis of the General War in India MDCCLXXXIV Defended Mangalore During a Siege of Eight Months against the United Arms of Mysore and France, And after extorting from the inexorable Sultaun [sic] an involuntary Eulogy with honourable terms for his Small but Brave Garrison

sunk at the age of Thirty Three under the hardships Experienced in the Discharge of his Duty to his King and Country

Turning to Scots in Calcutta, another significant development has been the rediscovery and renovation of the Scottish cemetery, further along South Park Street from the original 'English' one. The latter, which contains many Scots, was first opened by the EIC in 1767, allegedly closed later in the century, though family lairs continued to be used until the 1830s or 1840s. It is regarded as one of the first non-ecclesiastical burial grounds in the Christian world.[23] The Scottish cemetery, extending to six acres, was opened in 1820 at just the time that the Presbyterians were asserting themselves as a separate denomination in the imperial setting, part of the new evangelical thrust. This cemetery was requested by the Kirk Session of the Scottish Church in Dalhousie Square, Calcutta. The reasons given for its creation were that it was appropriate for a different denomination to have its own cemetery and, in any case, it had become too expensive to take burials in the earlier so-called English one. From 2008, the cemetery became the responsibility of the Kolkata Scottish Heritage Trust and a project was developed to restore and, as far as possible, renovate it. The umbrella body became known as the UK–India Educational and Research Initiative (UKIERI) under the aegis of Presidency University of Kolkata and St Andrew's University in Scotland.[24] Over a period of ten years, volunteers have been working in the cemetery to preserve and archive the records of some 3,000 Scots buried there.[25] People involved include representatives from both Scottish and Indian architectural and archaeological organisations as well as from the Royal Commission on the Ancient and Historical Monuments of Scotland and the Scottish Highland Council.[26] The burial records are held in St Andrew's Church in Kolkata.

A historic graveyard which is freely open is the old Protestant cemetery in Penang. It is full of historic grave slabs and tombs and is now cared for by the Penang Heritage Trust. The first governor and founder of the territory, Francis Light, is buried there. The graveyard was opened soon after the British arrival and it inevitably contains the graves of many Scots, some of them significant figures. Since this cemetery has been little noticed and since it offers a remarkable picture of the early years of the territory, it will be used here as a significant case study for the deaths of the Scots in the East in a new colony created in 1786.[27] Among these is the grave of another governor, the inscription on which reads:

> Here rest the mortal remains of John Alexander Bannerman [of Lethendy, Perthshire], late Governor of this Island [Penang], and Lt Col. in the service of the HEIC, whom he faithfully served forty-three years with unwearied zeal and spotless integrity. He died on the 8 Aug. 1819 aged 60 years, after a life passed in the benevolent and active exercise of every virtue becoming a Christian and a Soldier, universally respected and [his death] deeply deplored by an affectionate family.

The Penang cemetery also contains the grave of Commodore Charles Grant (1770–1824), a Royal Navy officer, the son of a Scottish baronet, who was appointed to the command of the Cape of Good Hope in 1821 and then of the East Indies in 1822. In 1824 he was involved in the war in Burma, which concluded with the annexation of the south of the territory by the British, but he caught cholera, was taken to Penang and 'departed this life on 25 July 1824 aged 54 years'. Other Scots there include James Scott of Roxburghshire, James Richardson Logan of Hatton Hall, Berwickshire, Sir John Gordon, baronet,[28] and Eva Amy Grace, daughter of James Cameron and Florence Thompson (the latter dying in 1873). Although the others are readily identifiable, only the Logan grave indicated the place of birth.

Unlike contemporary graves in their native Scotland, the identification of women is difficult, not least because on gravestones and monuments they tended in the tradition of the time to be identified as daughters and wives of men rather than in their own right (though this is not universally the case). Sometimes, the death of a wife is placed in a poignant position alongside that of the husband. A good example of this is that of 'Philip Dundas, Younger of Arniston', who is described as having died a few weeks after his wife, Margaret Wedderburn, 'a lady of the sweetest temper and the softest manners' (see Figure 8.3). In this description she is more prominent than her husband who had arrived as governor of Penang in 1805 and died in April 1807.[29] He was the nephew of the celebrated Henry Dundas, 1st Viscount Melville, one of the most powerful ministers in London.[30] Within the same tomb is John Hope Oliphant, a councillor in Penang, who died around the same time, and was married to Dundas's sister-in-law.

Another inscription which contains a significant encomium on the life of the deceased is that of another Scot from the Borders, James Scott. His inscription reads that he was the

> son of William Scott and Mrs Barbara McDougal. Born at Westermuirdean, Parish of Makerstown, County of Roxburgh, 6 Oct. 1746. Died 19 Sept. 1808. One of the original settlers of this Island, to the prosperity of which he mainly contributed, by an extensive influence with the Chiefs of the

Figure 8.2 The tomb of John Alexander Bannerman (1759–1819), Governor of Penang (1817–19), Penang Protestant Cemetery, Malaysia. (Photo: John MacKenzie)

surrounding Countries, and the devotion of his time, talents and fortune to the advancement of its trade and agriculture, securing thereby the respect and veneration of the various classes of inhabitants. This memorial over his remains erected AD1825 by Robert Scott (of Raeburn, Roxburghshire).

This gives the flavour of the manner in which Prince of Wales Island or Penang was seen as a significant 'coming' colony where reputations and fortunes could be made. It also reveals the ways in which a family encomium can obscure the reality. Scott was actually a friend and business partner of Francis Light, both of them having met as midshipmen in the navy. After many years in Asia (Scott may have arrived in India in 1774), they landed in Penang as business partners and in the 'free-for-all' spirit of the times set about enriching themselves with landholdings in order to establish plantations (pepper turned out to be the best prospect). Scott became the largest landowner in Penang and, on the death of Light in 1794, may have appropriated the latter's property, perhaps in a somewhat underhand way since the beneficiary of Light's will was his common-law wife. Such economic success seems to have given Scott considerable power.[31] He had proposed the case for a port on the eastern side of the Bay of Bengal to the East India Company and, it has been suggested, was just as influential as Light in the annexation of Penang.[32] He became a wealthy and powerful country trader and seems to have maintained a Malay lifestyle, adopting local dress and customs (he may have fathered over a dozen children with five different partners). It is, however, clear that he never forgot Scotland. He acquired estates with names like 'Killiecrankie' and 'Kelso' and eventually built a house for himself in the Malay style and sporting the name 'Scotland'. Light's successor as superintendent in Penang, Major Forbes Ross MacDonald, who served there from 1795 to 1799 and who came from Skye, greatly disapproved of Scott's lifestyle and clashed with him and other merchants who were clinging to the freewheeling days of the colony's foundation.[33] There is some evidence that county loyalties were important since Scott's business partner after the death of Light was David Brown of Longformacus in Berwickshire, very close to Scott's birthplace. The Browns have a family grave in the cemetery and David became the most powerful and wealthy settler after the death of Scott in 1808, owning the Glugor estate and renaming the company as Scott, Brown & Co. Brown is prominently displayed on the noticeboard to the cemetery as one of the most important people in the colony and there is also a good deal of information about the Brown family in general.[34] He donated a piece of land as a *padang* (open garden space) for the town

Figure 8.3 The tomb of Philip Dundas (1762–1807), Governor of Prince of Wales Island (Penang), 1805–7, Penang Protestant Cemetery, Malaysia. (Photo: John MacKenzie)

and a monument was placed there, 'erected by public subscription by European and native inhabitants':

> To the memory of the late David Brown esquire in testimony of their esteem and approbation of his character and for his unwearied zeal and usefulness as a member of the community during the long period of 25 years which he was resident on the island.

It is apparent that mores and interests were very much changing when we reach the days of the brothers Logan, also from the Borders, both of them lawyers and journalists with scholarly interests in the region. Their joint tomb in the cemetery simply indicates the dates of their deaths: James Richardson Logan (born 1819) in 1869 and Abraham (born 1816) in 1873, both of them from Hatton Hall in Berwickshire.[35] But a freestanding stone on Lebuh Light (the former Northam Road) elaborates:

> This monument is erected by the peoples of the Straits Settlements as a tribute of their respect and gratitude to James Richardson Logan, Advocate, FRGS, FES, whose death in the prime of his manhood they regard as a public calamity. He was always first, and sometimes stood alone, in every movement having the welfare of these settlements as its object, and the whole colony, and most especially Penang, owes much of its present welfare and success to his personal efforts and to his unflagging zeal and great ability. He was an erudite and skilful lawyer, an eminent scientific ethnologist and he has founded a literature for these settlements as the projector and editor of the Journal of the Indian Archipelago. Above all he was an upright, true and honorable [sic] man, held in the highest respect and esteem by his fellow countrymen and loved and implicitly trusted by all the native races around him.

It goes on to say that he arrived in the Straits Settlements in February 1839. As well as being an advocate, Logan was the editor of *The Penang Gazette* and founded the scholarly publication, *Journal of the Indian Archipelago and Eastern Asia*. His brother Abraham was prominent in Singapore, also as a lawyer and journalist, editing the *Singapore Free Press*. He served as the secretary of the Singapore Chamber of Commerce and moved to Penang in 1869 after his brother's death. The brothers Logan represented a very different era from that of the rapacious Scott. They also reflected the extraordinary dominance of Scots in the operation of the press in the British Empire in the period.[36]

The tombs in Penang reveal a number of other interesting phenomena of the day. One is the fact that there were already a number of monumental sculptors active in the supply of these carved stones. The Dundas–Oliphant tomb is ascribed to Coombs and Company of

Calcutta, while others include Simpson and Llewellyn also of Calcutta, as well as Yeathere (precise spelling unclear) and Brown and Company. It is clear that Christian and imperial funerary practices had already stimulated the development of a considerable British immigrant sector of sculptors at least partly thriving on the prevalence of European death and commemoration in Asia. It is also interesting to note the range of donors of the costs of such commemorations.

As we have seen, in the early days prominent figures might have their tombs or monuments paid for by the EIC. Other donors included brother officers (a common tribute in the case of the military), family members, the father of the deceased, or fellow citizens. In the case of the Scott memorial, it is interesting that a number of years elapsed between his death in 1808 and the erection of the tomb in 1825, presumably by a family member. While there were family burials of different social standing in the Penang graveyard, it is noticeable that, inevitably, a colonial elite was particularly prominent. It is apparent that the shift from EIC to Crown rule did not affect the scale of the memorials. Penang was very much in the orbit of Calcutta and it seems that the memorialisation to be found in Calcutta was matched by that in Penang. It is also apparent that upward social mobility could be achieved by entry into the professions, including trade, in the East. Missionary burials also indicate that enhanced social status could be achieved by missionaries in the Empire.

GRAVES AND COMMEMORATIONS WITHIN SCOTLAND

In commemorations back home, it may be that missionaries had a particular status in memorials erected to imperial service in Scotland. David Livingstone made the transition from poverty to considerable fame, crowned by burial in Westminster Abbey and many statues were erected to his memory around the world. His father-in-law, Robert Moffat (1795–1883), has a monument in his home village of Ormiston in Midlothian. Of humble origins, Moffat worked as a gardener before joining the London Missionary Society. His monument, unveiled two years after his death, consists of an obelisk on a plinth with a portrait head and an inscription which partially reads, 'He toiled amid the horrors of tribal warfare and through his Christian character won the friendship of the dreaded Matabele chief, Mzilikazi'.[37] It is a typical sentiment, stressing the supposed horrors and dread through which a figure like Moffat secured his triumphant immortality. Whereas other imperial sojourners, officials, planters or employees of commercial companies were in the Empire to benefit their careers or help to make a fortune, missionaries were seen as selfless individuals who travelled in order to bring indigenous people to the revelations and benefits of Christianity, who endangered themselves in order to benefit others. One of the most extraordinary of such gravestones can be found in the kirkyard at Abernyte, a small village near Dundee. Although he is not buried there, having died in Africa, it commemorates the Revd William Ross by giving a complete account of his career and of his achievements in conversions and other adherents. In the family grave, where his mother and father were buried, he is described as:

> Rev. William Ross, elder son of the above, Agent of the London Missionary Society in Central South Africa. He began his career as a farm servant & at the age of 21 became a joiner. At 30 he entered college & after full study was at 38 ordained a minister & appointed to foreign service. Ere long, with the same tools with which he had executed the finest of the woodwork in the parish church of Errol, he erected at Taung a temple to the living God which he afterwards filled with worshippers. He laboured unceasingly for nearly 23 years in the vast desert among abounding perils & died at Likatlong, 30 July 1863 at the age of 61, deeply lamented by the Bechuanas, the London Missionary Society & by the friends of missions. He left 731 church members, 85 enquirers after salvation, 370 scholars, & 11 native fellow teachers.

To have paid a memorial sculptor to carve such a long inscription must have been very costly, but the labours and heroism of the subject were no doubt judged to have justified it. He was surely seen as a classic case of upward mobility, from farm servant to joiner to ordained minister. Ross had laboured among the Tswana-speaking peoples at places which are now in South Africa – Taung in the North-West Province and Likatlong in the (Orange) Free State – so the notion of a 'vast desert' involved a certain degree of geographical licence.

It is clear that missionaries were particularly celebrated in Scotland. Among women missionaries we find Mary McNab (died 1974) of the Church of Scotland Mission in Calabar (the mission made famous by Mary Slessor) and Agnes Gray MA of the Gold Coast Mission who died in 1878 at the age of ninety, both of whom died in the village of Dull near Aberfeldy. Agnes Gray's MA degree is proudly proclaimed on her gravestone. Further north at Urray, near Dingwall, is the grave of Helen Barbara Kennedy Maclean, 1894–1983, a missionary of the China Inland Mission. These women survived to return and die at home in old age. But a number of missionaries were not so lucky. In Fettercairn Churchyard in Angus, the death of Alexander Bruce is recorded on the family headstone. He died at Cheng-Yuan-Kway, working for the

Figure 8.4 The gravestone of the missionary Revd William Ross (1802–63), Abernyte Kirkyard, Perthshire. (Photo: John MacKenzie)

China Inland Mission, in 1891, aged twenty-seven. At Garvald in East Lothian we find John Linton, described as an 'artisan missionary' who 'died at his post' in Kibwezi working for the East African Free Church Mission in 1893, aged twenty-one. Alexander Duff, one of the most celebrated missionaries in India, is commemorated several times. Buried in the Dean Cemetery in Edinburgh, he has a memorial in Moulin, his birthplace, where his honorary degrees are displayed as 'DD, LLD', and he is described as the 'first missionary to India' while in Pitlochry he has a Celtic Cross where he is described as 'the first to kindle the light of higher education in India'.

This memorial to Duff is a reminder that, in addition to graves, there are significant imperial memorials in Scotland. One of the most extraordinary is a fountain which stands on the roadside opposite the gates of Gordon Castle at Fochabers in Moray. The inscription reads:

> Erected by the natives of Fochabers and others to commemorate the heroic stand made against the forces of the King of Matabeleland by Major Allan Wilson of this town who with a small band of gallant comrades fell fighting bravely against overwhelming odds near the Shangani River in South Africa on the 4th December 1893.

This event constituted one of the most iconic moments in the history of the white community in Southern Rhodesia.[38] It took place during the Anglo-Ndebele War as part of the land grab for the region between the Limpopo and the Zambezi (now Zimbabwe) by Cecil Rhodes and his chartered British South Africa Company. Wilson and his small contingent became cut off from the main white column and fought until the last man fell. Images of this event were to be seen in many white settler homes in the country before independence. This memorial reflects a different level of commemoration from those of families in the public space of a cemetery. Wilson was celebrated by the community from which he sprang in this most obvious of locations just outside his home town. The fountain and its inscription (erected in 1895) remains, long after the positive, heroic attitudes towards the ideology surrounding his death have dramatically changed.

Some imperial monuments are even more apparent in the landscape. General Sir Hector Macdonald ('Fighting Mac') boasts no fewer than three highly public monuments. One is an imposing tower which stands outside the cemetery at Dingwall in Easter Ross, another tower (in a telescope shape) at Millbuie on the Black Isle, close to his birthplace, and finally, he has an impressive grave at the Dean Cemetery in Edinburgh. Macdonald, who rose from private to major general in the Gordon Highlanders, played a vital role in the reconquest of the Sudan in 1896–8, perhaps proving to be the key figure in the victory over the Khalifa (successor of the Mahdi) at the Battle of Omdurman. He also served in the Anglo-Boer War, after which he was appointed commander-in-chief in Ceylon (Sri Lanka). Despite the accusation of a sexual scandal and his subsequent suicide, he remained a household name and a major hero in Scotland.[39] His monuments bear inscriptions testifying to the power of the imperial ideology of the day.

The historical significance of the inscriptions on gravestones and memorials in imperial territories such as India and Penang (later part of the Straits Settlements and of Malaysia) is considerable. They unquestionably offer added value to the bare textual record in other sources. They provide a more direct contact with the lives of those commemorated, as well as evidence of donors, of the sentiments of those who commissioned them, of their alleged position in colonial societies, and even of the monumental sculptors who created them. They also reflect the pride of relatives in the achievements and courage of family members in a manner amenable to useful deconstruction. As we have seen in the case of James Scott, there may well be a rather different reality lying behind the funerary encomium, but the gulf between polite rhetoric and reality is itself highly significant. Above all, so many of these inscriptions reflect the ubiquity of imperial propaganda illustrating the central ideology of the day and indicating the social, economic and spiritual changes effected by the movement of individuals to colonial territories. The revelatory content of such inscriptions should never be ignored.

Acknowledgments

I am grateful to Professor Angela McCarthy, Professor Sir Tom Devine, and Dr Nicholas J. Evans for the invitation to speak at the Edinburgh 'Diasporic Deaths' conference. I am also grateful to Professor Liz Buettner for discussion about her work on BACSA and to Dr Nigel Dalziel for help in the compiling of databases.

NOTES

1. General Patrick Duff (1742–1803) from Aberdeenshire went back and forth to India four times in his career, between 1760 and 1792, but that was unusual and there were special circumstances, including his dismissal and efforts at rehabilitation. See Alistair Mutch, *Tiger Duff: India, Madeira and*

Empire in Eighteenth-Century Scotland (Aberdeen: Aberdeen University Press, 2017).
2. John M. MacKenzie, *Propaganda and Empire* (Manchester: Manchester University Press, 1984) and John M. MacKenzie (ed.), *Imperialism and Popular Culture* (Manchester: Manchester University Press, 1986).
3. From a considerable literature, see, for example, Edwin R. Nye and Mary E. Gibson, *Ronald Ross: Malariologist and Polymath* (Basingstoke: Macmillan, 1997).
4. John M. MacKenzie, 'Empires of travel: British guide books and cultural imperialism in the 19th and 20th centuries', in John K. Walton (ed.), *Histories of Tourism: Representation, Identity and Conflict* (Clevedon: Channel View Publications, 2005), pp. 19–38; and John M. MacKenzie, 'Empire travel guides and the imperial mind-set from the mid-nineteenth to the mid-twentieth centuries', in Martin Farr and Xavier Guégan (eds), *The British Abroad since the Eighteenth Century*, Volume 2: *Experiencing Imperialism* (Basingstoke: Palgrave Macmillan, 2013), pp. 116–33.
5. There are now many websites relating to this cemetery. See, for example, <https://macaomagazine.net/old-protestant-cemetery> (accessed 12 July 2019).
6. John M. MacKenzie, 'Scottish Orientalists, administrators and missions: A distinctive Scots approach to Asia?', in T. M. Devine and Angela McCarthy (eds), *The Scottish Experience of Asia, c. 1700 to the Present: Settlers and Sojourners* (Cham: Palgrave Macmillan, 2017), p. 63.
7. There are few specifically Scots cemeteries in the former British Empire, although they did exist in the major Indian centres of Calcutta, Bombay and Madras. The surviving one in Kolkata is now the subject of an archaeological project. See endnotes 18 and 19.
8. Barbara Groseclose, *British Sculpture and the Company Raj* (Newark: University of Delaware Press, 1995) and Mary Ann Steggles and Richard Barnes, *British Sculpture in India* (Kirstead: Frontier Publishing, 2011).
9. Robert Travers, 'Death and the nabobs, imperialism and commemoration in eighteenth-century Calcutta', *Past and Present*, 196 (August 2007), pp. 83–124, 118.
10. Gordon T. Stewart, *Journeys to Empire: Enlightenment, Imperialism and the British Encounter with Tibet, 1774–1904* (Cambridge: Cambridge University Press, 2009).
11. David Anderson was a Persian translator for the EIC while Claud Alexander was Paymaster General to the EIC Army. The epitaph is recorded in *Asiaticus* (Calcutta: Telegraph Press, 1803), part 2, pp. 74–5. Asiaticus was also the nom de plume of John Hawkesworth.
12. Stewart, *Journeys to Empire*, p. 77.
13. Holmes and Company, *The Bengal Obituary* (London and Calcutta: W. Thacker & Co., 1851). This remarkable source is available on the

web at <https://archive.org/details/bengalobituaryo00calgoog/page/n14> (accessed 12 July 2019)
14. There is once again nothing new in this. Analysis of inscriptions on Roman tombstones and monuments reveals a great deal about Roman, imperial, social and cultural history, including conflicts and concepts of 'othering'. Mary Beard pioneered such studies. See <https://www.eagle-network.eu/story/putting-ancient-inscriptions-in-the-limelight> (accessed 25 October 2017).
15. Theon Wilkinson, *Two Monsoons: The Life and Death of Europeans in India* (London: Duckworth, second edition, 1987), p. 78. The examples of Park and Duncan can be found respectively on p. 79 and p. 81.
16. Wilkinson, *Two Monsoons*, p. 95.
17. Elizabeth Buettner, 'Cemeteries, public memory and raj nostalgia in post-colonial Britain and India', *History and Memory*, 18:1 (2006), pp. 5–42.
18. Much of this is detailed in the BACSA website, <http://www.bacsa.org.uk> (accessed 21 May 2019).
19. This material is taken from the Kabristan website, <https://www.kabristan.org.uk> (accessed 21 May 2019).
20. Personal observation and knowledge. See Wilkinson, *Two Monsoons*, preface, p. ix.
21. Dr Vijaya Gupchup, edited by T. Thomas, *St. Thomas' Cathedral, Bombay: A Witness to History* (Bombay: Eminence Editions, 2005), particularly chapter VI. The fine monument to Jonathan Duncan can be seen on p. 115. Duncan was, however, brought up as an adherent of the Church of Scotland, baptised in Lethnott and Navar parish church. There was no Presbyterian Church in Bombay at this period. See John M. MacKenzie, 'Presbyterianism and Scottish identity in global context', *Britain and the World*, 10:1 (2017), pp. 88–112.
22. P. Nightingale, 'Duncan, Jonathan (bap. 1756, d. 1811), administrator in India', *Oxford Dictionary of National Biography* <https://doi.org/10.1093/ref:odnb/8224> (accessed 12 July 2019).
23. <http://kolkatacitytours.com/park-street-cemetery> (accessed 12 July 2019). In Britain, company and municipal cemeteries, as distinct from ecclesiastical graveyards, date only from the early nineteenth century. See <http://thefuneralsource.org/cemhist.html> (accessed 12 July 2019).
24. <http://www.scotscemeteryarchivekolkata.com> (accessed 21 May 2019).
25. <http://scotscemeteryarchivekolkata.com> (accessed 21 May 2019) contains a search facility so that names may be followed up. It is a well-known fact that Calcutta, unlike many areas of India, lacked stone. Apparently, gravestones of sandstone or granite were imported from Scotland: <https://en.wikipedia.org/wiki/Scottish_Cemetery_at_Calcutta> (accessed 21 May 2019).
26. <https://scottishcemeterykolkata.wordpress.com> (accessed 21 May 2019).

27. I visited this cemetery in April 2011, compiling a database of the graves there. But see also Alan G. Harfield, *Christian Cemeteries of Penang and Perak* (London: BACSA, 1987)
28. Among many Gordon baronetcies, this can be identified as Sir John Gordon of Embo, Sutherland, who died in 1804. He is mentioned on the sign at the gate of the cemetery as one of the significant figures buried there.
29. Dundas was described as being 'Governor of this Presidency' on his tomb because Prince of Wales Island or Penang was seen as potentially the capital of a presidency, Province Wellesley, equal in status to the presidencies in India.
30. See, for example, Michael Fry, *The Dundas Despotism* (Edinburgh: Edinburgh University Press, 1992).
31. For information on James Scott, see one of the many websites which contain information on the history of Penang: <https://www.penang-traveltips.com/james-scott.htm> (accessed 26 May 2019).
32. Sharon Oddie Brown, 'The sizzle of connections', 11 March 2014 <http://sharonoddiebrown.blogspot.com/2014/03/the-sizzle-of-connections.html> (accessed 16 April 2020).
33. For the wider context, see Anthony Webster, *Gentlemen Capitalists: British Imperialism in South-East Asia, 1770–1890* (London: I. B. Tauris, 1998).
34. <https://notjustanyfamily.wordpress.com/2015/04/11/david-brown-of-penang>. Brown was born in 1778, studied law at Edinburgh University (a common trajectory, as with the Logan brothers below) and arrived in Penang at the age of twenty-one. He built a fine residence, Glugor House, on his estate and seems to have followed a similar lifestyle to that of Scott with a local wife called Nonia Ennui and a second wife called Inghou.
35. Hatton Hall or Castle was owned, after 1916, by Sir William Burrell, the Glasgow shipowner and art collector.
36. John M. MacKenzie, '"To Enlighten South Africa": The creation of a free press at the Cape in the early nineteenth century', in Chandrika Kaul (ed.), *Media and the British Empire* (Basingstoke: Palgrave Macmillan, 2006), pp. 20–36. This article also contains some material on the struggle for press freedoms in India.
37. This and the succeeding inscriptions come from a personal database collected over many years, although the more famous ones can now be found online.
38. Lewis H. Gann, *A History of Southern Rhodesia* (London: Chatto & Windus, 1965), pp. 118–19.
39. Trevor Royle, *Fighting Mac: The Downfall of Major-General Sir Hector Macdonald* (Edinburgh: Mainstream, 1982). Royle suggests (chapter 16, 'Aftermath') that Macdonald remained a tragic hero in Scotland who, it was felt, had been 'stabbed in the back' by his superiors. He remained 'the darling of Scotland'.

9

Conclusion

Angela McCarthy and Nicholas J. Evans

This multidisciplinary collection has attempted to identify how and why British and Irish migrants and their families and friends sought to display – or not – attachment to 'home' from multiple sites in the British Empire, and whether such memorialisation differed between groups. Spanning both time and space, the contributors reveal that there was a revolution in death culture from the seventeenth century onwards, and especially during the eighteenth and nineteenth centuries. Textual analysis of diaspora gravestones reveals collectively the stories of mainly men, but also women and children, who are often written out of history. But so too are the contributors alert to the material composition of the stones they analyse, their locations, their symbolism, the continuity in traditions of remembrance, and their cross-cultural adaptation. Ultimately, gravestones were very public statements about an individual or family's religious, geographic, economic, political or ethnic identity, and are therefore potentially problematic sources to analyse centuries after they were erected.

Throughout the volume, the chapters highlight the diverse strategies individuals and groups used to preserve the identity of English, Scottish and Irish diasporas overseas. The collective findings suggest not just the evolution of a global death industry – accommodating every cultural whim of each generation – but also the transfer of cultural practices by most societies wherever they settled. Symbols and phrases associated with 'home' were transferred overseas, especially by the Highland Scots, Irish and Cornish. As Laurie Stanley-Blackwell and Michael Linkletter discuss in their chapter, diasporic memorialisation was not carried out in isolation since thistles and other symbols associated with Scots on both sides of the Atlantic were inscribed on headstones that presented a shared identity. As Harold Mytum shows, the thistle and lion rampant were also features of gravestones in Pennsylvania and New South Wales. Such cultural power transcended ever larger distances during the late nineteenth centuries for, as Janine McEgan outlines in her chapter, Britishness was not universal among migrants from Great Britain and Ireland. A noticeable use of shamrocks and Celtic crosses was adapted by Irish Catholics and Irish Protestants settling in South Australia. Yet, in some places, symbolism adapted to new worlds, such as the use of the crown in Pennsylvania or the emulation of Mughal mausoleums in India. Elsewhere, we find the continuation of mortality and heraldry symbolism of European established traditions. Specific references to local, regional and national places also testified to homeland connections, and the accompanying emotional bonds unbroken by settlement, whether temporary or permanent, abroad. The absence of ethnic symbolism or specific references to origin, however, did not necessarily reflect a lack of interest in national and ethnic identities, as Angela McCarthy and Philip Payton reveal in their chapters on the Scots in Ceylon and Cornish memorialisation practices in South America and Australia. Rather, an absence of engagement was likely a reflection of loose connections in the new land, an emphasis on factors such as occupation or the material achievements of the deceased, or a lack of financial resources to erect costly monuments to the dead.

Despite the impressive range of places covered in this volume, only a limited number of mnemonic devices were identified within remembrance during three centuries of British imperialism. Aside from the physical form of the memorial gravestone or tablet and the use of the English language, flowers carved into stone were a key device for identifying the rural backgrounds of migrants. Occasionally, religious or Celtic symbols were deployed to denote Irish or Scottish settlers. Yet no English device, such as a rose, or Welsh symbol such as a leek or daffodil, was popular, especially in the white settler colonies considered here. Although the graves of north-eastern Scotland during the eighteenth and early nineteenth century continued to use symbols on gravestones to convey the working identity of the deceased, this was not a practice exported overseas. Indeed, it is striking how few memorials to trades that dominated local economies – whether mining in South Australia or plantation slavery in the Caribbean – were noted on gravestones. Such elision is important too, as Nicholas Evans suggested in the case of Barbados. More often than not, only language was used. Overseas death markers therefore show some discernible differences to the gravestones that marked their counterparts who remained at 'home'.

Intergenerational messages and identities archived in stone present to successive generations the achievements of their antecedents. This suggests two things: a degree of literacy among the family unit, and also the possibility of 'return' to the memorials over time. While this latter point may have been probable for those dying in Britain and Ireland, for those dying, often alone, in diaspora the stones also needed to 'speak' to the people living around them to ensure they were invested in preserving the memorials of earlier generations. This was especially the case in the Caribbean, where, as Evans demonstrates in his chapter, notions of Englishness on Christian and Jewish death markers demonstrated a shared heritage in the increasingly English memorials erected on Barbados between 1627 and 1838. Similarly, in Nova Scotia during the nineteenth century, Stanley-Blackwell and Linkletter point to burials signifying more than simple respect for the dead: rather, gravestones ensured an emotional hold of the dead over the living. Descendants could also add information to death markers at later dates in acts of ancestral pride.

Throughout the studies here, each of the authors attempts to analyse what we, as twenty-first-century readers, can observe from those memorial devices that have survived. No one has sought to analyse how many people had memorials that have since been eroded through environmental damage or political conflict. Resistance to British settlement overseas invariably meant that in some places the British did not seek to erect memorials for fear of antagonising their hosts. Similarly, it is impossible to discern what form the deceased wished to have as their final memento mori or what they wished to tell the public about their life. Those memorials examined here are perhaps atypical because those who mourned them – including religious communities, fraternal organisations or fellow nationals – spent sufficient money that their life was documented in detail on a form of memorial that stood the test of time. Such texts from around the world were exceptional.

Without doubt, the British and Irish diasporas sought to secure individual and collective memory through memorial erection. Yet memory was selective. As Mytum suggests in his chapter, different strategies were used by the Scots and Ulster Scots in different spaces, whether across the Atlantic, or further south in Australasia. Elision, also discussed by Evans for Barbados, was a central part of this memory-making. Overseas, migrants selected key aspects of their identity that they wanted to remember – or forget. Typically, the British and Irish abroad focused upon only some aspects of their identity. Some aspects, such as their origin, was known to onlookers, as Payton notes in his chapter, concerning the unique Cornish surnames that were displayed on graves.

Alternatively, the trades associated with a time and group, such as the mining central to Cornish overseas identity in Australia, triggered interest from overseas groups and this became a byword for the reader 'knowing' the memorial displayed one of their kith and kin. Relying on surnames as indicators of origin is, however, not always reliable. In her study of Scottish gravestones from five cemeteries in Ceylon, McCarthy probes explicit references to place of birth and family ties on migrant headstones to examine the importance – or not – of national and ethnic identities. She reveals that such identities were just one aspect of Scots migrants' lives abroad, with their occupations and new localities also significant.

The significance of place to both the bereaved and the mourner is also an important aspect of death studies that has received scant attention by scholars. It was not only a story being publicly retold, but also a key part of the deceased's lived identity that was 'normally' remembered as one of their most discerning features. While many scholars have discussed how death levels everyone, remembering origins, whether national, regional or specific places, revealed both the geographic reach of remembrance practices during the nineteenth century and the knowledge of imperial geography. Crucially, someone's geographic identity was arguably more important than their religious identity in memorials, perhaps replicating a degree of secularisation in death.

A key contribution of the chapters throughout this volume is their comparative agenda, whether within or between countries and/or ethnicities. Such comparison exposes striking religious contrasts. At Barbados, Evans compares English and Jewish headstones, with the latter exhibiting more than one language and omitting until the 1800s reference to their places of origin, perhaps due to fears of persecution and anti-alienism. Jewish graves also lay flat rather than erect and exhibited various Judaic symbols. Catholic Scots at Antigonish in Nova Scotia also preferred to exhibit religious symbols rather than document their local, regional and national origins as did their Protestant counterparts at Pictou. Similar contrasts can be found among the Irish in South Australia where McEgan highlights the greater use of Christ and the cross on Irish Catholic graves compared with their Protestant counterparts.

Notable also from the preceding chapters is the long tradition of cemeteries as sites of tourism, with several contributors utilising transcripts of headstone inscriptions compiled by others. Such undertakings have proven vital in light of the deterioration and in some cases the destruction and disappearance of graves. John MacKenzie points to such recorded inscriptions at home and abroad celebrating imperial service while McCarthy reminds us that such previous compilations are not always accurate or comprehensive. The ongoing appeal of cemeteries for tourists as well as the horrendous ways in which some graveyards are subject to graffiti and other forms of desecration points to their ongoing social relevance. Even so, the preservation of gravestones over time also demonstrates, especially in Asia, Africa and the Caribbean, serious commitment to preserving the memory of people long since departed. The memorials must have been deemed worth preserving, despite the people they recall often being seen less positively by later residents in remote former colonies. The creation of ethnic spaces within cemeteries in the twenty-first century – whether of Poles in Glasgow, Scotland, the Chinese in Cardiff, Wales, or Tongans in Auckland, New Zealand – likewise testifies to the enduring importance of ethnic origins for some individuals and communities beyond the chronological focus of this book. How far these more recent memorialisation practices differ from those undertaken among British and Irish migrants during Britain's imperial phase awaits investigation. Future studies might situate the analysis of British and Irish diaspora gravestones within a more extensive comparative agenda with other ethnicities than what has been achieved in the chapters in this volume.

Overall, the volume demonstrates that cultural imperialism was being expanded not only through political and economic means but also through overriding pre-existing practices of remembering the dead at home and abroad. The practices associated with the remembrance of British and Irish people rapidly became the predominant way all people in overseas colonies remembered rich and poor alike. Through imposing the English language, they anglicised the death landscapes. Eurocentric ways of ordering the dead, and their death markers, thereby attained a global influence.

Index

accidents, 89, 157, 161, 164
afterlife, 2, 3, 138, 140
Anderson, James, 182–3
Anglicans, 56
 their burial and memorial practices, 5, 23, 56, 74, 118
archaeological approaches, 14–15, 18, 19, 128, 148, 178, 187
Arnold, William, 52, 54
Asiaticus, 178, 180–2
assimilation, 32, 55, 67, 69–74, 128, 135
Australia, 43
 Cornish migrants and memorials in, 157, 163–72, 202, 204
 Irish memorialisation in, 40–2, 128–9, 133–4, 135–49, 156, 202
 Irish migrants in, 35–6, 40, 127–8, 129–33, 134–5, 144, 146, 148, 149, 171, 202, 204
 Moonta Cemetery, 165–6, 171–2
 Rookwood Cemetery, 35, 36
 Ulster Scots migrants and memorials in, 16, 17, 18, 35–43, 44–5, 203

Bagot, Charles, 130
Bannerman, John Alexander, 188, 189
Barbados, 55
 Anglicisation of, 52–6, 58, 66–7, 74–5
 Carib and African inhabitants of, 52, 53, 55–6, 57, 74, 76n5, 77n27, 203
 English memorials in, 52–5, 56–67, 74–5, 203, 204
 Jewish migrants and memorials in, 53, 55, 67, 69–74, 203, 204
belonging, 82, 99, 111
Bengal Obituary, 178, 182
Bigham family carvers, 25, 29
Bogle, George, 181–2
British Association for Cemeteries in South Asia (BACSA), 178, 182–3
Britishness, 55, 101, 202
Brown, David, 190, 192, 200n34
burial practices, 3, 6–8, 57, 72, 83–4, 85, 99, 113, 163–4, 193, 203
burial spaces, 2–3, 57, 69, 72, 82, 85, 111, 113, 165

Campbell, John, 186–7
Campbell, Malcolm, 135
carvers, 18–19, 20, 24–5, 26, 29, 32–3, 43, 45, 88, 89, 94, 97, 106n54
Catholics, 16, 127, 129, 132
 symbols and motifs on their headstones, 25, 41, 43–4, 57, 88–90, 99, 101, 102, 128–9, 133–4, 135–40, 142, 149, 156, 204
 their burial and memorialisation practices, 2, 3, 6, 23, 24, 83, 86, 99, 113
cemeteries, 7–8, 81–2, 85, 99, 178, 183, 185–6
 as markers of territorial possession, 86, 155–6, 171, 197
 as places of reflection and retreat, 166, 168
 as sites of tourism, 53, 109, 111, 177–8, 204–5

ethnic cemeteries, 1, 157–9, 173, 187, 198n7
public and municipal cemeteries, 3, 8, 156, 187, 199n23
segregated sections in, 8, 36, 99, 123, 157, 160, 205
see also graveyards, war cemeteries
Ceylon, 113, 116, 120, 122
  English migrants and memorials in, 118–19, 120
  Garrisons Cemetery, 112, 114, 116
  Scottish headstones and memorials in, 108–13, 114–18, 122, 123–4, 202, 204
  Scottish migrants in, 108–9, 111, 112–14, 116, 118, 119–22, 123–4, 197, 204
Chapman, Montague, 130
Chinese migrants
  their burials and memorials, 8, 123, 171, 205
Chisholm, Caroline, 132
Cille Choirill graveyard, 81, 103n2
class, 2–3, 4, 9, 16, 17, 57
commemoration, 102, 111, 123, 156, 172, 178–80, 193, 196
  commemorative festivals, 157, 169, 171–2
  commemorative practices, 2–8, 18, 20, 21, 23–5, 44
conformity, 18, 25, 40, 57, 93, 101
Cornish diaspora, 156–7, 162–3, 169, 171–2, 201, 203–4
  Cornish identity, 156–7, 158–60, 169, 173, 204
  in Mexico and North America, 157–62
  in South Australia, 157, 163–72
  their funeral and burial practices, 158, 160, 163–6, 168, 172
  their gravestones, 157–8, 159–60, 161–2, 163, 164, 165, 166, 167, 168–70, 172–3, 202
crosses
  Celtic, 119, 122–3, 135–6, 140–2, 148, 156, 196, 202
  cross motifs, 88–9, 94, 98, 101, 122, 138, 140, 144, 156, 204
  iron, 142, 159, 186
  plain and carved, 109, 110, 113, 133–4, 135
cultural change and adaptation, 2, 4, 7, 14, 15, 16, 18–20, 24, 29, 32–3, 35, 40, 44–5, 81, 102, 128, 168, 180, 201, 202
cultural identity, 18–19, 82–3, 86–8, 89, 91, 93, 99, 101–2, 156, 201–2
cultural imperialism, 6, 52–3, 55–6, 74–5, 205
cultural practices and traditions, 14–19, 20–3, 25, 29, 32, 33, 43–4, 52–3, 55, 102, 106n54, 128, 142, 148–9, 201

de Piza, Angel, 72, 74
death culture, 2–6, 8–9, 52, 53, 56, 72, 74–5, 201
death markers, 1–3, 4, 53, 56–7, 67, 75, 202–3, 205
  and social identity, 55, 56–8, 60–3, 66, 67, 69, 72, 75
  as a mnemonic tool, 4, 53, 67, 68, 202
Decoration Day, 160, 171
desecration (of graves), 1, 9n5, 205
designs, 7, 15, 19, 20, 21–2, 25, 29, 36, 144
diasporic deaths, 162–3, 177
disease, 3, 59, 114, 116, 157, 164, 166, 168, 169, 171, 176, 177, 182, 183, 188
'Dressing the Graves', 157, 169, 171–2
Duff, Alexander, 196
Duncan, Jonathan, 182, 184–5, 186, 199n21
Dundas, Philip, 188, 191, 200n29
Dutch mortuary traditions, 29, 32, 33, 44
dùthchas, 82, 103n8

East India Company (EIC), 7, 122, 181–2, 186–7, 193
elision, 16, 35, 52–3, 67, 122, 202, 203, 204
English (language), 6, 57, 70, 72–4, 91, 93, 101, 202, 204, 205
English migrants and settlers, 6, 52, 87, 201
  'English' cemeteries, 157, 158, 187
  'English' identity, 53, 55, 57–67
  in Australia, 43, 127, 129, 132, 133
  in Barbados, 52, 53, 55–6, 58, 60–3, 66–7, 74–5
  in Ceylon, 118–19, 120
  their memorial practices, 6–7, 52–5, 56–67, 74–5, 203, 204
  see also Cornish migrants

INDEX

'Englishness', 55, 74–5, 203
Enright, Alexander, 60
epitaphs, 1, 3, 4, 52–3, 63, 138, 168, 180–2; *see also* inscriptions
ethnicity, 8, 9, 16, 19, 82, 103n5, 111, 113, 118, 123–4, 128, 204, 205
 absence of on headstones, 109, 111–12, 119–23, 124, 202
exoticism, 176–7

forgetting, 14, 15, 16, 17, 18–19, 20–1, 29, 32, 35, 41, 45, 203
Freetown, 7, 12n47

Gaelic, 6, 82–3, 88, 89, 91–3, 101–2, 106n54
Galbraith family memorials, 24
Gleeson, Edmund B., 130, 133
Grant, Charles, 188
graves, 2, 69, 72, 113, 114, 128–9, 135, 155, 204
 desecration and disappearance of, 1, 9, 9n5, 26, 85, 112, 183, 185, 203, 204–5
 family graves, 16, 23, 24, 25, 26, 113, 176, 190, 194
 grave markers, 5, 16, 56–7, 74, 87, 118, 122, 142, 144, 148, 166
 visiting graves, 4, 23, 53, 109, 111, 158–9, 161–2, 165–6, 177–8, 186
gravestones *see* headstones
graveyards, 2–3, 5, 6–7, 21, 24, 56, 81, 158–9, 161–2, 177–8, 182, 185–6, 187, 193

Hancock, Sarah, 164
Hawkesworth, John, 180–1, 198n11
headstones, 1–2, 3, 4, 5–6, 8–9, 21–2, 52–3, 128, 172–3, 179, 201–2, 203
 Classical revival headstones, 36, 39, 40
 production of, 4, 8, 146, 148
 shapes, 7, 18, 21, 29–32, 33, 44, 57, 63, 142, 144
 see also inscriptions, materials, motifs, symbols
Hebrew (language), 70–2, 123, 204
Hewson, Eileen, 113, 116

identity, 1–2, 16, 17, 55, 75, 86, 202–3, 204

British and North British identity, 40, 86–8, 101, 112, 116, 203
Cornish identity, 156–7, 158–60, 169, 173, 204
English identity, 53, 55, 57–67, 201
ethnic and national identity, 60, 72, 87, 101, 111, 113, 123–4, 135, 201, 202, 204
family identity, 9, 16, 18, 22–3, 24, 25, 43, 44, 63, 83, 86, 93–4
Irish identity, 122–3, 128–9, 135, 140–2, 144, 146, 148–9, 156, 201, 203
new identities, 16, 44–5, 124, 135, 149, 204
religious identity, 16, 83, 88–9, 94, 99, 101–2, 128, 201, 204
Scottish identity, 16, 20, 40–1, 82–3, 86, 87–8, 93–4, 99, 101–2, 111–12, 116, 119–24, 201–2, 203, 204
social identity, 15–17, 18–19, 22–3, 43, 44–5, 63, 144, 149
Ulster Scots identity, 16, 17, 19, 20–1, 25, 33, 40, 43
see also cultural identity
imperial deaths and memorials, 176–8, 180–5, 186–97
India
 memorials and Scots migrants in, 8–9, 111, 176, 177, 178, 180–5, 186–7, 190, 196, 197, 198n7, 199n25
inscriptions, 16, 18, 19, 40–1, 43, 86–8, 101, 118, 136–8, 157, 172–3, 197, 201
 age, 9, 38–9, 40, 112, 113–16, 148, 158, 161, 166–8, 194–6
 dates, 26, 38–9, 40, 148, 192
 familial pride and encomium, 86, 176, 179, 188, 190, 197, 202–3
 familial ties, 22–3, 24, 25, 43, 44, 63–5, 66, 72, 86, 93–4, 116, 119, 123–4, 144, 148, 161, 176, 193–4, 204
 fraternal ties, 62–3, 75, 159, 168, 203
 friendship, 63, 65–6, 74, 108–9, 116, 118, 122, 124n5, 181–2
 ideological content, 176, 178–80, 186–93, 196–7
 language of, 4, 5, 6, 57, 70–4, 82–3,

89, 91–3, 101–2, 123, 136, 182, 202, 204, 205
  military ties, 62, 66–7, 118, 156, 176, 180, 186–7, 188, 193, 196–7
  occupation, 43, 52, 61–2, 63, 75, 87, 109–10, 116, 118, 122, 124, 176, 181, 185, 187–90, 191, 192, 202, 204
  place of birth, 41, 44, 58, 70, 87–8, 103n8, 118, 122–4, 136, 140, 144, 166, 178, 188, 204
  place of origin, 36, 40–1, 58–61, 66, 70, 87–8, 112, 114–16, 122–4, 148, 176, 202, 203–4
  place of residence, 43, 58, 118, 124, 204
  records and transcriptions of, 36, 53, 67, 112–13, 116, 178, 180–3, 185, 187, 204–5
  religious affiliations and quotations, 5, 72, 85, 88, 101, 138, 149, 157, 164–5, 168–9, 170, 201, 204
  social statements, 4, 62–3, 86, 101, 122, 176, 185, 192, 193–7
Ireland
  commemorating death in, 4–5, 6, 17, 20, 23–5, 26, 185, 203
Irish migrants and settlers, 201
  and memorials in Barbados, 58, 60
  and memorials in Ceylon, 111, 116, 118, 120, 122, 123
  in Australia, 35–6, 40, 127–8, 129–33, 134–5, 144, 146, 148, 149, 171, 202, 204
  Irish Catholic migrants and memorials, 17, 36, 40, 41–3, 127, 128–30, 132–3, 134, 135–8, 139, 140–2, 144–9, 202, 204
  Irish Protestant migrants and memorials, 35–6, 40, 41, 43–4, 127, 128–30, 132, 133–4, 136–8, 140, 142, 149, 202, 204
  their memorials in Australia, 40–2, 128–9, 133–4, 135–49, 156, 202
  see also Ulster Scots
Irish nationalism, 134–5
'Irishness', 122–3, 128–9, 146, 148, 156
Irvine, Alexander, 62

Jamestown settlement, 6, 7, 52
Jewish migrants, 55, 69, 70
  their burial and memorialisation practices, 53, 55, 67, 69–74, 123, 203, 204

Kabristan Archives, 113, 178, 183, 185

Lewis, J. Penry, 112–13
Light, Francis, 187, 190
Logan, Abraham, 192, 200n34
Logan, James Richardson, 188, 192, 200n34

MacDonald, Alexander, 82
MacDonald, Alexander the Ridge, 82–3
MacDonald, Angus, 83
MacDonald, Hector, 196–7, 200n39
MacDonald, John the Hunter, 81
McDougall's Cemetery, 83–4
MacKinnon, Archibald 'The Big Bachelor', 85
MacLean, John, 91, 92, 101–2
McPherson, James, 114–16
Malaysia
  Scots migrants and graves in Penang, 177, 187–93, 197, 200n29, 200n34
material culture, 6–7, 14, 15, 16–17, 18, 19, 81–2, 148
materials, 7, 18, 201
  granite, 4, 5, 8, 108–9, 124n9, 199n25
  imported, 4, 5, 7, 18, 56–7, 63–6, 77n23, 199n25
  marble, 4, 5, 7, 8, 52, 56–7, 63–6, 67, 68, 69, 71, 73, 109, 160, 185
  new and locally sourced, 5, 7–8, 19–20, 52, 56, 77n23
  sandstone, 4, 8, 9, 35, 199n25
  slate, 4, 5, 8, 29–30, 32, 33, 56–7
  stone, 4, 16–17, 19–20, 23, 52, 69, 114–16
  wood, 8, 113, 166
memorialisation, 2, 8, 63, 66, 122, 148, 155–6, 163, 172–3, 176, 177, 201–2
  rituals and practices, 3–5, 6, 52, 53, 57, 67, 70, 74, 128–9, 202, 205
memorials, 1–2, 3, 5, 8, 9, 16–21, 203
  antiquarian and genealogical interest in, 2, 8, 23, 45, 67, 113, 155, 178, 183, 185
  donors to, 62, 108–9, 111, 193, 197
  imported, 4, 7, 18, 63–6, 180

memorials (*cont.*)
  of pioneers, 82, 84, 86, 104n23, 104n25, 104n26, 155–6, 166, 171
  styles, 4, 5, 16, 17–18, 19, 23–4, 36, 40, 63–6, 69, 71, 123, 142–4, 148
  visiting memorials, 23, 53, 177–8, 182, 203
  see also inscriptions, materials, motifs, symbols
memory, 203
  of the deceased preserved, 2, 4, 56, 66, 161, 162–3, 205
  see also social memory
Methodists, 156, 164–5, 168, 170
Mexico
  Cornish migrants and memorials in, 157–9
migration, 14–16, 18, 36, 113, 124, 127, 133
missionaries, 178, 193–6
Moffat, Robert, 193
Moir, David, 112, 114
motifs, 21, 23, 29, 99, 135, 144, 146, 148
  crosses, 88–9, 94, 98, 101, 122, 138, 140, 144, 156, 204
  crowns, 22, 32–3, 34, 44, 202
  doves, 29, 44, 88, 89, 101
  floral motifs, 21, 32, 93, 94, 96, 99, 136, 202
  hands, 26, 29, 32, 72, 89, 94, 96, 99–101
  hearts, 6, 21, 22, 99, 139, 144, 156
  heraldic devices, 22–4, 25, 26, 28–9, 32, 33, 44, 57, 201–2
  of affection and grief, 129, 136–8, 142, 148–9
  religious motifs, 129, 136, 138–40, 142, 148–9
  stars, 26, 32, 34
  thistle, 26, 29, 35, 38, 40, 43, 93–4, 95–6, 97, 98, 101–2, 201–2
  tulips, 29, 32, 44
  see also symbols
Mytum, Harold, 8, 53, 138, 140

Nairn, Margaret, 109
necroethnicity, 82, 103n5
New Zealand
  memorials and cemeteries in, 7–8, 113, 122, 123, 205
  Southern Cemetery, 122, 123
Nonconformists, 5, 6, 8

North America
  British and Irish migrants in, 6, 7, 8–9, 16, 17, 44, 60–1, 66, 127, 134, 148, 159–62
  British and Irish memorials in, 18, 20, 53, 56, 67, 102, 156, 160
  see also Pennsylvania
North Britain (NB), 40, 87–8, 101, 112, 114–16
Nova Scotia
  Scottish deathways in, 81–6, 87, 88–9, 93, 94, 99, 101, 102
  Scottish immigrants in, 81–3, 84–9, 97, 99, 101–2, 106n54

Orange Order, 35–6, 43

Patterson, Daniel, 20, 29, 33
Patterson, Robert, 87
Pennsylvania
  Dutch settlers and memorials in, 26, 29, 32, 33
  Ulster Scots migrants and memorials in, 16, 17, 20–1, 25–35, 40, 43, 44–5, 201–2, 203
place, 23, 40–1, 43, 58, 81–2, 83–4, 87–8, 103n8, 124, 144, 202, 204
Presbyterians
  Presbyterian settlers, 16, 17, 25, 27, 35–6, 43, 44, 84, 101
  symbols on their headstones, 23, 29, 32–3, 99, 102
  their burial and memorial practices, 24–5, 36–43, 44, 85–6, 99, 113, 123, 187
preservation, 178, 180, 182–3, 185–7, 205
Protestants
  Protestant Reformation, 2, 5
  Protestant settlers, 26, 35–6, 43–4, 83, 127, 129–30
  their burial and memorialisation practices, 2, 3, 6–7, 23–4, 40, 43–4, 113, 128–9, 133–4, 136–8, 140, 142, 149, 202
  see also Anglicans, Methodists, Presbyterians

relief carvings, 33–5, 63–6, 67–8, 89
religion, 83, 180, 185
remembering, 14, 16, 17, 18–19, 20, 26, 29, 32, 33, 35, 40–1, 43–4, 45, 203, 204

remembrance, 1–2, 4, 7, 8, 21, 43, 72, 74, 128, 136, 156, 157
  traditions and practices of, 6, 52–3, 55, 57–8, 74–5, 201, 204, 205
Robertson, Mary MacGillivary, 83
Ross, William, 194, 195
Rowse, A. L., 159, 161, 162
Rowse, 'Cheelie', 162

Sansum, Ann, 66–7
Scotland, 4–5
  commemorating imperial life and death in, 111, 176–7, 178–80, 193–7
  graves and memorials in, 5–6, 8, 15–16, 17, 19, 21–3, 24–5, 32, 43, 44, 138, 202
Scots dialect, 6
Scott, James, 188, 190, 193, 197
Scottish migrants and settlers
  and place, 40–1, 43, 81–2, 83–4, 87–8, 103n2, 103n8, 124, 202, 204
  and place names, 84, 119–20, 122, 126n27, 190
  and religious identity, 16, 83, 88–9, 99, 101–2, 187, 204
  British and North British identity, 40, 86–8, 101, 112, 116, 203
  commemorating Scots in Ceylon, 108–13, 114–18, 122, 123–4, 202, 204
  ethnic and national funerary markers, 26, 38–40, 82, 87, 93–8, 101–2, 113, 119, 123–4, 201–2, 204
  ethnicity absent on some headstones, 109, 111–12, 119–23, 124, 202
  Highland Scots, 82, 88, 99, 101–2, 114, 119, 123, 201
  in Ceylon, 108–9, 111, 112–14, 116, 118, 119–22, 123–4, 197, 204
  in Nova Scotia, 81–3, 84–9, 97, 99, 101–2, 106n54
  Lowland Scots, 84, 86–7, 123
  Scottish Catholics, 16, 82, 83, 84, 86, 88–90, 94, 99, 101–2, 204
  Scottish identity, 16, 20, 40–1, 82–3, 86, 87–8, 93–4, 99, 101–2, 111–12, 116, 119–24, 201–2, 203, 204
  Scottishness, 93, 97, 99, 101, 102
  symbols on their headstones, 6, 23–5, 26, 32, 85, 88–9, 90, 93–4, 95–8, 99, 101–2, 109, 123, 201–2, 204
  their housing, 97, 106n54, 190
  their imperial lives and deaths, 8–9, 108–11, 113–18, 119–22, 176–7, 178–80, 181–3, 184–5, 186–97, 200n34
  their cemeteries and burial customs, 6, 81–5, 99, 101–2, 103n2, 183, 187, 198n7, 203
  see also Ulster Scots
sculptors, 63, 180, 192–3, 194, 197
sculptures, 63–6, 111
secularisation, 2, 4, 7, 56, 57, 75, 204
settlements, 8–9, 19–20, 52, 127, 155–6, 171, 177, 182, 192, 201–2, 203
Shipton, Henry Noble, 61–2
social memory, 15–16, 18, 33, 43–4
social mobility, 101, 180, 193, 194
sojourners, 9, 55, 157, 176, 177, 182, 193–4
Somerville, Phyllis, 172–3
South Africa
  British migrants in, 111, 162–3, 169, 194, 196
Stiven, Henry, 113–14
Stiven, Margaret, 114, 125n20
stone ledgers, 21, 24, 26, 29, 35, 44, 88
symbols, 19, 201–2
  cherubs, 21, 22, 32, 33, 34
  ethnic and national symbols, 26, 38–40, 41–2, 93–8, 101–2, 122–3, 128–9, 134, 140–9, 156, 201–2, 204
  folk symbols, 22, 99, 100
  Irish symbols of identity, 41–2, 122–3, 128–9, 134, 140–9, 156, 202, 204
  Masonic insignia, 157, 159–60
  mortality symbols, 21, 22, 23–5, 32, 33, 34, 44, 202
  religious symbols, 29, 32–3, 43–4, 57, 72, 88–9, 90, 93, 94, 99, 101, 102, 109, 133–4, 136–40, 142, 148–9, 202, 204
  shamrocks, 41, 42, 122, 134, 140, 142, 148, 156, 202
  trade symbols, 22, 23, 43, 118, 202

Taylor, James, 108–11, 112, 113, 114, 120, 122, 124n5

Thomas, D. M., 161–2
Thomas, Eliza, 165
Todd, A. C., 158–9, 160
Trevithic[k], Annie, 167
'two monsoons' syndrome, 182, 183

Ulster Scots, 6, 14–15, 16, 17, 19, 20, 43, 203
  and their memorials in New South Wales, 16, 17, 18, 35–43, 44–5, 203
  migrants and memorials in Pennsylvania, 16, 17, 20–1, 25–35, 40, 43, 44–5, 201–2, 203
  their memorials in Ulster, 6, 17, 20–1, 23–5, 43–5
Urquhart, James, 116

waisted headstones, 29–32, 44
Wakefield, Edward Gibbon, 129
Walters, W. H., 108–9, 124n5
war cemeteries and memorials, 1, 9n5, 156, 177–8, 186–7, 196–7
Welsh (language), 5
Whitburn, James Michael, 169
Wilkinson, Theon, 182–3
Wilson, Allan, 196
Withers, Thomas, 63–6
women
  female migrants and remembrance, 72, 74, 132, 156–7, 172, 188, 194, 201
Woolcock, Thomas, 168
Wyndham, George, 130

Yelland, Thomas, 166, 168

EU representative:
Easy Access System Europe
Mustamäe tee 50, 10621 Tallinn, Estonia
Gpsr.requests@easproject.com